BED & BREAKFAST
ireland

Published in the United States in 2002 by Chronicle Books LLC

Text copyright © 2002 by Elsie Dillard and Susan Causin
Illustrations copyright © 2002 by The Appletree Press Ltd.
Published in asociation with the K.S.Giniger Company, Inc.,
New York, NY 10107, USA
For further up-to-date-information, please visit
www.irelandseye.com/breakfast.htm

Library of Congress Cataloging-in-Publication Data available.

ISBN: 0-8118-3272-4

Printed in India

Cover design by Anna Coluthon

Distributed in Canada by Raincoast Books
9050 Shaughnessy Street
Vancouver, BC V6P 6E5

10 9 8 7 6 5 4 3 2 1

Published by Chronicle Books LLC
85 Second Street
San Francisco, CA 94105

www.chroniclebooks.com

BED & BREAKFAST

ireland

REVISED & EXPANDED 4th EDITION

a trusted guide to *over 400* of Ireland's best bed and breakfasts

ELSIE DILLARD & SUSAN CAUSIN

CHRONICLE BOOKS

SAN FRANCISCO

Appletree Press

Contents

Our Favourite Bed and Breakfasts

Ashbrook House, Castleknock, Dublin 15

Ballaghtobin, Callan, Co. Kilkenny

Ballyknocken House, Ashford, Glenealy, Co. Wicklow

Barnageeha, Ardmillan, Killinchy, Co. Down

Delphi Lodge, Leenane, Co. Galway

Glendine Country House, Arthurstown, Co. Wexford

Greenmount House, Gortonora, Dingle, Co. Kerry

Joyville, Drumcondra, Dublin 9

Killeague Lodge, Coleraine, Co. Derry

The Moat Inn, Donegore Hill, Templepatrick, Co. Antrim

Moy House, Lahinch, Co. Clare

Primrose Cottage, Castlebar, Co. Mayo

Rahard Lodge, Cashel, Co. Tipperary

South Lodge, Portmarnock, Co. Dublin

Springview House, Urlingford, Co. Kilkenny

St John's Country House, Fahan, Inishowen, Co. Donegal

Temple Country House, Horseleap, Moate, Co. Westmeath

Tyrella House, Downpatrick, Co. Down

Whispering Pines, Bellheight, Kenmare, Co. Kerry

Woodtown House, Athboy, Co. Meath

INTRODUCTION

The exceptional warmth and hospitality of the Irish would be reason enough to visit Ireland, but combined with the scenic beauty of the countryside, Ireland is a perfect choice for a holiday.

Our research has covered the four seasons and we highly recommend a visit to Ireland in the off-season, when it is easy to get around and there is still plenty to interest the visitor. Each property listed in this guide has been personally visited by us, and there are no charges for inclusion. Our criteria for entry are based upon the warmth of the welcome and cleanliness of the property, with many other factors being taken into consideration. We have covered every county, and included areas not considered as tourist regions to accommodate business travellers, visiting friends and family gatherings.

Restrictions on pets have been noted. Most establishments are completely non-smoking and many have restrictions on where smoking is allowed. Children are welcome unless stated otherwise. Sometimes the location or style of a house makes it unsuitable for children; however, houses which provide facilities for children are noted. Parking is always available unless mentioned otherwise. We have included details on the number of ground floor rooms, which is helpful for older guests or visitors with disabilities. Unlicensed premises often allow guests to bring their own wine.

At the time of publication, price guides were correct, but please be aware of seasonal variations, and you should refer to the 'Important Note' below. When booking, it is advisable to verify specifics, such as child reductions, single supplements, special break prices, opening times, meals and dietary requirements. Obtaining driving directions is also recommended.

Most entries include the owner's name, but it is possible that a change in ownership may have occurred, which could lead to significant changes in the standard of accommodation.

At the time of publication, and to the best of our knowledge, the details in this book were correct. However, changes do occur for which we cannot be responsible. We would like to thank Bord Fáilte and the Northern Ireland Tourist Board for their help in making this book possible.

We would welcome any comments you have on your personal experiences about properties in this book. We would be delighted to receive your recommendations for consideration as future inclusions. Please send your comments and recommendations to Elsie Dillard and Susan Causin, 48 Nursery Road, Great Cornard, Sudbury, Suffolk, England CO10 3NJ or in North America to PO Box 54107, Redondo, WA 98054.

Important Note:
All Bed and Breakfast prices are per person. A "single supplement" refers to the practice of charging a single visitor who stays in a double room the single room rate plus an additional charge.

The prices listed for accommodation in the Republic of Ireland are given in Euro currency (€). The prices listed for accommodation in Northern Ireland are given in pounds sterling (British pounds) (£). At the time of going to press Euro prices could only be given as a guide, so check the rates when you book your room as well as the method of payment. Some establishments might not accept credit cards.

COUNTY DUBLIN

From above Killakee, on the northern slopes of the Dublin Mountains, there is a wonderful view of both city and county. You can see to the northeast of the majestic sweep of Dublin Bay, the beautiful peninsula of Howth Head, and to the south of the bay, South Killiney Head. The city stretches across the plain, divided by the River Liffey, and the large green patch in the northwest is Phoenix Park, one of Europe's finest city parks, covering some 116 hectares.

The county north of Howth has long sandy beaches and fishing villages, which in spite of their proximity to the city, still retain their character and charm, as well as a wealth of archaeological sites. The castle at Howth dates from 1464, but has been altered over the centuries. The gardens, which are open to the public, are famous for their rhododendrons and eighteenth-century formal garden. Malahide Castle belonged to the Talbot family from 1185 to 1976, when the property was sold to the Dublin County Council. It now houses a large part of the National Portrait Collection.

To the south of the Liffey, Blackrock and Dalkey retain their village identity, and the popular Victorian holiday resort of Dún Laoghaire is one of the main sea-gateways to Ireland. The city of Dublin is beautifully situated and the people have a friendliness and wit that captivates most visitors. Relatively speaking, it is a small and compact city. The city centre, stretching between Parnell Square and St Stephen's Green north to south, and Dublin Bay and Phoenix Park east to west, can be covered easily by foot. Most points of interest in the city lie between these boundaries. Like most European capitals, there is so much to see in the city that it would take weeks to do it full justice, taking in not only the principal sights of churches, museums and galleries, but taking the time to browse and absorb the atmosphere, the people, shops, theatres and pubs as well. Amongst the sights on the top of the list to visit are the National Museum, the National Gallery and the Municipal Gallery, as well as St Patrick's Cathedral dating from 1190; Christchurch Cathedral, restored in the nineteenth century; St Michan's, where intact bodies still lie in vaults; the fine eighteenth-century church of St Anne's; and St Werburgh's Church – which are amongst the most noteworthy churches to visit.

Dublin Castle, with its beautifully decorated State Apartments, was used by the British for state functions, and since 1938 has been the scene of the inauguration of the Presidents of Ireland. The General Post Office in O'Connell Street is where the Free Republic was proclaimed in 1916. The Custom House is one of the most impressive buildings in Dublin. Parliament House, now the Bank of Ireland, was built in

1785 by James Gandon, Dublin's most famous architect. The Book of Kells is kept in the Library at Trinity College, which is a restful spot away from the bustle of the city.

DALKEY

Tudor House

Castle Lane, Dalkey, Co. Dublin
Tel: 01 285 1528 Fax: 01 284 8133

This impressive Victorian house can be found at the end of a quiet lane right in the middle of Dalkey. It is surrounded by gardens and has glimpses of the sea through the trees that ring the end of the garden. The Haydons poured a lot of energy, love and work into restoring this interesting building, which was constructed for a Dr. James Richard Parkinson, a well known Dublin surgeon. The individually decorated bedrooms all have telephones, TVs, trouser presses and hairdryers. The DART line runs through the end of the garden, and Dalkey's attractions — Norman castles, a quaint harbour, great restaurants and pubs — are but a few minutes walk away. Tudor House has become very popular with business visitors, who can easily commute into Dublin on the DART. Major credit cards accepted. No pets. No smoking in the bedrooms.

OWNER Katie & Peter Haydon OPEN all year ROOMS 6 double en suite. TERMS €57–101.50

DUBLIN 2

Number 31

31 Leeson Close, Dublin 2
Tel: 01 6765011 Fax: 01 6762929 Email: number31@loo.ie
Website: www.number31.ie

Number 31 is an unusual place to find in the heart of Georgian Dublin off busy Leeson Street. Built by the famous Dublin architect Sam Stephenson as his home it is an oasis of peace and quiet, hidden behind a high creeper-covered wall. The house has many interesting features; the low entrance opens up into a spacious drawing room with a sunken sitting area, featuring a bar, fireplace, high ceilings and tall windows. There are terracs, patios and different levels, and the comfortable en suite bedrooms all have hairdryers, telephones, TVs and tea and coffee making facilities. From the back of the house a winding path leads through gardens to the back door of Fitzwilliam Place — a total contrast of architecture and style, it's a beautiful, classical building with ornate ceilings and enormous rooms. Fitzwilliam Place has no public rooms — guests that stay here cross the garden to make use of Number 31's drawing room, and for breakfast, which is quite a feast and is served in either the upstairs dining room or in the enclosed conservatory. Guests experience the very best of Irish charm and welcome from the Comers. Noel is a never ending font of knowledge of Dublin and all things Irish. Supplied with maps and advice, the visitor cannot go wrong. Off-street, secure parking is available. It is not suitable for children under 10. No pets. American Express, Visa and Mastercard accepted.

OWNER Noel and Deidre Comer OPEN All year ROOMS 18 twins, doubles, family; all en suite. TERMS €57–95; single supplement €20

Trinity Lodge
12 South Frederick Street, Dublin 2
Tel: 01 6795044 Fax: 01 6795223 Email: trinitylodge@eircom.net

Trinity Lodge is probably one of the most centrally located guest houses in Dublin, almost next door to Trinity College and surrounded by shops, restaurants, cafes and pubs. A Georgian town house, it has been interestingly renovated and decorated in the original strong, bright, old Irish colours, to match the colours of the paintings by the artist Knuttel (who lives close by). The walls are hung with prints of his work, and an original depicting the sinking of the 'Titanic' hangs over the staircase. The house is eleganty furnished and beautifully equipped, each bedroom or suite having a hairdryer, trouser press, telephone, TV, air conditioning, safe and tea and coffee making facilities. Some rooms also have desks and modem points. The three suites can sleep up to six people and include a bedroom, sitting room, bathroom and small kitchen. No pets. All major credit cards accepted. Although Trinity Lodge does not have its own parking, the staff will make sure parking is available.

OWNER Peter Murphy, MD OPEN January 2 – December 22 ROOMS 2 double, 3 twin, 2 single, 3 family, 3 suite; all en suite. TERMS €89; single supplement €51; reductions for children

DUBLIN 3

Kincora Lodge
54 Kincora Court, Clontarf, Dublin 3
Tel: 01 8330220

Caroline and Paul extend a warm welcome to their immaculate red brick townhouse house close to the city, airport and ferry. The spacious, en-suite rooms, have TV, tea makers, hospitality tray, hairdryers, new modern furnishing, comfortable beds, colourful bed covers and co-ordinated curtains. Bedrooms are non-smoking areas.

Guests arriving by car would be well advised to leave their car at the house and take the bus to the city centre. Although convenient to most amenities, this is a quiet location, and guests will be comfortable and well taken care of here. Excellent breakfasts are served, and there are several venues for evening meals close by. Golf Courses and the beach are within walking distance. All major credit cards accepted.

OWNER Caroline & Paul Connolly OPEN All year ROOMS 3 double/twin/family; all en suite. TERMS €33; child reduction; single supplement from €12.50

Willowbrook
14 Strandville Avenue East, Clontarf, Dublin 3
Tel: 01 8333115 Fax: 01 8333115 Email: willowbrook@ireland.com Website: willowbrookbandb.com

Joe and Mary Mooney set up in business here five years ago – to 'semi-retire' from a larger guest house operation. They adapted Willowbrook, which was built 15 years ago, to accommodate bed & breakfast guests. The compact, comfortably furnished bedrooms were made en suite, and they each have tea and coffee making facilities, water and fruit, and TVs. Guests have use of a long sitting room cum breakfast room which overlooks the quite substantial back garden, and the décor and furnishings are in keeping with the style of the house. There is car parking in the front driveway area of the house. Willowbrook is very conveniently located in a quiet residential street in the old part of Clontarf, and is close to Dublin Port and Point Depot - a venue for concerts. The DART station is three minutes away. No smoking and no pets. Minimum stay of two nights.

OWNER Joe & Mary Mooney OPEN All year except for Christmas ROOMS 1 double/twin, 1 triple/family; all en suite. TERMS €31.50–38; single supplement €12.50–19

DUBLIN 4

66 Townhouse
66 Northumberland Road, Dublin 4
Tel: 01 6600333 Fax: 01 6601051

An elegant refurbished Victorian house, situated in the Diplomatic area, with all the facilities of a first class hotel. The house is furnished in keeping with the period, and the good size bedrooms have attractive floral bed covers and are immaculately maintained. All, have en-suite facilities, direct dial phone, TV, tea makers and hairdryers. There is separate dining room, where a delicious breakfast is served, and a sitting room. Susan and Paul are a great couple, who work as a team to maintain their high standards, and who have thought of everything for guest's needs, including umbrellas for rainy days. This is a popular venue with business people and tourists, early reservations suggested. Non-smokers preferred. A ten minute walk has you in the city centre, and buses run frequently.

OWNER Susan & Paul Keane OPEN All year except for Christmas ROOMS 7 double/twin/single; all en suite. TERMS €70–95; child reduction; single supplement negotiable

Aberdeen Lodge
53 Park Avenue, Ballsbridge, Dublin 4
Tel: 01 2838155 Fax: 01 2837877 Email: aberdeen@iol.ie
Website: www.greenbook.ie/aberdeen

Aberdeen Lodge is a substantial, brick built Edwardian house in an elegant residential area, easily accessible both to the centre of Dublin and Dun Laoghaire. Considerable renovation work has been done here over the years and a lot of the original features have been saved, such as the ceiling work and fireplaces. The décor is elegant and tasteful and it is nicely furnished. All bedrooms have hairdryers, telephones, trouser presses and TVs The drawing room and dining room are comfortable, pleasant rooms, and a 'drawing room' menu is available offering light snacks and wines to residents in the afternoons and evenings. The house has a large garden, beyond which is the cricket ground, and it is peaceful and quiet. There is off-street car parking in front of the house. No pets. Some bedrooms are designated for smokers. Major credit cards accepted. Central Dublin can be reached in a few minutes on the DART railway.

OWNER Pat Halpin OPEN All year ROOMS 6 twin, 3 triple, 2 family, 7 double; all en suite. TERMS from €57; single supplement €25.50; reductions for children

Burkes
26 Waterloo Road, Dublin 4
Tel: 01 668 1085

The restoration of this Victorian town house took the Burkes a few years. The end results are comfortable, very spacious bedrooms, a 'home from home' atmosphere, and good Irish hospitality. Guests have use of a large drawing room and breakfast is served in the formal dining room. Waterloo Road is very well located for the centre and close to many restaurants and pubs, and Burkes offers excellent value for money. There is off-street parking in front of the house.

OWNER Marie Burke OPEN March – October ROOMS 1 triple, 3 twin/double, 1 double; all en suite. TERMS €47.50; single supplement €10; reductions for children

Elva
5 Pembroke Park, Ballsbridge, Dublin 4
Tel: 01 660 2931 Fax: 01 660 5417

An impressive Victorian residence in a central location, just five minutes from the town centre. The house continues to maintain its high standards; it is freshly decorated and spotlessly clean. There is a good bus service into town; guests with a cars would find it less stressful to leave the car at the B&B and take the bus. The front door has some beautiful stained-glass work and leaded windows, and other original features include decorative ceiling cornices and fireplaces in the bedrooms and lounge. There are antique furnishings throughout the house and the atmosphere is warm and friendly. Pleasant and personal attention guaranteed.

OWNER Sheila Matthews OPEN February 1 – November 30 ROOMS 1 double, 1 family; all en suite; TERMS €34.50; single supplement €19

Glenogra Guesthouse
64 Merrion Road, Dublin 4
Tel: 01 668 3661 Fax: 01 668 3698
Email: glenogra@indigo.ie

Glenogra is a beautifully appointed Georgian residence in an excellent location, close to the city centre, DART and all amenities. The house has been furnished to a high standard of comfort in pleasing fabrics and colours. The good sized bedrooms all have TVs, telephones, hairdryers and tea and coffee making facilities. The dining room, where breakfast only is served, is quite ornate with pillars, a decorative ceiling and a fireplace. Seamus and Cherry McNamee offer all the faciltiies of a hotel, combined with the warmth and personal service of a private residence. No pets and no smoking. Visa, Mastercard and American Express accepted. Glenogra is opposite the Four Seasons Hotel in Ballsbridge. There is off-street parking in front of the house.

OWNER Seamus & Cherry McNamee OPEN January 20 – December 20 ROOMS 10 double, 2 twin; all en suite TERMS €50; single supplement €25 reductions for children

Glenveagh

31 Northumberland Road, Ballsbridge, Dublin 4
Tel: 01 668 4612 Fax: 01 668 4559

Glenveagh is an impressive Victorian house retaining many
original features, including beautiful cornices and a ceiling rose.
There are antique furnishings, including a grandfather clock in
the hallway. The well-appointed bedrooms are decorated and
furnished to a high standard, providing all the comforts of a
first-class hotel in an inviting atmosphere. Improvements are
continually ongoing, the kitchen has now been moved upstairs,
and two additional bedrooms have been added.

The house is spacious, beautifully maintained, extremely comfortable, and retains the warmth and friendliness of a private
house. Joe and Bernadette are a gracious couple who enjoy
welcoming people to Dublin and are happy to offer advice on
what to see. Freshly prepared breakfasts are presented on fine
china at separate tables in the elegant dining room, which has a
fireplace, soft, restful wallpapers and matching curtains. The
lounge has soft furnishings and a fireplace. A quiet spot in which
to relax after a busy day, with plenty of information provided for
guests. Glenveagh is delightful in every way, a good choice for
visitors wanting first-class accommodation in a convenient location. There is an excellent bus service to town, and the house is
minutes from the DART station. There are several venues for
evening meals within walking distance. Visa, Access accepted.

OWNER Joe & Bernadette Cunningham OPEN All year ROOMS
5 double, 3 twin, 3 family; all en suite TERMS €51; reduction for
children; single supplement (seasonal)

Haddington Lodge

49 Haddington Road, Dublin 4
Tel: 01 660 0974

A Georgian house in a good location, 15 minutes' walk from the
town centre. Mary Egan has been running her B&B for over 12
years and the house has recently been freshly decorated with
soft pastels and new carpets installed. Each bedroom has an
electric blanket, and some rooms overlook a pretty courtyard
with shrubs and trees. Ground floor rooms are available.
Haddington Lodge started life as two separate houses, but they
were cleverly converted to one house 12 years ago, when Mary
Egan opened up the premises for business. The lounge area is
quite small, and leads onto the dining room, which has a soft
yellow and orange décor. Breakfasts only are served, and
vegetarians catered for if pre-arranged. There is a self-catering
unit available.

OWNER Mrs Mary Egan OPEN February 1 – December 1
ROOMS 3 double/twin/family; all en suite TERMS €33; single
supplement (seasonal)

Merrion Hall
54 Merrion Road, Ballsbridge, Dublin 4
Tel: 01 6681426 Fax: 01 6684280
Email: merrionhall@iol.ie
Website: www.greenbook.ie/merrion

This substantial Victorian brick built house is set back off the
main road, opposite the Royal Dublin Showground (RDS) in the
heart of Ballsbridge, one of Dublin's elegant suburbs. The building
has been elegantly furnished and the comfortable bedrooms all
have TVs, hairdryers, telephones and trouser presses. The dining
room has a bay window overlooking the garden, and the large,
comfortable drawing room has high ceilings with the original
plasterwork. The centre of Dublin can easily be reached by the
DART railway, or regular bus service. No pets. Some designated
smoking bedrooms. Major credit cards accepted. Off street
parking available in front of the house.

OWNER Pat Halpin OPEN All year ROOMS 3 family, 4 triple, 2
single, 9 double, 6 twin; all en suite. TERMS from €57; single
supplement €25.50; reductions for children

Northumberland Lodge

68 Northumberland Road, Ballsbridge, Dublin 4
Tel: 01 660 5270 Fax: 01 668 8679
Email: info@northumberlandlodge.com

Northumberland Lodge is a gracious, comfortable Victorian
residence with many original features remain, such as the leaded
light windows in the front door, ceiling coving and fireplaces. The
house is furnished in keeping with its character, has pine floors in
the entryway, lounge and dining room and is in excellent
decorative order. There are several watercolours of local scenes
on display by a local artist. Bridget and Tony Brady are excellent
hosts, who work as a team to provide visitors with a high
standard of accommodation in an informal, welcoming
atmosphere. The bedrooms are well-appointed and of a good
size, with non-smoking rooms available. Plenty of information for
visitors can be found in the spacious lounge, which has satellite
TV and video. Breakfasts include a buffet choice of cereals and
juice, followed by a full cooked breakfast. Bridget Brady is happy
to make recommendations of local establishments for evening
meals. The well-tended gardens are available to guests.
All major credit cards accepted.

OWNER Bridget & Tony Brady OPEN All year ROOMS 2 double,
2 twin, 4 family; all en suite. TERMS €45.50–76; reduction for
children; single supplement from €12.50

Raglan Lodge

10 Raglan Road, Ballsbridge, Dublin 4
Tel: 01 660 6697 or 087 2257789 Fax: 01 660 6781

In a quiet residential road within walking distance of the centre,
Raglan Lodge is a welcoming, peaceful place, with a friendly,
charming owner. Dating from 1861 iit is an impressive Victorian
house, which, in its more recent past was turned into flats and
allowed to deteriorate. It has now been restored back to its
original character of well proportioned rooms and high ceilings.
The bedrooms all have TVs and telephones. The poet, Patrick
Kavanagh, lived on Raglan Road in the 1940s, and one of his
poems is entitled 'On Raglan Road'. There is off street parking on
the premises, and major credit cards are accepted.

OWNER Helen Moran OPEN All year except for Christmas
ROOMS 5 doubles, 2 singles; all en suite. TERMS €51–63.50;
single supplement €12.50

Simmonstown House

Sydenham Road, Ballsbridge, Dublin 4
Tel: 01660 7260 Fax: 02 660 7341
Email: info@simmonstownhouse.com
Website: www.simmonstownhouse.com

Down a quiet side street off busy Merrion Road, Simmonstown House exudes elegance, comfort and tranquillity. Beautifully furnished and decorated, and with a charming owner, this Victorian homse offers its guests a restful stay. The comfortable bedrooms have TVs and telephones. The centre can be reached in ten minutes either by bus or DART, and it is a short walk to Ballsbridge's restaurants and pubs. Off street parking. No smoking in bedrooms. Major credit cards accepted.

OWNER Finola Curry OPEN Mid-February – mid-December ROOMS 4 doubles/twins; all en suite. TERMS €76; single supplement €12.50

DUBLIN 7

Belcamp Hutchinson

Carr's Lane, Malahide Road, Balgriffin, Dublin 7
Tel: 01 846 0843 Fax: 01 848 5703

This superb, ivy-clad Georgian house is hidden away down a narrow lane off the main Malahide road, It is named after Francis Hely-Hutchinson, third Earl of Donoughmore. The house has been renovated with the utmost care, preserving its features and elegance, whilst introducing the best of twentieth century comforts, It stands in seven hectares of fields and gardens, including a walled garden and a maze. The house is superbly furnished and extremely comfortable, and has an easygoing, relaxed atmosphere. Each spacious bedroom has been decorated with a different colour scheme and has a hairdryer, TV, telephone and tea and coffee making facilities. Copious breakfats, are served at the

enormous table in the elegant dining room, and the large, long drawing room has an honesty bar. The owners are very proud of the latest addition - a downstairs loo (which had some plumbing problems to overcome). The attractive little seaside village of Malahide is close by, Dublin can easily be reached by bus, and it is only a few minutes' drive to the airport. Belcamp Hutchinson is a peaceful and relaxing place to stay, on arrival or departure from Ireland, or as a base for visiting Dublin. Neither pets nor smoking are allowed in the dining room. Visa, Access, Mastercard accepted.

OWNER Doreen Gleeson & Karl Waldburg OPEN All year except for Christmas ROOMS 3 double, 3 twin, 2 single; all en suite. TERMS €56

DUBLIN 9

Egan's House
7/9 Iona Park, Glasnevin, Dublin 9
Tel: 01 830 3611 Fax: 01 830 3612
E-mail: eganshouse@tinet.ie

Egan's House is an attractive red brick turn-of-the-century house that has been refurbished to a high standard. It started out as two separate houses, which have been tastefully converted to provide comfortable accommodation. The bedrooms have good-sized bathrooms, quality furnishings and are individually decorated in soft shades and rich colours of blue, grey, green and wine. There are 12 ground floor bedrooms. The house is impeccably maintained and retains many original features, including covings and fireplaces. Two lounges provide comfortable areas in which to relax, and are furnished in keeping with the character of the house, with rich green velvet curtains. The house is situated in a quiet residential area, 1.6 km from the city centre, the bus stop is just a few minutes' walk; guests who have a car would be well advised to leave it behind and take the bus. All major credit cards accepted.

OWNER John & Betty Egan OPEN All year ROOMS 25 double/twin/family; all en suite. TERMS €38; reduction for children; single supplement (seasonal)

Iona House
5 Iona Road, Dublin 9
Tel: 01 830 6217 Fax: 01 830 67632

This attractive red brick residence was built at the turn of the century and is situated in one of Dublin's unique Victorian quarters. Jack and Karen Shouldice bought the property in 1963, which they have refurbished to provide comfortable accommodation with a taste of luxury. The décor and furnishings are rich and tasteful, and several original features remain, such as attractive coving, a ceiling rose and a marble fireplace. Fine prints adorn the walls, and the spacious lounge, with a predominantly green décor, is available to guests, as is a furnished patio. The bedrooms are of a good size, well-appointed and colour-co-ordinated. Breakfasts are served in the dining room, which has booth-style tables, and there are several venues for evening meals within walking distance. The house is well situated for the airport and convenient to the city centre.

OWNER Jack & Karen Shouldice OPEN All year ROOMS 4 double, 1 twin, 2 single; all en suite. TERMS €44.50; reduction for children; single supplement (seasonal)

Joyville
24 St Alphonsus Road, Drumcondra, Dublin 9
Tel: 01 830 3221

Roma Gibbons is a delightful, kindly lady who extends a warm welcome to her immaculate red brick Victorian house, situated opposite St Alphonsus Convent and Church 2 km from the city centre. There is a good local bus service; guests would be well advised to take local transport to avoid the parking and traffic problems. The bedrooms are average in size with orthopaedic beds.

There are no en suite rooms, but there are two shower rooms and two WCs exclusively for guests' use. The family lounge has a marble fireplace, which guests are welcome to share. Roma Gibbons enjoys meeting people and would be happy to recommend pubs and restaurants for evening meals. Joyville is a good value accommodation and is a popular B&B. Visitors to Dublin should reserve in advance.

OWNER Roma Gibbons OPEN All year ROOMS 1 double, 3 twin TERMS €24; reduction for children; single supplement (seasonal)

Moyne Guest House
17 Botanic Road, Dublin 9
Tel: 01 830 9337

Mrs Susan Forde has been in business for 24 years offering good value accommodation. Many of her visitors return; advance reservations are advised. Susan is interested in crafts. One of her tapestries hangs in the lounge, and her embroidered cushions reflect a Celtic design. The house is immaculate and the bedrooms have country diary bedspreads. Substantial breakfasts are served; guests help themselves to starters, followed by a traditional cooked breakfast. Vegetarians can be catered for if pre-arranged. Botanic House is across the road, the city centre bus stop is a two-minute walk, and the airport is 9 km. Plenty of establishments within walking distance serve evening meals.

OWNER Mrs Susan Forde OPEN All year ROOMS 2 double, 2 twin, 1 single, triple; 3 en suite. TERMS €20.50–23; reduction for children; single supplement €6.50–12.50 (seasonal)

Parknasilla
15 Iona Drive, Drumcondra, Dublin 9
Tel: 01 8378036

Teresa Ryan runs a clean and bright house, with easy reach of the city centre and the airport. The rooms are of a good size in this detached, large red brick Edwardian House. Families are welcome and baby sitting services are available. It is well maintained and spotlessly clean. A fresh cooked breakfast is well presented, and Teresa is happy to assist visitors in any way she can. This is good value accommodation, and a non-smoking house. If arriving by car, guests would be well advised to take the bus to the city centre.

OWNER Mrs Teresa Ryan OPEN January 1 – December 21 ROOMS 4 double/twin/family; 2 en suite. TERMS €24–29; child reduction; single supplement from €6.50

DUBLIN 15

Ashbrook House
River Road, Ashtown, Castleknock, Dublin 15
Tel: 01 838 5660 Fax: 01 838 5660

Out in peaceful countryside, Ashbrook is a quiet oasis, yet very close to Phoenix Park and the city centre. Given its proximity to urban life it comes as a delightful surprise. Imagine arriving at night by taxi to a city address, and waking up in the morning to birds singing, surrounded by fields and gardens, and not a building in sight! Ashbrook is a beautifully maintained Georgian house, on a more manageable smaller scale than some, decorated in bright welcoming colours and with comfortable furniture. The spacious bedrooms have telephones. The two sitting rooms have rounded ends, as does one of the bedrooms, and the dining room, where breakfast is served, easily seats twelve people. The grounds include a grass tennis court and walled garden. Ashbrook is popular with business people, and Eve Mitchell, who is a delightful hostess, runs a busy establishment. No pets and no smoking. Visa, Access, Mastercard accepted. Suitable for children. To reach

Ashbrook exit the N3 at the roundabout with the Halfway House Pub, cross the railway line, and turn on to River Road. Directions might be advisable.

OWNER Stan & Eve Mitchell OPEN All year except for Christmas ROOMS 4 double/twins; all en suite. TERMS €44.50; single supplement €19

DÚN LAOGHAIRE

Rosmeen House
13 Rosmeen Gardens, Dún Laoghaire, Co. Dublin
Tel: 01 2807613

This turn of the century, Spanish style villa is set in its own grounds in a quiet cul-de-sac, minutes from the ferry, bus and train terminals. The good size bedrooms are prettily decorated and have comfortable beds and hairdryers. There is one ground floor en suite room. Joan Murphy and her sister Maureen are friendly hosts, and serve a good breakfast in the dining room. There is also a well furnished, comfortable lounge with TV. No pets and no smoking. There is car parking in the street.

OWNER Joan M. Murphy OPEN 1 February – 1 December ROOMS 1 single, 3 double/twin, 2 en suite, 1 public bathroom. TERMS €31.50; single supplement €6.50; reductions for children

The Cumberland Lodge
54 York Road, Dún Laoghaire, Co. Dublin
Tel: 01 280 9665 Fax: 01 284 3227
Email: cumberlandlodge@tinet.ie

David and Mariea Jameson have done a fine job of putting back together this attractive Georgian house. They have chosen strong, rich colours, and have interesting pictures and furniture. The breakfast area is at one end of the comfortable drawing room, and a quiet back garden is also available for guests' use. The bedrooms have TVs, tea and coffee making facilities and telephones. A warm welcome, and delicious breakfast await the visitor here. It is just up the hill from the ferry terminal and a few minutes walk to the DART station. No pets, no smoking in bedrooms. All major credit cards accepted. Secure parking.

OWNER David & Mariea Jameson OPEN All year ROOMS 6 doubles, twins, families; all en suite. TERMS €38; single supplement €12.50

King Sitric

East Pier, Howth, Co. Dublin
Tel: 01-832 5235/832 6729 Fax: 01-839 2442
Email: info@kingsitric.ie
Website: www.kingsitric.com

At the extreme eastern end of Howth stands the King Sitric Restaurant, a gaily painted, modest building with nothing to obstruct 90 degree views from its windows to the harbour, the southern cliffs and out across the Irish sea. Originally the old Harbour Master's house, the MacManus' have owned King Sitric since 1971 and built up a reputation for a first class fish restaurant. Then just two years ago they virtually rebuilt the whole premises, creating 8 very comfortable bedrooms, all with telephones, hairdryers, TVs and tea and coffee making facilities. Each one has a sea view and they are named after lighthouses. The cleverly designed first floor restaurant ensures that every table can enjoy the view, and an atmospheric bar on the ground floor incorporates the cellar, which is stocked with a superb selection of wines, of which Aidan and Joan are justifiably proud. Apart from its proximity to the centre of Dublin and the airport, Howth is a delightful place to visit, with its fishing harbour, marina, cliff walks and golf courses. Major credit cards accepted.

OWNER Aidan & Joan MacManus OPEN All year except for Christmas & last 2 weeks January ROOMS 8 double/twins; all en suite. TERMS €57–95; single supplement €26 MEALS dinner €41, & a la carte. Lunch Monday–Friday

Druid Lodge

Killiney Hill Road, Killiney, Co. Dublin
Tel: 01 285 1632 Fax: 01 284 8504

Built in 1832, this delightful family home stands in an old fashioned garden with beautiful views over Killiney Bay. The main rooms have lovely carved pine door surrounds, painstakingly stripped by the owners, as was the staircase. The McClenaghans have lived here 20 years and brought up six chlidren. The two front bedrooms are enormous, with two or three beds apiece, and they have cleverly hidden, small en suite bathrooms which in no way detract from the original shape of the rooms. Smaller rooms on the ground floor do not have sea views, but are comfortable, and all rooms have TVs. Guests eat breakfast at one large table in the dining room, and there is a lovely, comfortable drawing room. No pets and no smoking. Killiney Hill Road is above the centre of Killiney and Druid Lodge is located between Druid's Chair Pub and Killiney Avenue. It is a 10 minute walk from the DART station, with trains running every 15 minutes into central Dublin. Visa and Mastercard accepted.

OWNER Ken & Cynthia McClenaghan OPEN All year except for Christmas ROOMS 2 double, 2 family; all en suite. TERMS €44.50–51; reductions for children

PORTMARNOCK

South Lodge
Portmarnock, Co. Dublin
Tel: 01 8461356 Fax: 01 8461366

This very attractive compact brick building stands just inside an impresssive gateway right next to the golf course, beyond which is the sea. It has been the family home of Pat and Colin Burton for the last thirty years, and just three years ago they started a bed & breakfast business. To offer the best accommodation possible they cleverly redisgned the house, creating a small wing for themselves and rebuilding the first floor - which now provides four charming bedrooms. They are spacious, furnished and decorated with simplicity, and have beamed pitched, attic like ceilings. Some of the rooms overlook the golf course, and three are en suite. They have TVs, hairdryers, tea and coffee, books and packs of cards. There is a sitting area in the breakfast room which has views of the golf course beyond the small attractive garden, and a nice place to enjoy fine weather is on the patio in front of the house. South Lodge, built in 1873, was a gate lodge to the James family home, of distiller fame, now the Portmarnock Links Hotel,. This is a fabulous location for the golf lover, has great access to Dublin (bus stop just outside) and the airport, and the lovely sandy beach of Portmarnock is two minutes away. No credit cards, smoking or pets.

OWNER Pat & Colin Burton OPEN All year except for Christmas ROOMS 1 double/twins; 3 en suite. TERMS €34.50; single supplement €23

Newtown House
St Margaret's, Co. Dublin
Tel: 01 834 1081

This delightful old Georgian farmhouse is surrounded by a golf course, driving range and various other enterprises. In spite of all the activity, the house is completely private and has a peaceful outlook overlooking the golf course. It is beautifully furnished in a very traditional manor, and guests have use of a drawing room and TV sitting room. Only minutes from Dublin Airport, Newtown House makes a great starting off or ending point for visitors. Sheila Wilson-Wright only takes guests who have pre-booked. The gates from the road to the golf course and house are closed at midnight. No pets.

OWNER Mrs. Sheila Wilson-Wright OPEN All year except for Christmas ROOMS 2 twins, 2 public bathrooms (one with shower, one with bath). TERMS €51; single supplement €6.50

COUNTIES LOUTH AND MEATH

The Boyne Valley cuts right through the centre of this area – one of the most historic and evocative places in Irish history, and for thousands of years the centre of political power. Innumerable remains from every century lie scattered across this fertile, green valley.

Dominating the town of Trim are the ruins of King John's Castle, the largest Anglo-Norman castle in Ireland, dating from 1172. The Duke of Wellington's family came from here, as did the family of Bernardo O'Higgins, a prominent figure in Chilean history.

Apart from a few earthworks, there is not much left to see at the Hill of Tara, the seat of Ireland's kings since prehistoric times. Imagination is needed to conjure up the sight of great buildings and a mass of warriors and nobles who inhabited this place in days gone by.

At the attractive village of Slane, the old castle overlooks the river, and a little farther along the valley is Brugh na Boinne (the Palace of the Boyne), an enormous cemetery with graves dating back to the Neolithic era, the main sites of which are at Newgrange, Knowth and Dowth.

The pretty village of Kells, which is in the Blackwater Valley, was the site of the settlement of the Columban monks, who moved here from Iona in 807. St Columba's house still stands, and in the church is a copy of the famous Book of Kells. Monasterboice and Mellifont are the sites of the two ancient ecclesiastical centres, and at Drogheda, in the Church of St Peter, one can see the preserved head of St Oliver Plunkett, former Archbishop of Armagh.

The Cooley Peninsula is an attractive and unspoilt area with lovely views, and the old town of Carlingford has lots of historical sites, including King John's Castle.

COUNTY LOUTH

ARDEE

Red House
Ardee, Co. Louth
Tel: 041 6853523 Fax: 041 6853523
Email: redhouse@eircom.net
Website: homepage.eircom.net/-redhouse

This attractive, red brick Georgian house, just off the main Dundalk to Ardee road, is approached through park-like grounds. It was once the home of the politician Chichester Fortescue (Lord Carlingford) and the Countess Waldegrave, a famous hostess. It is relaxed, informal place with very friendly owners and a welcoming atmosphere. The house is grand and elegant, including a large entrance hall, formal dining room, comfortable drawing room and enormous bedrooms. Outside, one end of the stable courtyard has been turned into a swimming pool and sauna, and beyond is a hard tennis court that is floodlit at night. Guests have access to Slane Castle to fish for salmon and trout on the River Boyne, and racing, foxhunting, shooting and golf are all within easy access. Pets by arrangement. Smoking in the public rooms. American Express and Visa are accepted. Red House is 1 km north of Ardee on the N52.

OWNER Linda Connolly OPEN January 30 – December 15
ROOMS 1 double, 2 twin/double, 1 en suite, 2 private bathrooms.
TERMS €60–70; single supplement €15; reductions for children
MEALS by arrangement

CARLINGFORD

Viewpoint
Carlingford, Co. Louth
Tel: 042 9373149 Fax: 042 9373149
Email: paulwoodsviewpoint@hotmail.com
Website: www.omeath.net/viewpoint.htm

Enjoying spectacular views of the town and harbour and across to the Mourne Mountains, Viewpoint is a modern house standing above the road on the edge of Carlingford. All the bedrooms are motel-style, with their own entrances and en suite shower rooms, and most have a view. They are comfortably furnished with modern fittings. The large breakfast room with separate tables takes full advantage of the view, and visitors are invited to use the owner's sitting room. No pets, no smoking in the dining room. Visa and Mastercard accepted. The house is signposted off the N1.

OWNER Paul & Maria Woods OPEN All year except for Christmas ROOMS 4 double, 2 twin, 2 family; all en suite. TERMS €29; single supplement €10; reductions for children

DROGHEDA

Glebe House
Dowth, nr. Drogheda, Co. Louth
Tel: 041 9836101 Fax: 041 9843469

This attractive, whitewashed, small country house is covered in wisteria, clematis and roses. Surrounded by a pretty garden, and with lovely views over the tennis court to distant hills, it is set in the heart of the Boyne valley, between Newgrange and Drogheda. Mrs. Addison is a delightful welcoming person, who apart from her B&B business, specialises in small functions and private dinner parties. The reception rooms are welcoming and warm, with fireplaces in both the large formal drawing room and the small, cosy study/sitting room and mauve carpets cover the entire ground floor. The bedrooms are pretty and comfortable. Cream teas are served to the public. Pets outside only and no smoking. For those who wish to improve their art skills, there are art workshops. Visa, Access and Mastercard accepted.

OWNER Elizabeth Addison OPEN March – November ROOMS 4 doubles and twins; 3 en suite, 1 private bathroom TERMS €44.50–51; reductions for children

Harbour Villa
Mornington Road, Drogheda, Co. Louth
Tel: 041 9837441

Harbour Villa is an attractive, vine-covered old country house on the banks of the River Boyne, just three kilometres south of town. Eileen Valla offers her guests a warm welcome. The gardens are most attractive, and there is a garden house containing a sun lounge where guests can relax. The bedrooms are small, clean and simply furnished, and the comfortable lounge has the original marble fireplace. Harbour Villa is close to the beach, and golf and the possibilities for horse riding are nearby. No pets, smoking permitted in the TV lounge.

OWNER Eileen Valla OPEN All year ROOMS 1 twin, 2 double, 1 single; 2 en suite, 1 public bathroom. TERMS €25.50–28; single supplement €6.50; reductions for children

Cooley Lodge
Mountbagnal, Riverstown, Dundalk, Co. Louth
Tel: 042 9376201

Cooley Lodge itself is the bed & breakfast range of buildings, one of a disparate collection of converted old stone farm buildings which also include a row of self catering cottages and the owner's house. The property lies at the foot of the Cooley Mountains in lovely countryside and is only a short distance to the medieval town of Carlingford, a mecca of good restaurants and pubs. The bed and breakfast building was originally a cow shed and has five bedrooms on the first floor and five underneath. They are all very spacious, individually decorated in various motifs, such as Edwardian, Victorian, etc. and are equipped with telephones, TVs and hairdryers, and many have lovely mountain views. There is a sitting area at one end and a conservatory at the other end, adjoining which is a 25 metre indoor heated swimming pool. Breakfast is served in the galleried dining room. No pets. Cooley Lodge can be found just of the R173 approximately 9 miles from Dundalk.

OWNER Geraldine Lynn OPEN 1 May – 31 October ROOMS 10 twins or doubles; all en suite TERMS €44.50–51; single supplement €12.50

COUNTY MEATH

Woodtown House
Athboy, Co. Meath
Tel: 046 35022 Fax: 046 35022
Email: woodtown@iol.ie
Website: www.iol.ie/~woodtown

Way out in the countryside at the end of a long no-through road is this delightfully restored Georgian house, surrounded by mature gardens. It has a friendly, family lived in atmosphere and the house is full of knick-knacks, particularly in the lower level's cosy vaulted breakfast room, and where the old bells of the house can still be seen. Woodtown is a beautifully proportioned building with a bow fronted dining room where evening meals are served. These need to be booked in advance, and guests should bring their own wine. Of the three bedrooms, the double is a smaller room and its private bathroom has the original decorated loo and old-fashioned bath tub, the remaining two bedrooms are extremely spacious, each en suite and having double and single beds, and one has two old sinks and a fireplace. There are five acres of grounds, including a traditional walled garden -

currently derelict, but ripe for restoration! Fishing can be organised. No smoking. All major credit cards accepted. Woodtown is five miles south west of Athboy – directions are advisable.

OWNER Anne & Colin Finnegan OPEN April – September ROOMS 1 double, 2 double/twin; 2 en suite, 1 private bathroom TERMS €32 MEALS dinner €19

DULEEK

Annesbrook
Duleek, Co. Meath
Tel: 041 982 3293 Fax: 041 982 3024

An impressive gate and a long wooded drive bring you to Annesbrook, an interesting house, the core of which is seventeenth century with additions of different periods. The pedimented portico of the house and the ballroom were added on to impress George IV when he came here in 1821, and the front entrance hall is beautifully proportioned with a lovely winding staircase. Another distinguished visitor was William Thackeray. However, the formal hospitality of those days has been replaced by a relaxed and welcoming family atmosphere. All of the bedrooms are spacious and comfortable, with folders detailing events of local interest and suggested walks and drives to local attractions. Each bedroom has tea- and coffee-making facilities and hairdryers. The reception rooms have big log fires. Evening meals, which are available on some days, must be booked in advance. The ingredients feature home grown organic vegetables picked fresh daily from the walled garden. There is a wine licence. Smoking in the sitting room only. No pets. The house can be found seven kilometres north of Ashbourne.

OWNER Kate Sweetman OPEN Mid-April – end September ROOMS 5 double/twin/family, all en suite TERMS €38–51; single supplement €12.50; reductions for children; MEALS dinner €29

DUNSHAUGHLIN

The Old Workhouse
Dunshaughlin, Co. Meath
Tel: 01 8259251 Fax: 01 8259251
Email: comfort@a-vip.com
Website: travel.to/oldworkhouse

As its name implies, this was a workhouse first used in 1841, and later used as various factories. It is an imposing building which over the last ten years has been lovingly restored by the Colgans. It stands just off the main road, about one kilometre outside Dunshaughlin. There is still a wing to be renovated, and the derelict buildings to the rear of the house belong to the local authority. It is a very interesting building; it was used by the administrators of the workhouse, and the immense, lovely drawing room with a high beamed ceiling on the first floor was the board room. The house has been furnished with old pieces, some quite heavy and big, and there are five large, comfortable bedrooms, three on the ground floor, and one has a large four poster bed. Guests also have use of a small, cosy sitting room with TV. Meals are served at one table in the large entrance hall area. The bedrooms have TV on request, hairdryers, bathrobes, tea, coffee and mineral water. Proximity to the main road makes it somewhat noisy, alleviated by the new double glazed windows. Glebeland and Glebewood Gardens are nearby, there is an old famine graveyard at the back of the house up the hill, and Dublin is only 20 minutes away by car. No smoking. Pets are permitted. Visa and Mastercard accepted.

OWNER Niamh Colgan OPEN All year except for Christmas ROOMS 4 double, 1 twin; 3 en suite, 2 private bathrooms. TERMS €44.50–63.50; single supplement €12.50–19

KELLS

Lennoxbrook
Carnaross, Kells, Co. Meath
Tel: 046 45902 Fax: 046 45902
Email: lennoxbrook@unison.ie

Lennoxbrook is an old farmhouse standing just off the main road. The back part of the house is over 200 years old, and the surrounding farmland is let out. It's an old world family home with plain, but comfortable bedrooms and dinner is available if booked in advance. There is a croquet lawn and a pony for children, and there are also self catering facilities. Guests may use a laundry room. Pets outside only, and no smoking. Visa and Mastercard accepted. Lennoxbrook is three miles north of Kells on the N3

OWNER Pauline Mullan OPEN All year ROOMS 2 double, 1 twin/double, 1 single; 2 en suite, 1 public bathroom
TERMS €23–38; single supplement €9; reductions for children
MEALS dinner €20.50

Gainstown House
Navan, Co. Meath
Tel: 046 21448

This small country house dating from the early nineteenth century stands in peaceful lawned gardens surrounded by 80 hectares of farmland. The house is simply furnished and decorated, and the drawing room with open fireplace leads off the large entrance hall. Breakfast is served in the dining room. A patio at the rear of the house overlooks the garden. No pets and no smoking. Gainstown House is sign-posted in the N3 Navan to Dublin road at the Old Bridge Inn.

OWNER Mrs. Mary Reilly OPEN June 1 – September 1
ROOMS 2 family, 2 twin; 1 en suite, 2 public bathrooms.
TERMS €26.50; single supplement €6.50; reductions for children

Lios Na Greine
Athlumney, Navan, Co. Meath
Tel: 046 28092 Fax: 046 28092
Email: call@hotmail.com

Lios Na Greine, meaning "enclosure of the sun", is a modern house in a sunny location. It is set back off the road one and a half kilometres from the town centre on the Duleek to Ashbourne airport road. The house is immaculate and decorated with matching wallpapers, fabrics and cosy duvets. One room is on the ground floor and there is a comfortable TV lounge where tea is served in the evening. Breakfast is served in the bright and cheerful dining room, and evening meals are available by arrangement. The pleasant garden is a nice spot to sit after exploring Newgrange and the Boyne Valley, which are within easy reach. No smoking. Pets are accepted in the car or garage.

OWNER Mary Callanan OPEN All year ROOMS 4 double, twin, family; 3 en suite, 1 public bathroom TERMS €25.50; single supplement; €9 reductions for children; MEALS dinner €19

Mountainstown
Castletown, Kilpatrick, Navan, Co. Meath
Tel: 046 54154 or 54195 Fax: 046 54154

Standing in 750 acres of farmland Mountainstown is an impressive Queen Anne house with a Georgian wing, which has been in the Pollock family since 1730. It has enormous reception rooms, which lead from one into another - the library or small dining room, immense drawing room, massive dining room and the billiard room, which can be used by children. Breakfast is served in the kitchen, which has doors out to the terrace, a pleasant place to be on sunny days. In the basement the old shoot room with vaulted ceiling has been turned into a playroom, and the old bells of the house line the corridor. The massive master bedroom has a four poster bed, fireplace and enormous old fashioned bath tub. John and Diana's son lives to one side of the impressive stable block and takes care of the farm. The acreage includes parkland and woodlands, and there are horses, donkeys, peacocks, geese and poultry. Dinner is served if booked in advance, and Mountainstown is a popular place for wedding receptions and parties. Small dogs allowed.

OWNER John & Diana Pollock OPEN All year except for Christmas ROOMS 6 doubles or twins; 3 en suite, 1 public bathroom reductions for children. TERMS €40.50–89; single supplement from €12.50

OLDCASTLE

Loughcrew House
Oldcastle, Co. Meath
Tel: 049 41356 Fax: 049 41722
Email: snaper@indigo.ie

The Loughcrew estate has been in the Naper family for over 400 years, and Charles and Emily's home is a conversion of what used to be an elegant conservatory designed by Cockrell. It stands next to part of the ruins of the old house, and the estate comprises a lake, tennis court, the family church of St Oliver Plunkett and Loughcrew Gardens, which are open to the public. Emily Naper is an amazing woman, a friendly person with boundless energy, she is one of Ireland's leading gilders, and has a studio adjoining the house where she restores gilt furniture and frames and designs hand finished decorative furniture. She also runs a school for gilding and specialist paint finishes and courses in botanical watercolour painting and ceramic sculpture. This is all in addition to running the house, garden and tending to the needs of her children. Charles is the cook, producing fine meals from local produce and home grown herbs. Loughcrew is a lived in family home, an eccentric and unusual place, with whimsical décor, some frescoes and interesting pieces. Guests have use of a long room for breakfast combined with a sitting room, as well as a small cosy sitting room with wood burning stove. One twin bedroom is on the ground floor with private bathroom, and the upstairs double room also has a private bathroom. Visitors here enjoy the atmosphere and countryside, No smoking in bedrooms. Pets outside only. Visa accepted.

OWNER Charles & Emily Naper OPEN All year except for
Christmas ROOMS 1 double, 1 twin; both with private bathrooms.
TERMS €44.50; single supplement €12.50 MEALS dinner

Crannmór

Dunderry Road, Trim, Co. Meath
Tel: 046 31635 Fax: 046 38087
Email: cranmor@eircom.net
Website: www.crannmor.com

This old country house is in a peaceful setting surrounded by
pleasant gardens and 2.5 hectares of fields. The O'Regans took
over the house at the beginning of 2000 and have done a lot of
refurbishment. Three of the bright, cheerful guest rooms are on
the ground level in what was once the stable block, and one is
particularly suited for disabled guests. The fourth room is on the
first floor in the main part of the house. The breakfast/sitting
room is very charming with antique furniture and an open fire.
Anne O'Regan is a cheerful, capable woman, who has been in the
guest house business for many years, and Crannmór is a friendly
and comfortable place to stay. Historic Trim, which boasts the
largest Norman castle in Ireland is only 1 km away. One of Trim's
attractions is the annual Trim Fair, featuring "The Power and the
Glory" – a multimedia exhibition explaining the background of
Trim's medieval ruins. Pets in car only and no smoking.
Mastercard accepted. To reach Crannmor from Trim, leave Super
Valu on the right, take the next right, stay right at next junction
and the house is 400 yards on the right.

OWNER Marc & Anne O'Regan OPEN All year ROOMS
1 double, 1 twin, 2 family; all en suite. TERMS €25.50; single
supplement €7.50; reductions for children

COUNTY WICKLOW

Lying just to the south of Dublin, this is an area of hills and mountains, lakes and streams – a pleasant, peaceful place of escape after the bustle of the city.

From Dublin one comes first to Bray, a large seaside resort, and then to Enniskerry. Here one can visit the gardens of Powerscourt Estate. The house, which had been one of the most beautiful in Ireland, was destroyed in the 1950s, leaving only the shell still standing.

Glendalough is a beautiful, scenic place in the mountains, set between two small lakes near the ruins of St Kevin's Kitchen, the church and the cathedral founded by St Kevin in 520. Just beyond is the small twelfth-century priory of St Saviour. The county town, Wicklow, is on the coast, and farther south is Arklow, a popular resort and fishing centre.

At Blessington is Russborough House, a beautiful Palladian-style house, containing a marvellous art collection, and the Poulaphouca Reservoir, which has been formed by damming the River Liffey.

ARKLOW

Ballykilty House
Coolgreany, Arklow, Co. Wicklow
Tel: 0402 37111 Fax: 0402 37272
Email: ballykiltyfarmhouse@eircom.net

This 200 year old house stands in a lovely garden with a tennis court in peaceful countryside. It is part of an 80 hectare dairy farm with 100 milking cows. Anne Nuzum is a friendly lady and the house has a warm and welcoming atmosphere. There are two cosy sitting rooms with open fires each side of the front door, and one has a TV. The dining room was the original kitchen and still has the old beams and cooking pots. The bedrooms have hairdryers, and there are no tea- and coffee-making facilities in the rooms, but tea is readily available on request. This is a good base for exploring Powerscourt and Mount Usher gardens, Avondale House and Forest Park, Russborough House, Castleruddery Transport Museum, and the Vale of Avoca. No pets. No smoking. Visa and Mastercard accepted. Ballykilty can be found on the road between Coolgreany and Arklow, five kilometres from Arklow.

OWNER Mrs. Anne Nuzum OPEN 1 March – 1 November
ROOMS 2 doubles, 2 twins, 1 triple; all en suite. TERMS €31.50;
single supplement €10; reductions for children

Fairy Lawn
Wexford Road, Arklow, Co. Wicklow
Tel: 0402 32790

This brick and plaster house, set back off the main road, is located one kilometre from Arklow on the N11 road to Gorey. The comfortable bedrooms are regularly redecorated and are simply furnished. There's a comfortable guest lounge with a TV, and breakfast only is served in the dining room. Mr. Kelly is a keen gardener, maintaining the well landscaped gardens and colourful window boxes. No pets. No smoking. Visa, Mastercard and Eurocard accepted.

OWNER Rita Kelly OPEN All year except for Christmas ROOMS 4 double/twin/family; 3 en suite, 1 public bathroom. TERMS €28; single supplement €9; reductions for children

Moneylands Farm
Arklow, Co. Wicklow
Tel: 0402 32259 Fax: 0402 32438
Email: mland@eircom.net

This neat, small, whitewashed farmhouse is located down a quiet country lane on the outskirts of Arklow and has pleasant views. The ground floor family room has a small sitting area and French doors that open on to the garden. All bedrooms have hairdryers, and tea and coffee facilities are on hand in the conservatory. The comfortable lounge leads through to the large conservatory, where breakfast is served. Mr. And Mrs. Byrne, who are a kindly couple, have made many additions to the farm. They include an indoor heated swimming pool, gym, sauna and tennis court, which are available both to bed & breakfast guests, as well as to those staying in the self catering courtyard of renovated stone built coach houses. Pets in car only, smoking is permitted in the TV lounge. Visa, Mastercard and American Express accepted. Moneylands Farm is one kilometre south of Arklow off the N11.

OWNER Michael & Lillie Byrne OPEN February 1 – November 30 ROOMS 2 double, 1 twin, 1 family; 3 en suite, 1 private bathroom TERMS €38; single supplement €12.50; reductions for children

Plattenstown House

Coolgreaney Road, Arklow, Co. Wicklow
Tel: 0402 37822 Fax: 0402 37822

This old farmhouse was built in 1853 for Lady Jane O'Grady. It is set in 20 hectares of farmland, supporting cows and goats, and has a lovely, peaceful, mature front garden. The attractive, white-washed farm buildings are at the back of the house. The comfortable drawing room is for non-smokers, while smokers can use the small sitting room with fireplace and TV. Additionally, there is a conservatory and bicycles for use. There are beaches 5–7 kilometres away and pleasant forest walks. No pets. Visa, Mastercard, Eurocard and Access accepted. Plattenstown House is five kilometres from Arklow on the Coolgreaney road.

OWNER Mrs. Margaret McDowell OPEN 1 March – 31 October ROOMS 3 double, 1 twin; all en suite. TERMS €26.50–34.50; single supplement €7.50; reductions for children MEALS dinner €23

AVOCA

Keppel's Farmhouse

Ballanagh, Avoca, Co. Wicklow
Tel: 0402 35168 Fax: 0402 30950
Email: keppelsfarmhouse@eircom.net

Built around 1880, Keppel's Farmhouse is set in quiet country-side with beautiful views over the Vale of Avoca. A recently added wing contains a large dining room, where breakfast including home made bread and preserves is served, a lounge, and two first floor bedrooms. Not suitable for children under 10 years. The bedrooms are spacious, clean and bright and full of fresh country air; all have hairdryers, TV and tea- and coffee-making facilities. An ironing board and trouser press are available if needed. Guests are welcome to walk around the farm, watch the cows being milked and observe the famous Avoca handweavers nearby. A woodland path is now in use giving visitors the option

of walking to Avoca, a pleasant 20 minute stroll. Avoca was the setting for the BBC TV series *Ballykissangel*. No smoking. No pets. Visa, Mastercard, Eurocard and Access accepted. To reach Keppel's turn right in front of 'Fitzgerald's Bar' having crossed the bridge into the village. Follow the road uphill for two kilometres where there is a sign.

OWNER Charles & Joy Keppel OPEN 1 April – 31 October ROOMS 2 twin, 2 double, 1 triple; all en suite. TERMS €28.50; single supplement €19

DUNLAVIN

Rathsallagh House
Dunlavin, Co. Wicklow
Tel: 045 403112 Fax: 045 403343
Email: info@rathsallagh.com
Website: www.rathsallagh.com

Set in 214 hectares of beautiful, mature parkland, the house is reached up a majestic, long, sweeping driveway across the Rathsallagh Championship Golf Course which, were it not for the odd sign to stop and watch for golfers, one would hardly be aware of. The original house was built in the early 1700s and was burnt down in the rebellion of 1798. Not being able to afford to rebuild the house, the family moved into the Queen Anne stables, which now form Rathsallagh House. Its long rooms and comparatively lower ceilings give it a relaxed, country house feel, in comparison to the more formal, high ceilinged ornate Georgian houses. It is built around a courtyard, the bedrooms arranged off one side of the long narrow corridors. Not suitable for children. Some rooms are very spacious with lovely parkland outlooks and are comfortably and unfussily furnished. They have every amenity including hairdryer, iron and ironing board, telephone, TV, DVD computer connection, and tea- and coffee-making facilities. The food at Rathsallagh is an experience - beautifully presented dishes are served in the light panelled dining room, and there is an extensive buffet at breakfast time and excellent menus in the evening using organically produced food, fresh fish and game when in season. There are any number of activities within the estate for guests to enjoy, including golf, tennis, croquet, snooker, swimming in the indoor pool, sauna and massage. Arrangements can be made for riding, shooting, deer stalking and archery. Major credit cards accepted. Pets can be accommodated in the stables, smoking permitted in one dining room, the bar and drawing rooms. Rathsallagh is sign-posted in Dunlavin village.

OWNER O'Flynn family OPEN All year except for Christmas & 2 weeks mid-January ROOMS 29 doubles & twins; all en suite. TERMS €70–134; single supplement €38–63.50 MEALS dinner from €44.50, bar lunches

Tynte House

Dunlavin, Co. Wicklow
Tel: 045 401561 Fax: 045 401586
Email: info@tyntehouse.com
Website: www.iol.ie/-jclawler

Built in the early 1800s, Tynte House is a tall, whitewashed building standing right in the middle of town. In its later days it was a
pub until 1930. John Lawler's father bought the house and there
was still a lot of work to be done on it when John and Caroline
took it over. It has been furnished and decorated appealingly in
keeping with its style and age. The bedrooms, some of which are
on the second floor, have telephones, TV, hairdryers and tea- and
coffee-making facilities, and they are unfussily furnished and decorated. There is a cosy snug room, and the dining room is in two
different areas - separate tables in a darker, inner room, and one
big table in a large, bright room with a sitting area at one end.
There is also a games room. Caroline is friendly and welcoming,
and also offers eight self catering mews cottages in the courtyard, which were originally stables and lofts. There is a hard
tennis court, a children's playground and golf courses and riding
nearby. Pets by arrangement, smoking permitted in the snug
room. Mastercard, Visa and American Express accepted.

OWNER Mrs. Caroline Lawler OPEN All year except for
Christmas ROOMS 6 twin or double, 2 family; all en suite.
TERMS €25.50; single supplement €9; reductions for children
MEALS packed lunch €5.50, dinner €18

ENNISKERRY

Ferndale

Enniskerry, Co. Wicklow
Tel: 01 2863518 Fax: 01 2863518
Email: ferndale@tinet.ie

This attractive, 160 year old house stands right in the centre of
Enniskerry and has been in Noel Corcoran's family for a good
part of its life. He and his wife, Josie, took it over a few years ago
and did up the whole house, almost to the extent of rebuilding
it. There is a relaxing drawing room, and elegant bedrooms with
brass and old iron beds, all of which have TV, hairdryers and tea-
and coffee-making facilities. The dining room, with one large table
covered with a white linen tablecloth, is in the basement and
leads into the conservatory, which in turn has doors out to the
pleasant terraced rear garden with a gazebo. Beyond is the car
park. Pets outside only. Smoking is permitted in the
conservatory. Dublin is only 12 miles away, served by a regular
bus service, and Ferndale is close to Powerscourt.

OWNER Noel & Josie Corcoran OPEN 1 April – 31 October
ROOMS 1 twin, 1 family, 2 doubles; all en suite.
TERMS €25.50–35

GLENDALOUGH

Carmel's Bed & Breakfast
Annamoe, Glendalough, Co. Wicklow
Tel: 0404 45297
Email: carmelsbandb@eircom.net

The house was built by the Hawkins in 1970, and has been
added on to a few times, most recently to enlarge the
lounge/dining area and bedrooms. Carmel's is a warm and
welcoming house, set back off the main road in half a hectare of
immaculately kept garden, where everyone is treated as a family
friend and plied with cups of tea or coffee on arrival. All the bedrooms are on the ground floor, have hairdryers, and two of the
bedrooms have two toilets. Mr. And Mrs. Hawkins are local
people, willing to assist with sightseeing and local events. The
Glendalough Fun Park is close by, and hiking and walking can also
be enjoyed. No pets. No smoking. Carmel's is on the R755 from
Glendalough to Dublin.

OWNER Carmel Hawkins OPEN March – November ROOMS 4
double, twin, family; all en suite. TERMS €25.50; single supplement
€9; reductions for children

GLENEALY

Ballyknocken House
Ashford, Glenealy, Co. Wicklow
Tel: 0404 44627 Fax: 0404 44696
Email: cfulvio@ballyknocken.com
Website: www.ballyknocken.com

Ballyknocken House, built in the 1850s, is set in a pretty wooded
valley below Carrick Mountain. The Byrne family acquired the
house in the 1940s and today Catherine Byrne Fulvio is the third
generation of the family to own Ballyknocken. She and her Italian
husband, Claudio, have carried out renovation work, including
transforming the old kitchen with its original inglenook fireplace
into an additional dining room, and decorating and finishing the
bedrooms in keeping with the period of the house. The rooms
are fresh and bright, and some have brass beds, and the
bathrooms claw foot baths. However, the main feature of
Ballyknocken is the warmth of an unhurried welcome and its
casual informality. Catherine exudes an infectious special warmth
and enthusiasm and makes her guests feel immediately at home.

She and Claudio between them are experts in food and wine, and those staying enjoy wonderful culinary experiences at dinner and breakfast. Guests are welcome to use the tennis court and wander around the gardens and the adjoining forest. Mastercard and Visa accepted. No pets. No smoking. To find Ballyknocken from the N11 in Ashford turn right (from the Dublin direction) after the Texaco station and continue for three miles. The house is on the right.

OWNER Catherine Fulvio OPEN 15 March – 30 November ROOMS 1 triple, 2 double, 4 twin; all en suite. TERMS €44.50; single supplement €24; reductions for children MEALS dinner €24

KILTEGAN

Barraderry House
Kiltegan, Co. Wicklow
Tel: 0508 73209 Fax: 0508 73209
Email: jo.hobson@oceanfree.net
Website: www.barraderrycountryhouse.com

On the western edge of the Wicklow Mountains, Barraderry is an attractive Georgian house, surrounded by its own farmland with lovely mountain views, and is set in a peaceful location. It has been the Hobson family home since 1950 and was farmed by John until recently Now, one of their daughter's has a few sheep and horses, and the rest of the land is leased. With the children gone, Olive started a b&b business just five years ago, and offers a warm and friendly welcome. The four large bedrooms are comfortable and have TV, hairdryers and tea- and coffee-making facilities. Guests have use of a sizeable drawing room, with breakfast served in the dining room. A feature of the grounds is an unusual 250 year old twin grafted beech tree. Barraderry is approached up a long driveway through a park-like setting off the Baltinglass to Kiltegan road. Golf and racing are well catered for, with 6 golf courses within 30 minutes, and for the race horse lover Punchestown, Naas and The Curragh racecourses are nearby. No smoking and no pets. Children welcome

OWNER Olive & John Hobson OPEN Mid-January – mid-December ROOMS 1 twin, 1 single, 1 double, 1 double/twin; all en suite. TERMS €31.50; single supplement €6.50 reductions for children

Humewood Castle

Kiltegan, Co. Wicklow
Tel: 0508 73215 Fax: 0508 73382 Email: humewood@iol.ie
Website: www.humewood.com

This imposing, magic-like castle was the last of its kind to be built in Ireland. Dating from the 1860s it is a masterpiece of Victorian architecture and is said to be the "finest and most important 19th century castellated mansion in Ireland". Right on the edge of the village of Kiltegan, it is approached up a long avenue. Its 500 acre walled estate, which includes two small lakes, is considered one of the best duck shoots in Ireland. Additional acreage on nearby properties offer pheasant shooting as well. The interior is majestic and palatial with enormous rooms and painted, beamed ceilings. The public rooms include a ballroom, dining room, drawing room and cosy sitting room attached to the bar. Humewood is a luxurious family home and can be booked for individuals on a nightly basis, and also caters for conferences and corporate entertainment. Each bedroom is a different shape and size and decorated and furnished in a unique style. The castle tower, reached by a narrow winding staircase, contains one of the honeymoon suites. The bathroom on the lower level is the same size as the bedroom above, and with windows all around affords a 360 degree view of farmlands and the Wicklow Mountains. A wealth of activities can be arranged for the visitor, including clay pigeon shooting, horse riding, fishing, deer stalking, polo, golf, hunting, hill walking, falconry and tennis. No smoking in bedrooms. Major credit cards accepted. Humewood Castle offers a unique experience – enjoy a night being treated like royalty!

OPEN All year ROOMS 14 doubles/twins; all en suite. TERMS €158–285 (depending on room and time of year)

RATHNEW

Hunter's Hotel

Newrath Bridge, Rathnew, Co. Wicklow
Tel: 0404 40106 Fax: 0404 40338
Email: reception@hunters.ie
Website: www.hunters.ie

This attractive, long, low building, covered with climbing plants, was originally an old coaching inn. Built in 1720, it stands on what used to be the main road, though now it is one kilometre off the new Dublin road, five kilometres outside Wicklow. Owned and run by the Gelletlie family, it has been in the same ownership since 1840. It is comfortable and old-fashioned, combining a lot of old world charm with modern comforts. Several rooms overlook the beautiful, colourful garden, and others on the ground floor are suitable for disabled guests. Tables and chairs are dotted around the garden, which lies along the banks of the River Vartry, a delightful place for afternoon tea or a pre-lunch or dinner drink. The garden room is available for small conferences or private parties. Smoking in public lounges only. All major credit cards accepted. Mount Usher Gardens are nearby.

OWNER The Gelletlie family OPEN All year except for Christmas ROOMS 16 doubles and twins; all en suite. TERMS €82.50–101.50 MEALS lunch €21, dinner €38, tea €5.50

Tinakilly Country House
Rathnew, Co. Wicklow
Tel: 0404 69274 Fax: 0404 67806
Email: wpower@tinakilly.ie
Website: www.tinakilly.ie

Built in 1883, Tinakilly, meaning "house of the wood", was con-structed for Captain Robert Halpin, who as Commander of 'The Great Eastern' , was responsible for laying most of the world's transoceanic telegraph cables. A fine print of 'The Great Eastern' hangs in the house, together with a collection of sea faring pictures in ornate frames. The British Government footed the considerable bill for the mansion's construction, and the best architects, materials and craftsmen were used in the creation of this splendid Victorian building. William and Bee Power acquired the house in 1982, adding more wings to it in 1991 and 1997, and today Tinakilly belongs to their son and daughter-in-law, Raymond and Josephine, who continue the tradition of maintain-ing the atmospheric Victorian character of the building, and the high standard of food and service. The house is surrounded by gardens and parkland and has magnificent views over the Irish sea. There is a tennis court, croquet lawn and heliport, and near-by are excellent golf courses, as well as riding and walking in the Wicklow Mountains. All major credit cards accepted. The entrance to Tinakilly is on the R750 on the Wicklow side of Rathnew.

OWNER Raymond & Josephine Power OPEN All year ROOMS 52 doubles, twins, junior suites, 5 suites; all en suite. TERMS €94–132; single supplement €61 MEALS dinner €49.50

Saraville
Redcross, Co. Wicklow
Tel: 0404 41745 Fax: 0404 41745

Right in the middle of the little village of Redcross, Saraville is a small, modernised house with some farm buildings at the back. The Flemings, a young couple with two children, farm in a small way and keep horses. The house is immaculately clean, the cooking fresh and wholesome, with freshly squeezed orange juice for breakfast and home-made food using local produce available by request for dinner and lunch. The bedrooms have TV and there is a living room with TV. Pets outside only, and no smoking in the bedrooms. Children are very welcome, the hostess is charming, and the atmosphere is friendly and relaxing.

OWNER Henry & Sarah Fleming OPEN March 17 – September 30 ROOMS 3 double, 1 twin; 2 en suite, 1 public bathroom. TERMS €23; single supplement €5; reductions for children MEALS dinner €18, packed lunch, light tea

Park Lodge
Clonegal, Shillelagh, Co. Wicklow
Tel: 055 29140

This charming, whitewashed Georgian farmhouse is in a peaceful, rural setting enjoying lovely views of the Wicklow Mountains. It is surrounded by its 200 acre mixed farm, and sheep, geese and guinea fowl roam close to the house. Guests here enjoy genuine Irish farmhouse hospitality with home baking, fresh farm produce, and a cheerful, friendly atmosphere. The house offers old fashioned comfort with large rooms and pretty, quilted bedcovers. Local amenities include horse riding, fishing, golf and walking. Park Lodge stands just above the very minor road from Shillelagh to Clonegal. Pets outside only. No smoking. Major credit cards accepted.

OWNER Mrs. Bridie Osborne OPEN Easter – end October ROOMS 4 double or twin, 3 en suite TERMS €31.50; single supplement €6.50

Lissadell House

Ashtown Lane, Wicklow, Co. Wicklow
Tel: 0404 67458
Email: lissadellhse@eircom.net

Built in the Georgian style, Lissadell is a modern house surrounded by its own grounds on the outskirts of Wicklow, and is part of a mixed farm. The Klaues, who built the house themselves, are a most friendly couple, and the house has a welcoming, warm atmosphere. The rooms are plainly decorated and furnished, and there is a pleasant sitting room and dining room where home cooked meals are served. Both rooms have French windows that open onto the lawn and garden. Pets outside only. No smoking. To reach Lissadell House turn off the N11 Wicklow to Wexford road at the Beehive Pub on to the R751. There is a sign at the first turning to the left.

OWNER Patricia Klaue OPEN March 1 – November 1 ROOMS 3 double or twin, 1 famil; 2 en suite, 2 public bathrooms. TERMS €25.50–28.50; single supplement €10; reductions for children MEALS dinner €20.50

Silver Sands

Dunbur Road, Wicklow, Co. Wicklow
Tel: 0404 68243
Email: lyladoyle@eircom.net

This modern, friendly bungalow is on the coast road just outside the town centre. It has a reputation for its warm welcome and has lovely sea views. The bedrooms are on the small side, immaculately clean and simply furnished. They have hairdryers and tea- and coffee-making facilities, and three are on the ground floor. Guests share the family lounge and breakfast is served in the bright dining room overlooking the sea. Mr. & Mrs. Doyle are a down to earth, friendly couple, always willing to help plan outings to local events and places of interest. Pets outside. Smoking permitted in the lounge.

OWNER Mrs. Lyla Doyle OPEN All year except for Christmas ROOMS 3 triple, 1 double, 1 twin; 4 en suite, 2 public bathrooms. TERMS €29; single supplement; reductions for children

COUNTY CORK

Cork, Ireland's largest county, has a spectacular coastline alternating between long, sandy beaches and wild, rugged cliffs, high, rocky mountains, corn-covered farmland and subtropical gardens.

Cork city is a bustling, cosmopolitan, friendly place founded by St Finbar in the sixth century on some dry land in the Great Marsh of Munster – Cork meaning "a marsh." The appearance of much of the city is nineteenth-century, with elegant, wide streets.

The famous Blarney stone-kissing – it gives you the gift of the gab – is at the castle, one of the largest and finest tower houses in Ireland.

Nineteenth-century Cóbh, with its Gothic cathedral, is Cork's harbour, some 24 km from the city. Beyond, westward along the coast, is Kinsale, an attractive old town, popular with yachtsmen, and packed with people enjoying its many restaurants and old buildings. There are marvellous cliffs at the Old Head of Kinsale and the remains of a fifteenth-century castle, plus a lovely sandy beach at Garretstown.

Youghal, which is a most attractive seaside town, has many interesting things to see, including the Clock Gate and St Mary's Collegiate Church, and is known for its association with the potato. Sir Walter Raleigh is said to have planted the first potato in his garden during the time he was mayor of the town. Nearby is Shanagarry with its pottery, where William Penn lived, and Ballycotton, a small fishing village.

The coastal scenery west of Skibbereen is particularly beautiful, and the view from Gabriel Mountain, which can be easily climbed, is spectacular. Garnish Island has a wonderful garden, which can be visited most days. Bantry House is a most interesting house with a superb view; and Castle Hyde, a Georgian house close to Fermoy and former home of Douglas Hyde, first President of the Irish Republic, is one of the most beautiful houses in Ireland. Macroom is set in glorious country-side, and the road across the pass of Keimaneigh and through the forest of Gougance Barra is particularly beautiful.

BALLYCOTTON

Spanish Point Seafood Restaurant
Ballycotton, Co. Cork
Tel: 021 4646177 Fax: 021 4646179

It is the food and the splendid location just above the sea that attract visitors to Spanish Point. It was originally a nuns' holiday home and was bought and renovated by the Tattans in 1992. The staff and atmosphere are friendly and there is excellent food prepared by a gourmet French chef and Mary Tattan, using fish caught from the Tattans own trawler. The restaurant extends into a larger, built-on conservatory overlooking the sea and the cosy sitting room has an open fire and small bar. All the comfortable bedrooms have some sort of a sea view as well as hairdryers, TV, telephone and tea- and coffee-making facilities. Spanish Point has its own private beach and sun deck, and there is also a tennis court for guests' use. It is located on the edge of Ballycotton, which is a great area for walking, swimming, bird watching or angling. Pets OK. Smoking is permitted in the lounges and one part of the dining room. Visa, Access and Mastercard accepted.

OWNER Mary Tattan OPEN February – December ROOMS 5 doubles; all en suite. TERMS €44.50; single supplement €6.50; reductions for children MEALS lunch €19, dinner €33.50 & a la carte

BALLYLICKEY

Ballylickey Manor House
Ballylickey, Co. Cork
Tel: 027 50071 Fax: 027 50124
Email: ballymh@eircom.net
Website: www.ballylickeymanorhouse.com

On the boundary of Cork and Kerry, amidst sheltered lawns, flower gardens and parkland and bordered by sea, river and mountains, stands Ballylickey House, commanding a magnificent view over Bantry Bay. Built some 300 years ago by Lord Kenmare as a shooting lodge, Ballylickey has been the home of the Graves family for over four generations. Robert Graves, the poet, was an uncle of the present owner. The house was burnt down in recent years, but was rebuilt incorporating the best of the old features with a new standard of comfort. This elegant residence is exquisitely decorated with many pieces of antique furniture. One of the main features of a stay at Ballylickey is the food, which is superbly prepared and presented, and served with great elegance in the attractive dining room. The bedrooms are luxurious and all have TV, telephone, hairdryer and trouser press.

The suites include a bedroom, sitting room and bathroom. Some of the rooms are in the manor house, and others are delightful garden cottages around the swimming pool and gardens. A restaurant by the pool is open for lunch. The four hectares of grounds include another Georgian home for self-catering and a croquet lawn. There are two golf courses nearby, miles of mountainous coastline, fishing, and two of the finest botanical gardens to visit. No pets. No smoking in the restaurants. Visa and American Express accepted. The house is between Bantry and Glengarriff on the N71.

OWNER Mr. & Mrs. Graves OPEN April – November ROOMS 7 suites, 7 doubles; all en suite. TERMS €101.50–153.50 MEALS lunch, a la carte dinner €45.50

BANDON

Glebe Country House
Glebe House
Ballinadee, Bandon, Co. Cork
Tel: 021 4778294 Fax: 021 4778456
Email: glebehse@indigo.ie
Website: indigo.ie/~glebehse

Set next to the church in the centre of Ballinadee, Glebe Country House is a very pretty Georgian rectory, which was carefully renovated by the Brackens and then redecorated after extensive damage during the 1997 Christmas storm. The bedrooms are spacious and attractively decorated and furnished and some have views of the river. All have hairdryers, telephones, irons and tea- and coffee-making facilities. Guests have the run of the house, which includes a large drawing room with television and open fire, and the dining room where good home cooked dinners are served featuring organically home grown salads and herbs. Guests should bring their own wine. Gill Good is a bright, cheerful person, and the atmosphere is friendly and informal. The attractive garden contains a croquet lawn and "fun" grass tennis court. Three self catering units are available. Ballinadee is a 15 minute drive from Kinsale. There are several nearby golf courses, and river fishing and sea angling can be arranged. Pets by arrangement. Smoking permitted in the lounge. Visa and Mastercard accepted.

OWNER Gill Good OPEN All year except for Christmas ROOMS 2 double, 2 family; all en suite. TERMS €44.50; single supplement €12.50; reductions for children MEALS dinner €25.50

St Anne's

Clonakilty Road, Bandon, Co. Cork
Tel: 023 44239 Fax: 023 44239
Email: stannesbandon@eircom.net

This attractive Georgian house was in need of work when Anne Buckley bought it. She did a great job renovating it, and now the house offers bright and attractively furnished bedrooms, equipped with TV and tea- and coffee-making facilities. Both the dining room, where breakfast only is served, and the sitting room have their original fireplaces, and guests can enjoy the pretty garden at the back of the property. Anne, who is an ex-school teacher, is very charming and attentive to the needs of her guests. No pets. No smoking in the bedrooms. St Anne's is one kilometre from Bandon on the N71 to Clonakilty.

OWNER Anne Buckley OPEN All year except for Christmas ROOMS 2 doubles, 2 family, 1 twin, 1 single; all en suite. TERMS €27; single supplement €6.50; reductions for children

BANTRY

Bantry House

Bantry, Co. Cork
Tel: 027 50047 Fax: 027 50795
Website: www.hidden-ireland.com/bantry

Bantry House, overlooking Bantry Bay, is one of the finest stately mansions in Ireland. Purchased by the White family in 1739, it is furnished with the most wonderful collection of pictures, furniture and works of art. The White family were also responsible for laying out the formal gardens. Both the east and west wings of Bantry House provide newly refurbished en suite accommodation, all with telephones, hairdryers and tea- and coffee-making facilities. Residents have use of a sitting room, bar, library and a balcony TV room overlooking the Italian garden with its fountain, parterres and "stairway to the sky". There is a wine licence, and guests are welcome to help themselves to drinks from the bar. Bantry House is open to the public and overnight guests are admitted at no extra charge. There is also a tennis court, tea room and craft shop on the premises. Evening meals are sometimes available, but must be booked by noon. No pets. Smoking permitted in the bar and lounge. Visa, Mastercard and American Express accepted.

OWNER Egerton Shelswell-White OPEN March 1 – October 31 ROOMS 5 double, 2 twin, 1 family; all en suite. TERMS €108–120.50; single supplement €12.50 MEALS dinner €31.50

Dunauley
Seskin, Bantry, Co. Cork
Tel: 027 50290 Fax: 027 50290
Email: rosemarymcauley@eircom.net
Website: www.dunauley.com

Dunauley stands in a spectacular position with magnificent views of Bantry Bay and the Caha Mountains. It is located above the town of Bantry in its own garden. Rosemary McAuley is a warm and welcoming host and serves a wonderful breakfast, including freshly squeezed orange juice and drop scones, in the spacious lounge-cum-dining room, which takes full advantage of the view. Three of the bedrooms are on the ground floor, and they are furnished simply and comfortably and have hairdryers and tea and coffee making facilities. There is also a self catering unit available. Dunauley is an ideal base for hill walking, cycling and exploring the gardens and west Cork bays. No pets. No smoking. Upon arriving in Bantry, follow signs for the hospital until you see Dunauley signposted

OWNER Rosemary McAuley OPEN May 1 – September 30 ROOMS 3 double, 2 twin; all en suite. TERMS €31.50–51; single supplement €6.50; reductions for children

Grove House
Ahakista, Bantry, Co. Cork
Tel: 027 67060

This 250 year old whitewashed stone farmhouse is set amidst beautiful scenery on the Sheep's Head Peninsula. It is an idyllic setting, perfect for nature lovers, with beautiful walks, bird-watching and a private beach for swimming or boating (a boat is provided); with advance notice, bicycle hire can also be arranged. There is a huge old log fireplace, and the dining room has been extended to include a conservatory with a stone floor that also enjoys the lovely view. The bedrooms are bright and simply furnished. Down to earth Mary O'Mahoney is a good cook, using home grown vegetables from the garden, and when the fishing is good, fresh seafood. Light meals, as well as evening meals, can be provided by arrangement. Honey fresh from the hive, soda scones and home baked breads are all on the menu here. Pets outside only. No smoking in bedrooms. Grove House is signposted in Durrus, 8 kilometres away.

OWNER Mary O'Mahoney OPEN May 1 – October 1 ROOMS 2 double, 2 family; 3 en suite. TERMS €25.50; single supplement €8.50; reductions for children MEALS dinner by arrangement

Hillcrest House
Ahakista, Bantry, Co. Cork
Tel: 027 67045 Fax:
Email: agneshegarty@oceanfree.net

Hillcrest is an attractive, old stone dairy farm that was renovated a few years ago, and stands in a lovely position on top of a hill overlooking Dunmanus Bay on the 'Sheeps Head' peninsula. An extension was built onto the house, linking it with the old barn which now houses the games room, where guests can play table tennis and darts. There are flagstone floors, peat fires and simply furnished and decorated bedrooms, which have hairdryers and tea- and coffee-making facilities. Fresh farm produce is used for evening meals and breakfast, as is home baking. Hillcrest is a five minute walk to a sandy beach ; there is good sea fishing and mountain walking behind the house, and the Sheep's Head Way walking path runs by the property. Pets outside or in car only. Smoking allowed in games room. There are bicycles for hire. The house is sign-posted from Durrus.

OWNER Mrs. Agnes Hegarty OPEN April 1 – November 1 ROOMS 1 double, 1 twin, 2 famil; 3 en suite, 1 private bathroom. TERMS €23–25.50; single supplement €8.50; reductions for children MEALS dinner €19 high tea €15

The Mill
New Town, Glengarriff Road, Bantry, Co. Cork
Tel: 027 50278 Fax: 027 50278
Email: bbthemill@eircom.net

Tosca and Kees Kramer fell in love with Bantry while on an Irish holiday from their native Holland, so they stayed and made Ireland their home. The Mill is a chalet style house, set back from the road in colourful gardens. Most of the bedrooms are on the ground floor and have hairdryers and TV. Kees Kramer is not only a craftsman, making all the wardrobes, cabinets and dining room tables, but also an artist. A selection of his work can be found around the house. A conservatory in the front of the house furnished with cane pieces, is a warm, sunny spot for visitors to sit and relax. The Mill offers a laundry service and there are bicycles for hire. The house is on the main Bantry to Glengarriff road and the town centre is only a five minute walk away. There are plenty of excellent pubs and restaurants in the area, and close by are possibilities for golf, fishing and horseback riding. No smoking. No pets. Visa cards are accepted.

OWNER Tosca Kramer OPEN Easter – October ROOMS 3 doubles, 2 twins, 1 family; all en suite TERMS €31.50; single supplement €12.50; reductions for children

BLARNEY

Ashlee Lodge
Tower, Blarney, Co. Cork
Tel: 021 4385346 Fax: 021 4385726
Email: ashlee@iol.ie
Website: www.welcome.to/ashleelodge

Ashlee Lodge is a modern, whitewashed bungalow with a porticoed front porch standing in the village of Tower, three kilometres from Blarney. John and Anne, who used to be in the hotel business, are constantly striving to offer their guests top quality accommodation, and they will be extending and refurbishing the rooms for the 2002 season. This will provide larger bedrooms. Ashlee Lodge is professionally run and immaculately clean, and has a pleasant open plan sitting/dining room with cathedral

ceilings and a fireplace. No smoking. No pets. Mastercard, Visa and American Express cards are accepted. The house can be found on the R617 Blarney to Killarney road.

OWNER Anne & John O'Leary OPEN All year except for Christmas ROOMS 3 doubles, 3 twins, 2 family; all en suite. TERMS €31.50–44.50; single supplement €12.50; reductions for children

Traveller's Joy
Tower, Blarney, Co. Cork
Tel: 021 4385541

Traveller's Joy is an unassuming little bungalow set in a pretty garden, but what makes it special is the friendly welcome from warm-hearted Gertie O'Shea and the atmosphere of a home away from home. The rooms are basic and spotlessly clean and there is a cosy guest lounge with TV, off of which is the small breakfast room where breakfasts "to last you the day" are served. A recent extension to the front of the house has enlarged the lounge area and one of the bedrooms. The O'Sheas are happy to offer advice on local sightseeing and where to find the best traditional entertainment. Pets outside only, and smoking is permitted in the lounge. Visa and Mastercard are accepted. Traveller's Joy is in the village of Tower, three kilometres from Blarney.

OWNER Sean & Gertie O'Shea OPEN 1 February – 20 December ROOMS 1 twin, 2 family; all en suite. TERMS €25.50–29; reductions for children

BUTLERSTOWN

Sea Court
Butlerstown, Co. Cork
Tel: 023 40151 & 023 40218 or 513 961 3537 (U.S.A.)
Fax: 513 721 5109 (U.S.A.)
Email: seacourt_inn@yahoo.com

Set in four hectares of wooded parkland, Sea Court is a handsome Georgian country house, built in 1760 by the Longfield family. David Elder, an American, acquired it on a visit to Ireland some 20 years ago - a daunting project as he spends the greater part of the year practising law in Kentucky, and the house was in serious need of repair. Restoration took place, gradually but meticulously, and eventually it was opened up to overnight visitors during the summer, and for self-catering parties at other times of the year. It has been furnished simply with antiques and has comfortable bedrooms, one of which used to be the Edwardian ballroom wing, and four have sea views. Breakfasts are quite a feast and include scones made from the owner's own recipe. Gourmet dinners served for a minimum of four are available if booked in advance - guests are welcome to bring their own wine. Pets in car, or outbuilding. No smoking in bedrooms. Sea Court lies between Courtmacsherry Bay and Dunworley

Bay and is within walking distance of the Coolim Cliffs, said to be the second highest in Ireland, Timoleague with its monastic ruins is 7 kilometres away, Kinsale and the Old Head Golf Course is a 40 minute drive and Clonakilty within easy reach. The house can be found a couple of hundred yards from the centre of Butlerstown.

OWNER David A. Elder OPEN June 8 – August 20 ROOMS 3 doubles, 2 twins, 1 family; 5 en suite, 1 private bath. TERMS €33; reductions for children MEALS dinner €30

CASTLELYONS

Ballyvolane House
Castlelyons, nr. Fermoy, Co. Cork
Tel: 025 36349 Fax: 025 36781
Email: ballyvol@iol.ie
Website: www.ballyvolanehouse.ie

In a magnificent parkland setting, Ballyvolane is a gracious, beautifully restored country house. It is surrounded by its own farmland, wooded grounds (quite spectacular in bluebell time), formal terraced gardens and three restored lakes stocked with trout. It was built in 1728 on the site of an older house and later altered to the Italianate style. Guests experience here a blend of elegance, informality and charming hosts. Jeremy and Merrie Green have done a superb job, gradually furnishing and restoring the house, which offers six very comfortable and spacious bedrooms, all with hairdryers and TV, and one of the bathrooms has a wonderful old bathtub, encased in wood and raised on two steps. The lovely pillared hall has a baby grand piano and plenty of comfortable chairs in front of the open fire. Beautifully

presented delicious food is served in the elegant dining room at the long dining room table, the open fire is lit both in the evening and at breakfast time. Guests serve themselves drinks from the honesty bar by the sitting room. Salmon fishing is available by arrangement on Ballyvolane's own stretch of the River

Blackwater; there is trout fishing in the lakes and a croquet lawn. Pets in car only. Smoking is allowed in the sitting room. Visa, Mastercard and American Express accepted. There are signs for the house on the N8 at River Bride and the R628 just before Rathcormac coming from Cork.

OWNER Jeremy & Merrie Green OPEN All year except for Christmas ROOMS 3 double, 3 twin; all en suite TERMS €63.50–71; single supplement €23; reductions for children MEALS dinner €35

CASTLETOWNSHEND

Bow Hall
Castletownshend, Co. Cork
Tel: 028 36114

Dating from the late seventeenth century, Bow Hall is right in the centre of the picturesque village of Castletownshend, whose one steep street leads to the harbour and sea. The Vickerys are a delightful retired couple from New York state who have lived here in excess of 20 years and have created a charming home. The bedrooms are light and spacious, with some American furniture. Breakfast is a grand affair, with home-made sausages and pancakes a particular treat. Good home cooked dinners are served in the dining room and the large drawing room-cum-library has floor to ceiling bookshelves at one end with a fireplace at the other; all kinds of ornaments and knick-knacks are found throughout the house. The slate-faced front of the building overlooks a very large and immaculately kept walled garden. No smoking. No pets.

OWNER Dick & Barbara Vickery OPEN All year except for Christmas ROOMS 3 double; 1 en suite. TERMS €44.50; single supplement €6.50 MEALS dinner €31.50

CLONAKILTY

An Garran Coir
Rathbarry, Clonakilty, Co. Cork
Tel: 023 48236 Fax: 023 48236
Email: angarrancoir@eircom.net

The original family farmhouse is close to the old farm buildings, some 200 metres up the lane, where guests like to wander and watch the cows being milked. An Garran Coir was built by the Calnans and then extended to accommodate bed & breakfast guests. It offers clean and comfortable rooms equipped with TV, tea- and coffee-making facilities and hairdryers, one of which has interconnecting rooms and a jacuzzi, a smartly decorated lounge with plush red chairs, and a dining room with both a piano and a "help yourself" tea and coffee area. Evening meals using fruit and herbs from the herb garden are available by arrangement, and you can pick your own free-range eggs for breakfast. Children are well catered for with their own play area, and they can go for rides with a leading rein on the farm pony. Adults can use the tennis court, play croquet or take a lovely walk to the award winning village of Rathbarry. Pets outside only. Smoking only in reception bar area. The farm is sign-posted off the Skibbereen to Clonakilty road.

OWNER Michael & Jo Calnan OPEN All year ROOMS 2 double, 2 twin, 1 family; all en suite. TERMS €28.50–31.50; single supplement €8.50; reductions for children MEALS dinner €19–25.50

Ard Na Greine
Ballinascarthy, Clonakilty, Co. Cork
Tel: 023 39104 Fax: 023 39397
Email: normawalsh1@eircom.net
Website: www.ardnagreine.com

Ard Na Greine is a working dairy farm set in pleasant farming countryside and enjoying lovely views. The atmosphere is friendly and informal, and guests immediately feel at home, many return-ing year after year. Norma Walsh is hospitable, warm-hearted and offers simple farmhouse comfort, and copious amounts of good home-cooked food. The bedrooms are comfortable and have hairdryers, and there is a cosy TV lounge and dining room with separate tables where both breakfast and dinner or lighter meals are served. There is no licence, but guests are welcome to provide their own wine. Ard Na Greine is well placed for Kinsale and visiting the attractive south and west Cork coastlines, and some guests like to watch the cows being milked. Pets can be accommodated in an outhouse. No smoking. Visa and Mastercard accepted. The farm is sign-posted on the N71 near Ballinascarthy, 8 miles from Bandon and 4 miles from Clonakilty.

OWNER Norma Walsh OPEN All year ROOMS 6 doubles/twins; 5 en suite, 1 private bathroom. TERMS €31.50; single supplement; reduction for children MEALS dinner €15–26.50

Duvane Farm
Ballyduvane, Clonakilty, Co. Cork
Tel: 023 33129 Fax: 023 33129

This Georgian farmhouse was built around 1870 and has been in the McCarthy family for quite a while; before that it belonged to a bishop. It is beautifully furnished and has some brass and half tester beds, and all the bedrooms have hairdryers. The farm supports cattle, and the attractive farm buildings lie behind the house. Breakfast includes honey from the farm's own bees. Pets can be accommodated in the stables. Smoking is permitted in the lounge. Visa accepted. Duvane Farm can be found on the N71, two kilometres west of Clonakilty.

OWNER Noreen McCarthy OPEN March – November ROOMS 4 double/twin/family; 3 en suite, 1 private bathroom. TERMS €31.50; single supplement €8.50; reductions for children

CORK

Garnish House
Western Road, Cork, Co. Cork
Tel: 021 4275111 Fax: 021 4273872
Email: garnish@iol.ie Website: www.garnish.ie

Conveniently located on the western edge of town opposite University College Cork, Garnish House is a double fronted Victorian town house, set back from the main road by its parking area. It is a comfortable house, efficiently run in a businesslike fashion by pleasant, helpful staff and offering such facilities as a night porter and a 24-hour service for arrivals and departures. The bedrooms vary in size, some being quite spacious, and quite a few have Jacuzzi baths. They all have hairdryers, trouser presses, telephones, TV and tea- and coffee-making facilities, as well as fresh fruit and flowers. Guests have use of a small TV lounge, and breakfast with its extensive menu is served in the dining room from 6 a.m. until 11 a.m. or midday. No pets. Smoking permitted in some rooms and sitting area. All major credit cards accepted.

OWNER Johanna Lucey OPEN All year ROOMS 8 twin, 5 single, 5 double, 5 family; all en suite. TERMS €25–44.50; single supplement €12.50; reductions for children .

River View
Douglas East, Cork, Co. Cork
Tel: 021 4893762
Email: edwardsc@eircom.net

River View, which is a Georgian style house built in the Victorian era, can be found right in the centre of Douglas village. Mr. and Mrs. Edwards are a charming couple who offer their guests a personal service, and the atmosphere is warm and welcoming. The lounge/dining room has the original fireplace and is interestingly furnished, and the bedrooms are a good size with comfortable beds, TV, hairdryers and tea- and coffee-making facilities. No pets and no smoking. The house is 100 metres from Barry's Pub, next to the Garda Station, and about one and a half kilometres from the centre of Cork, which can be reached by bus.

OWNER Catherine Edwards OPEN All year except for Christmas
ROOMS 1 double, 2 twin; all en suite. TERMS €26.50; single
supplement €9.50; reductions for children

Seven North Mall
Cork, Co. Cork
Tel: 021 397191 Fax: 021 300811
Email: sevennorthmall@eircom.net

This terraced, 240 year old listed building is in a tree-lined mall
facing the River Lee, right in the middle of Cork. When the
Hegartys bought the property it was derelict. Their hard work
has successfully transformed the building into comfortable and
tastefully decorated accommodation. The bedrooms are spacious
and have telephones, cable TV, trouser presses, hairdryers and
tea- and coffee-making facilities, and overlook either the river or
the rural aspect at the back of the house. Both the sitting room
and breakfast room have original 1740 fireplaces. There is
wheelchair access to the house, and one room is equipped for
disabled guests. There is a private car park. No pets. Smoking in
the sitting room only. Children over 12 are welcome. Access and
Visa cards accepted. Seven North Mall is convenient to theatres,
art galleries, Shandon, the University and some great restaurants
and pubs.

OWNER Hegarty Family OPEN January 8 – December 1
ROOMS 4 double/twin, 1 double, 1 twin, 1 single; all en suite.
TERMS €44.50 –57; single supplement €12.50

DONERAILE

Creagh House
Main Street, Doneraile, Co. Cork
Tel: 022 24433 Fax: 022 24715
Email: creaghhouse@eircom.net Website: www.creaghhouse.ie

Michael O'Sullivan and Laura O'Mahony, both environmental
engineers, were looking for a small house in Co. Cork, and
ended up with 10,000 square feet of Creagh House! – room for
themselves and guests. Renovation was a mammoth task, but the
results are quite spectacular. Built in the early 1800s, Creagh
House, is considered to be one of the finest and largest
Georgian townhouses outside Dublin. The magnificent ceiling
cornices have been painstakingly restored, and the sheer size of
the rooms is almost overpowering. The hallway, broken down
into two halves by double doors, the drawing and dining room
are each 600 square feet in size. The house has many literary
associations, including Thackeray (whose wife was a Creagh),

Elizabeth Bowen, Canon Sheehan and Daniel O'Connell. For those interested in history or literature Michael is an enthusiastic expert. Off street parking. Major credit cards accepted. Supper needs to be booked by noon and is served from 8–10 p.m. Creagh House is adjacent to the Golf Club and Doneraile Court.

OWNER Michael O'Sullivan & Laura O'Mahony OPEN February – November ROOMS 3 doubles, en suite TERMS €70; single supplement €13 MEALS supper €13

FARRAN

Farran House
Farran, Co. Cork
Tel: 021 733 1215 Fax: 021 733 1450
Email: info@farranhouse.com
Website: www.farranhouse.com

When Patricia Wiese and John Kehely bought Farran House it was a bigger undertaking than they had imagined. Restoration work took five years, and they opened for business in 1997. It is a gracious Georgian residence, built in 1750 and remodelled in 1806, standing in lovely grounds with wonderful views of the hills of the Lee Valley and overlooking the medieval castle and abbey of Kilcrea. In later years the house was divided into seven flats, and Patricia and John were lucky enough to have the drawings of the 1806 house, which they've restored back to the layout of that era. They have sympathetically left large rooms intact and converted whole rooms into bathrooms. The result is four exceptionally large bedrooms, one of which is a four-poster, each one having windows on two sides affording a lot of light and different aspects of the surrounding countryside. The rooms have TV, phones and hairdryers, and all have very large bathrooms, one with a claw foot bath and fireplace. Downstairs there is a drawing room, billiard room and dining room with patio off for fine weather breakfasts. The house retains its wooden floors, and the furniture and decor is simple, tasteful and unfussy. Tea and coffee are available in the dining room, and a kitchen adjacent to the dining room can be used if the whole house is let to one group. The coach house, which used to be the old kitchen with servants' quarters above, is now a delightful self catering unit with one enormous open room downstairs and three bedrooms above. Smoking allowed only in drawing room. No pets. Major credit cards accepted. Farran House can be found off the N22 15 kilometres west of Cork.

OWNER Patricia Wiese & John Kehely OPEN April 1 – October 31 ROOMS 4 double/twins; all en suite. TERMS €70; single supplement €15; reductions for children; MEALS dinner €31.50

Ghillie Cottage
Kilbarry Stud, Fermoy, Co. Cork
Tel: 025 32720 Fax: 025 33000
Email: flyfish@eircom.net
Website: www.ghilliecottage.com

Ghillie Cottage takes its name from the previous owner, who was ghillie to the Duke of Devonshire, owner of nearby Lismore Castle. Built around 1903, it is a converted "high cottage" – an original council cottage built on half a hectare of land. The cottage lies on a minor country road overlooking the River Blackwater with 10 hectares of land stretching up the hillside behind. Kilbarry is a working stud farm, crossing traditional Irish cobs with thoroughbred mares and supporting three stallions. There are livery stables for visiting riders and horseback riding can be arranged. As well as, or perhaps above, the interest in horses is Doug and Joy's passion for fishing. Doug is a fly fishing instructor and guide and can arrange fishing on the Blackwater. The décor of the attractively furnished small house reflects these interests. There is an informal and relaxed atmosphere, and guests share the TV lounge with the owners. Good home cooked evening meals are available by prior arrangement and packed lunches can be ordered. Ghillie cottage is not suitable for children. Pets by arrangement. Smoking in lounge only. Access, Visa and Mastercard accepted. To reach Ghillie Cottage take the N72 east from Fermoy in the direction of Tallow. After one and a half miles take first left turn to Clondulane – look for the sign for Ghillie Cottage.

OWNER Joy Arnold-Lock & Doug Lock OPEN April 1 – September 30 ROOMS 2 twin, 1 single, 1 public bathroom and 1 WC. TERMS €38 MEALS packed lunch, dinner €25.50

Glanworth Mill
Glanworth, Co. Cork
Tel: 025 38555 Fax: 025 38560
Email: glanworth@iol.ie
Website: www.iol.ie/glanworth

This late eighteenth century mill below the ruins of medieval Glanworth Castle and beside the narrow fifteenth century bridge is in an idyllic setting. Lynne Glasscoe and Emelyn Heaps have done wonders renovating the old building, which they acquired in September 1997 and opened for business 22 weeks later. The restaurants are open to the public, as is the new craft shop. The Mill Tea Rooms, an attractive flag stoned room where the old mill wheel turns, offers light meals, and the charming restaurant, plainly furnished and decorated in fresh, bright colours is where dinner is served. A small cosy drawing room/library leads into the tea rooms, beyond which are the attractively laid out courtyard gardens - a popular place to eat when the weather is fine enough, and the site of the new leisure gardens. Each bedroom has its own theme and decor based on the literary figures associated with the area and with its name inscribed on a piece of slate on the door. One room – the Seamus Murphy room – has the exposed stone of the hillside into which it is built. Major credit cards accepted.

OWNER Lynne Glasscoe & Emelyn Heaps OPEN All year except for Christmas ROOMS 10 doubles; all en suite TERMS €57–64; single supplement €12.50. MEALS a la carte meals all day

GLENGARRIFF

Ardnagashel Lodge
Glengarriff, Co. Cork
Tel: 027 51687

Neither the original lodge, or the big house still stand. The Ronaynes built this replacement lodge in the early 1990s with bed & breakfast guests in mind. It is a neat, attractive, small whitewashed house standing in pretty gardens just inside a massive stone archway off the main road between Bantry and Glengarriff. The bedrooms are bright and simply decorated, there's an attractive small sitting room and breakfast is served in the conservatory like room overlooking the gardens. TV and tea and coffee can be put in the rooms by request. No smoking, no pets. Not suitable for children. 3% extra is charged if using a credit card for payment. Golf, fishing and good restaurants and pubs are nearby.

OWNER Eleanor Ronayne OPEN May – September ROOMS 2 twins, 1 double; all en suite. TERMS €28.50; single supplement €9.50

Cois Coille
Glengarriff, Co. Cork
Tel: 027 63202

This modern house is approached up a very steep driveway and stands in a commanding position overlooking Bantry Bay and Garnish Island, and is set in a lovely hillside garden. It is a peaceful spot by the woodlands of Glengarriff and within walking distance of the village. Rita Barry-Murphy is kind and welcoming

and offers comfortable accommodation and an extensive breakfast menu. The attractive bedrooms are all en suite, and have
hairdryers and tea- and coffee-making facilities. Pets to be kept in
the car. No smoking. Cois Coille is off the Bantry road on the
edge of the village.

OWNER Rita Barry-Murphy OPEN Easter – September ROOMS
4 double/twin/family; all en suite. TERMS €28; single supplement
€10; reductions for children

GOLEEN

Fortview House
Gurtyowen, Toormore, Goleen, Co. Cork
Tel: 028 35324 Fax: 028 3532

Although built only a few years ago by the Connells, Fortview
House has an air of rustic charm. It is a small, stone built farmhouse on a working dairy farm in an excellent location for
exploring the Mizen Head, Sheep's Head and the Beara
Peninsula. The interior of the house is very attractive. It is fresh
and bright and quite simply but comfortably furnished with pine
floors, antique country pine furniture, brass and iron beds and
comfortable sofas in the sitting room, where drinks are available
by donation. The bedrooms all have hairdryers and mineral
water. The dining room has a tiled floor, wood-burning stove and
white tablecloths; excellent breakfasts are served which include
freshly squeezed orange juice and pancakes. Evening meals are
available by arrangement. There is also a self-catering cottage. No
pets; smoking permitted in the lounge. Fortview House is
located 10 km from both Schull and Goleen on the R591 and is
sign-posted at Toormore.

OWNER Violet Connell OPEN March 1 – November 1 ROOMS
5 double, twin, family; all en suite. TERMS €31.50–38; single
supplement €12.50 MEALS dinner €25.50

KANTURK

Glenlohane
Kanturk, Co. Cork
Tel: 029 50014 Fax: 029 51100
Email: msb@iol.ie
Website: www.glenlohane.com

Glenlohane is a superb Georgian country house set in beautiful
parkland grounds with some wonderful old trees and views to
the distant mountains. The present owners are direct descendants of the family who built it in 1741. Desmond lived and

worked in the United States and Melanie is American, and between them they have combined the very best of modern comforts with the character and atmosphere of the past. Glenlohane is an informal house with good food and log fires to relax in front of. The large comfortable drawing room features a square bay window, a superb full-length mirror, baby grand piano, grey marble fireplace and interesting pictures and furniture. There is also a small study filled with books, a dining room and a country kitchen. A traditional stable yard is attached to the house, where visitors' horses can be housed by arrangement. There are plenty of animals around, and the farm includes sheep and cattle. Guests are welcome to watch the daily farm activities, to play croquet, or just relax in the old walled garden. With notice, riding, or hunting with the Duhallow Hunt, the oldest pack of hounds in Ireland, can be arranged. Fishing is available only one kilometre away on the River Blackwater, and there are a variety of golf courses and lovely walks nearby. Glenlohane is suitable for children under 12. Pets in car only. No smoking. Visa, Mastercard and American Express accepted. To reach Glenlohane from Kanturk take the R576 towards Mallow, bear left on the R580 towards Buttevant, then take the first right towards Ballyclough. Look for the first residential entrance on the left after 2.2 kilometres – there is no sign.

OWNER Desmond & Melanie Sharp Bolster OPEN All year ROOMS 2 double, 3 twin; all en suite. TERMS €82.50; single supplement €12.50 MEALS dinner €38

Ballymakeigh House
Killeagh, Co. Cork
Tel: 024 95184 Fax: 024 95370
Email: ballymakeigh@eircom.net
Website: www.ballmakeighhouse.com

The friendliest of welcomes, superb food and comfortable rooms make Ballymakeigh House a delightful place to stay. The 250 year old farmhouse is located in the rich farmlands of east Cork and guests are welcome to walk around the intensive dairy farm and watch the cows being milked. For the energetic there are bicycles available, a full-size hard tennis court and horseback riding with a variety of courses on offer at the new Equestrian Centre, run by the Browne's daughter. The conservatory offers lots of sunny sitting space, and the bedrooms are constantly being upgraded and are equipped with every comfort, including hairdryers. Margaret has won countless awards over the years, including Housewife of the Year, Guesthouse of the Year, AA Landlady of the Year, and has written a book containing some of her favourite recipes - 'Through my Kitchen Window'. Copies are available for sale at the house. Dinner is now available at the newly opened restaurant - Brownes - which is two miles away on the main road to Youghal, and transport is provided for those who don't want to drive. Margaret is a superb cook, and a stay at Ballymakeigh would not be complete without a meal at Brownes. This is a marvellous spot in peaceful and tranquil sur-roundings, convenient to beaches, Fota Wildlife Park, Trabolgan Leisure Centre and Blarney Castle. Pets outside only. Visa and Mastercard accepted. Ballymakeigh is sign-posted at the Old Thatch pub in the village of Killeagh on the N25.

OWNER Margaret Browne OPEN March – November ROOMS 2 double, 2 twins, 2 family; all en suite. TERMS €44.50; single supplement €12.50 reductions for children MEALS dinner, a la carte

Desmond House
42 Cork Street, Kinsale, Co. Cork
Tel: 021 773575 Fax: 021 773575
Email: DesmondHouse@compuserve.com
Website: www.dragnet~systems.ie/dira/deshouse

In a quiet spot, in the very centre of Kinsale, Desmond House is a nineteenth century town house, originally home to the parish priest. It has four exceptionally large en suite bedrooms and is comfortably furnished. The rooms have TV, hairdryers and tea-

and coffee-making facilities. The Scallys pride themselves on their breakfast, which includes home baking and home made preserves. It is served in the ground floor cheerful breakfast room. Some off street parking is available. No smoking.

OWNER Liam Scally OPEN All year except for Christmas ROOMS 4 twins/doubles; all en suite. TERMS €60–70; single supplement €15–20

Perryville House
Kinsale, Co. Cork
Tel: 021 4772731 Fax: 021 4772298
Email: sales@perryville.iol.ie
Website: www.perryvillehouse.com

This spectacular house stands right in the centre of Kinsale on the quay overlooking the marina and the colourful streets of the medieval fishing port. Laura Corcoran, who previously owned Albany House in Dublin, bought Perryville House in a very run-down state and transformed it into a place of elegance and comfort, opening for business in 1997. The house is run with a quiet air of friendly professionalism. It has lovely furniture and tasteful décor, the hessian covered floors offsetting colourful rugs. The bedrooms, which are luxuriously appointed, come in every shape and size, some overlooking the harbour, some in a new wing, but even the smallest room is a good size. They all have TV, hairdryers, telephones, trouser presses and mineral water, and the majority have separate baths and showers in the en suite bathrooms. The drawing room, where morning coffee and afternoon tea are served daily, is comfortable and elegant, and the large, open reception area is another place to sit and relax. Substantial buffet-style breakfasts are available in the dining room, including home baked breads and preserves, local cheeses and fresh fruit. No pets. No smoking. No children under 13. Visa, Access and Mastercard accepted.

OWNER Laura Corcoran OPEN April 1 – November 1 ROOMS 22 doubles and twins; all en suite. TERMS €101.50 MEALS Irish breakfast €10

Raheen House
Kilgobbin, Ballinspittle, Kinsale, Co. Cork
Tel: 021 778173 Fax:
Email: raheenhouse@tinet.ie
Website: www.dragnet-systems.ie/dira/raheen

Raheen House belonged to Maria Sweetnam's grandparents. Maria, a bright, cheerful mother of teenage children, and her builder husband, have added to and improved the house over the years. Guests now enjoy very comfortable accommodation, with three en suite rooms upstairs and a perfect family suite of two bedrooms and bathroom on the ground floor. All rooms have TV, tea- and coffee-making facilities and hairdryers. There is a sitting room and dining room, both facing the sweeping views over rolling farmland to the sea and Old Head of Kinsale. Breakfast includes home baking, and there is a conveniently placed restaurant at Ballinspittle for evening meals. The land surrounding the house is used for keeping and breeding show horses, which is an activity the Sweetnams are involved in. The house is sign-posted between Ballinspittle and Ballinadee, and is approximately ten kilometres from Kinsale. No smoking in bedrooms. Pets outside, or in stables only. Horseriding, fishing, sailing and golf are all available locally, as well as lovely beaches, historic forts and museums.

OWNER Mrs. Maria Sweetnam OPEN April 1 – end October
ROOMS 4 rooms – 1 family suite, 3 doubles/twins; all en suite
TERMS €25.50

MACROOM

An Cuasan
Coolavokig, Macroom, Co. Cork
Tel: 026 40018 Fax:
Email: cuasan@eircom.net
Website: www.welcome.to/cuasan

This small, modern, country house stands above the N22 in an attractive garden. It is comfortable and clean, and has a relaxed atmosphere, and traditional music for guests is played by family musicians. Two of the en suite rooms are on the ground floor, and all rooms have hairdryers. The large conservatory is used both as a lounge and to accommodate the overflow from the dining room. The patio is a nice spot to sit on sunny days, and a shed for the tackle and refrigeration of bait is available for the angler. An Cuasan is a good spot for visiting Kerry and western Cork, and for riding, fishing and walking. No pets. Smoking in lounge only. The house can be found 9 kilometres west of Macroom on the N22. Visa, Access, Mastercard and Eurocard are accepted.

OWNER Sean & Margaret Moynihan OPEN April – October
ROOMS 2 double, 3 twins, 1 family; 5 en suite, 1 public bathroom
TERMS €25.50; single supplement €8.50; reductions for children

Longueville House

Mallow, Co. Cork
Tel: 022 47156 Fax: 022 47459
Email: info@longuevillehouse.ie

This impressive, listed Georgian manor house is set in beautiful park like grounds with lovely views overlooking the Blackwater River valley, surrounded by 200 hectares of woods, farmland, a vineyard and gardens which include 1.2 hectares of kitchen gardens. Visitors flock to Longueville House primarily for its food, which mostly comes from the river, garden and farm and is under the direction of William O'Callaghan; its lovely peaceful setting; the salmon fishing on the Blackwater, which runs through the estate; and because it is a good touring base for exploring both the south and south west coasts. The bedrooms are supremely comfortable, ranging in shape and size, and seven have mini suites which include sitting areas and luxury bathrooms. All rooms have hairdryers, telephones in both bedroom and bathroom, TV and bath robes. In spite of the grandeur, the atmosphere is warm and welcoming and guests have use of the comfortable drawing room, the old conservatory, which has been completely weather proofed, and a games room with a full size billiard table. As well as breakfast and dinner, a snack lunch is available all week. There are some bedrooms allocated to smokers, and pets are welcome in the courtyard accommodation. All major credit cards accepted. Longueville House is three miles west of Mallow on the N72.

OWNER O'Callaghan family OPEN Mid-March – early November ROOMS 3 family, 1 suite, 2 singles, 8 doubles, 8 twins, all en suite or private bathrooms. TERMS €82.50; single supplement €51; reductions for children MEALS light meals, dinner

Barnabrow Country House

Cloyne, Midleton, Co. Cork
Tel: 021 4652534/4652776/4652749 Fax: 021 4652534
Email: barnabrow@eircom.net
Website: www.barnabrowhouse.com

Built in 1639, with two wings added later, Barnabrow – meaning a fairy fort – stands on a hill surrounded by its own 14 hectares and enjoys pleasant country views. The house was gutted and has been most interestingly restored with the four large second floor bedrooms having high raftered ceilings. Apart from one bedroom on the first floor, the remainder are in two ranges of converted farm buildings at the back of the house, one of which also houses the bar and restaurant above it. The rooms all have hairdryers, telephones and bottled water. The house has been unusually decorated and plainly and simply furnished with a mixture of old and new, and strong, vibrant and bright colours are used on the walls, reflecting the colours of Guatemala. A lot of the interestingly shaped furniture and the flooring are made from imported teak from Botswana. The restaurant's chef spent some time at the Ballymaloe cookery school which, together with Ballymaloe House, is just down the road. Organically grown vegetables from the walled garden are a part of the delicious food on offer, and the outside terrace is used for barbecuing. There is now an African furniture and crafts shop open daily, and the enlarged restaurant can cater for weddings, conferences and large parties. The cathedral at Cloyne was the seat of George Berkeley, the well-known philosopher after whom the Californian university was named. Pets are accepted in the courtyard rooms and smoking is permitted in the TV lounge. Visa and Mastercard taken. Barnabrow is one and a half miles from Cloyne on the Ballycotton road.

OWNER Geraldine O'Brien OPEN All year except for Christmas ROOMS 3 family, 7 twin, 11 double; all en suite. TERMS €42–60.50; single supplement €12.50 reductions for children MEALS Sunday lunch €19, dinner a la carte

Glenview House

Ballinaclasha, Midleton, Co. Cork
Tel: 021 4631680 Fax: 021 4634680
Email: glenviewhouse@esatclear.ie
Website: www.dragnet-systems.ie/dira/glenview

Dating from 1780, this Georgian house is in a lovely rural setting, and stands in 8 hectares of grounds and gardens. When the Sherrards bought the house some 30 years ago, it was derelict, with ivy growing through the floor. They added the bow shaped

end of the drawing room that faces south, and in the course of renovation and furnishing, bought the contents of 16 houses, using what they needed and auctioning off the remainder. One of these acquisitions is the old bath, which has a brass surround. Evening meals are served in the attractive dining room, and there is a wide hall with a fireplace at one end. Visitors to Glenview find it a relaxing and peaceful place, the ideal setting in which to paint or write. The ground floor double bedroom has outside access and is suitable for the disabled, and all the rooms have hairdryers and tea and coffee facilities. There are doors leading from the bar out onto the patio, which is a nice sunny spot to sit on fine days. Guests have use of the grass tennis court and croquet lawn, and there are also two coach house apartments, one of which is designed for wheelchair users. Pets in cars only, and smoking is permitted in the lounge by arrangement. American Express, Visa and Mastercard accepted. Glenview is sign-posted off the L35 Midleton to Fermoy road.

OWNER Ken & Beth Sherrard OPEN All year ROOMS 4 double, 1 family, 1 twin, 1 wheelchair accessible; all en suite. TERMS €57; single supplement €10; reductions for children MEALS dinner €31.50

Old Parochial House
Castlemartyr, Midleton, Co. Cork
Tel: 021 4667454 Fax: 021 4667429
Email: enquiries@oldparochial.com
Website: www.oldparochial.com

Built in 1784 by the Earl of Shannon for his land agent, this very attractive house stands in a small garden in the village of Castlemartyr. Later the house belonged to the Catholic Church and was home to the Bishop of Cloyne. It was in really bad shape when the Sheehys bought it in 1996, and they have done a splendid restoration job, furnishing and decorating the house with taste and care. There are pine floors and open fires in both the small sitting room and dining room. The dining room has one table, and a good choice of home-made produce is offered at breakfast served on local pottery. The spacious bedrooms have hairdryers, TV, tea- and coffee-making facilities and fresh flowers. The old conservatory off the sitting room is reputed to have one of the oldest vines in Ireland, which in summer is laden with fruit, and honey comes from home beehives. Kathy and Paul Sheehy are a very welcoming young couple with two small children, and like to offer their visitors coffee and scones on arrival, and a drink by the fire in the evening. No pets, smoking in the drawing room only. Visa and Mastercard accepted. To find the Old Parochial House take the Shanagarry sign in the village of Castlemartyr – it is the first house on the left.

OWNER Kathy & Paul Sheehy OPEN February – October
ROOMS 2 double, I double/twin; all en suite. TERMS €44.50–51;
reductions for children

Ballinatona Farm

Ballinatona, Millstreet, Co. Cork
Tel: 029 70213 Fax: 029 70940

Not your typical farm, this is a most unusual and wonderful
place, set in beautiful countryside, with outstanding views of
mountains, moors and farmland. But what makes it such a special
place is cheerful, welcoming Jytte Storm, who immediately makes
her guests feel at home. Jytte's Danish origins have a big influence on the décor and the house, which she and her husband
originally built 20 years ago, and then added on to. Ballinatona
was meant to be for their retirement, which is a pretty active
one, what with running a 40-hectare dairy farm and a six bedroom guesthouse. It seems every room in the house was built to
take advantage of the best views. The sitting room, conservatory
and dining room are all bright with large windows, as is the
honeymoon suite reached up a very narrow spiral staircase. The
décor and furnishings are simple, clean cut and very bright, and
the bedrooms all have hairdryer, TV and tea- and coffee-making
facilities. Ballinatona Farm is a walker's dream - from the
doorstep there are wonderful hikes, including this most remote
and beautiful part of the Blackwater Way, which is part of the
coast to coast walk and runs the other side of Clara Mountain,
one of the viewpoints from the house. Snacks are available. Pets
in cars only. No smoking. Visa and Mastercard accepted. Excellent
value are the tiny chalets in the grounds, which offer basic
accommodation; they have no inside water, but do have fridges
and small cookers. Water and a toilet are available
outside. They can be rented by the night. Ballinatona Farm is
three kilometres from Millstreet on the R582.

OWNER Jytte Storm OPEN All year ROOMS 6 double, twin,
family; all en suite. TERMS €25; single supplement €10; reductions
for children MEALS snacks

Rock Cottage

Barnatonicane, Schull, Co. Cork
Tel: 028 35538 Fax: 028 35538
Email: rockcottage@eircom.net
Website: www.mizen.net/rockcottage

Until a few years ago Barbara (who comes from Germany) was the head chef at Blairs Cove Restaurant, just a few miles away. She bought Rock Cottage - named for a small rock outcrop at the back of the house - and opened for business five years ago. Decidedly a Georgian house, it is a cottage by the standards of the 1800s, and was in fact built as a hunting lodge. It offers delightful simple, bright accommodation - pine has been used quite extensively - and the rooms have TV and hairdryers. There is an attractive sitting room, and superb meals are served at separate tables in the dining room. Apart from the three bed-rooms in the house, there are self catering units in the grounds, built of renovated attractive stone farm buildings. The house is beautifully positioned, on the Mizzen Head peninsula, within a short distance of the sea on either side, and stands in lovely park-like grounds, with sheep, horses, donkeys, geese and a pet pig. Dinner is served from 7 to 8 p.m. - bookings should be made previous day. Wine licence. Children welcome. Major credit cards accepted. Rock Cottage can be found on the R591 between Durrus and Toormore.

OWNER Barbara Klotzer OPEN All year ROOMS 2 family en suite, 1 double with private bathroom. TERMS €31.50–38; single supplement €12.50 MEALS dinner from €31.50

Stanley House

Colla Road, Schull, Co. Cork
Tel: 028 28425

Although it has a modern look, Stanley House is actually a renovated old farmhouse about one kilometre from Schull. Surrounded by 3 hectares of fields with deer and colourful gardens, it is in a wonderful position overlooking Schull harbour, Roaring Water Bay with its many islands, and Mount Gabriel. Nancy Brosnan has been doing bed & breakfast for 20 years and has a far-flung circle of guests who return again and again to this home away from home. Maeve Binchy is among her regular visitors and she has written "This is my fifth visit to the gleaming place where all the guests stare in wonder at the sparkling surfaces and shining windows and wonder do folk from another world come and do the housework at night." TV and tea- and coffee-making facilities are in all the bedrooms, and the small dining room has separate tables where breakfast is served. The comfortable TV lounge has a sun porch beyond which is the terrace – a great place to sit and take in the views. The Brosnans have quite a presence in Schull, with Nancy's husband running the Spar Supermarket and her son managing the restaurant and bar. They also have four houses for self catering, including a thatched cottage. It is a lovely walk into the village, which runs the length of one main street; there are ferries to the islands two or three times a day in summer; bicycles can be hired, or, for the energetic, a climb to the top of 412 metre Mount Gabriel is well worth it for the wonderful view. Visa, Mastercard and Eurocard accepted.

OWNER Nancy Brosnan OPEN 1 March – 31 October ROOMS 2 double, 1 twin, 1 family; all en suite. TERMS €25.50; single supplement €10; reductions for children

SHANAGARRY

Ballymaloe House
Shanagarry, Co. Cork
Tel: 021 4652531 Fax: 021 4652021
Email: res@ballymaloe.ie
Website: www.ballymaloe.ie

Famous as one of Ireland's top restaurants and the training ground (at Ballymaloe Cookery School) for many of Ireland's best chefs, it is undoubtedly food that lures many visitors to this lovely old family home. Set in 160 hectares of its own farmland, Ballymaloe is built around an old Geraldine castle, the fourteenth century keep still intact. The bedrooms, which vary in size and character, are located in the main house; around the old coach-yard, where there are four on the ground floor designed to take wheelchairs; in the gatehouse, with the twin bedded room up short steep stairs, and where, in an addition, there are five newer rooms. The bedrooms all have hairdryers, and on request TV, iron and ironing boards. Three small dining rooms open off the main room, and they have an interesting collection of modern Irish paintings, including works by Jack B. Yeats, brother of the poet William Butler Yeats. The Allens, in addition to Ballymaloe House, the Cookery School and the farm, also run a craft shop on the premises, and the restaurant in the Crawford Art Gallery in Cork. Facilities on the estate include a heated outdoor swim-ming pool (summer only), tennis court, small golf course, children's play equipment and the craft shop. There is kennel accommodation for pets, and smoking is permitted in some areas. All major credit cards accepted. Ballymaloe is three kilometres outside Cloyne on the Ballycotton road.

OWNER Mrs. Myrtle Allen OPEN All year except for Christmas ROOMS 3 singles, 16 doubles, 15 twins; all en suite. TERMS €133.50; single supplement MEALS lunch €28, dinner €47.50, children's menu

Grove House
Skibbereen, Co. Cork
Tel: 028 22957 Fax: 028 22958

Just a kilometre from Skibbereen, Grove House stands in two acres of wild gardens and fields in a peaceful spot. The Warburtons bought the property, a modest Georgian country house, in the early 1990s and spent a couple of years on renovation work, before opening for business. There's a pretty drawing and dining room where delicious home cooked candlelit dinners are served. The three bedrooms in the house, which vary in size, are simply furnished and have TV. Behind the house the pretty, old stables and barn buildings provide three very attractive, cleverly converted bedroom suites. There are also self catering cottages nearby. Three course dinners including wine, are available if booked in advance. Major credit cards accepted. Grove House can be found a kilometre off the N71 on the R593 in the Bantry direction.

OWNER Anna & Peter Warburton OPEN All year except for Christmas, except cottages ROOMS 3 four-posters; en suite. TERMS €38–57; single supplement €12.50 MEALS dinner €20.50

Aherne's
163 North Main Street, Youghal, Co. Cork
Tel: 024 92424 Fax: 024 93633
Email: ahe@iol.ie
Website: www.ahernes.com

The Fitzgibbon family have owned Aherne's for three generations. The inn started life as the family's pub and small grocery store that made sandwiches. It is the present generation of the family that made the transformation from sandwiches to a restaurant, and later built on an entire wing for accommodation. Located in the heart of the historic walled port of Youghal, Aherne's is a renowned seafood restaurant serving freshly caught local fish, including lobster, prawns, crab, salmon, oysters and sole. The restaurant is decorated in warm, glowing colours, and there are two small, cosy bars with prints and pictures. The bedrooms are exceptionally large, have very big beds and are restfully decorated. They each have TV, trouser press, telephone and hairdryer. The drawing room has an open fireplace, books and antique furniture, and the bright dining room in the new wing is where residents are served breakfast. River and deep-sea fishing, horseback riding, hill walking and visiting magnificent beaches are activities that can easily be undertaken from Youghal, not to mention the seven nearby golf courses. No pets. Some restrictions on smoking. The restaurant is open from 6.30 to 9.30 daily and bar food is available at lunchtime. Access, Visa, American Express accepted.

OWNER The Fitzgibbon Family OPEN All year except for Christmas ROOMS 12 double or twin; all en suite. TERMS €70–89; single supplement €31.50–38 MEALS dinner €38, bar food

Glenally House
Copperalley, Youghal, Co. Cork
Tel: 024 91628 Fax: 024 91628
Email: enquiries@glenally.com
Website: www.glenally.com

On the edge of Youghal and reached down a narrow lane, Glenally House was built in 1826, and stands in seven acres of gardens and fields. It is a plain, and somewhat austere looking building, greatly improved by Fred and Herta Rigney, who moved here three years ago. The house is simply furnished using a mixture of old and modern pieces and bright colours, and many of the rooms have the original wooden floors, some of which have been painted. The bedrooms have TV and tea- and coffee-making facilities. Breakfast, and dinner by arrangement, is served in the dining room, and for a larger number of people the morning room is also used for meals. Fred and Herta enjoy having guests, and make sure their stay in enjoyable. Not suitable for young children. No smoking or pets. Visa and Mastercard accepted.

OWNER Herta & Fred Rigney OPEN All year except for Christmas and January ROOMS 3 doubles en suite, 1 twin with private bathroom TERMS €31.50–51; single supplement €12.50 MEALS dinner €30.50

COUNTY KERRY

Every tourist wants to visit Kerry to see the beauty of the landscape. There is an inconsistency in the weather – wind and rain from the Atlantic, misty drizzle or bright light and sunshine – making each day or part of a day different from the next and projecting a constantly changing pattern over the mountains, lakes and streams. Each type of weather brings its own peculiar beauty to the landscape.

Killarney town caters to large numbers of tourists and is full of hotels, yet the lakes, mountains and woods of the surrounding countryside remain unspoiled. Close by is the ruined fourteenth-century Ross Castle. From here one can hire a boat to Inisfallen Island and visit the ruins of the twelfth-century Augustian Inisfallen Abbey. Muckross House is now a folk museum and has the most beautiful garden. From the Gap of Dunloe there is a marvellous view of the Black Valley where huge torrents of water poured through the Gap at the end of the ice age.

The Ring of Kerry is a famous scenic drive around the Iveragh Peninsula. Killorglin is known for its annual horse and cattle fair, Puck Fair, held for two days In August, a great event with pagan origins, when a wild mountain goat is captured and enthroned in the centre of the town. Waterville is the principal resort on the Ring of Kerry, and at Cahirsiveen one can see the magnificent police barracks, which were meant to have been built in the north-west frontier of India, but the plans got mixed up. At Ballinskelligs, which is an Irish-speaking area, there are the ruins of a monastery and a fine beach with wonderful views. The Skelligs are rocky islands off the Ring of Kerry, which can be visited to see wild birds, notably kittiwakes, guillemots, petrel, shearwater and fulmar. One can also see the ruins of the old monastery that stands 183 m above the landing place and is approached by long flights of stone steps. There are also beehive huts, stone crosses, the Holy Well, oratories and cemeteries to see. This is a beautiful, peaceful spot in fine weather, but terrifying in a storm.

The Dingle Peninsula is made up of beautiful mountains, cliffs, glacial valleys, lakes and beaches. Some 2,000 prehistoric and early Christian remains have been discovered, and a little old Gaelic culture can be observed at the tip of the peninsula. The little village of Ventry was the scene of a legendary battle, and at Fahan lies the greatest collection of antiquities in Ireland: stone beehive huts, cave dwellings, standing and inscribed stones and crosses, souterrains, forts, cahers and a church. There are spectacular views around Slea Head, and it was around here that the film *Ryan's Daughter* was made. Beyond Ballyferriter is Gallaurs, the most perfect example of early Irish building and dry-rubble masonry. The principal town of Kerry is Tralee, a trading and industrial centre. At Ardfert, the cathedral, which was built in 1250 and has the ruins of its Franciscan Friary, is the most striking building.

Four Winds
Anascaul, Co. Kerry
Tel: 066 915 7168 Fax: 066 9157174

Kathleen O'Connor has been running her B&B for about 17 years; she enjoys meeting people and sharing her house and is an accommodating host. There are views of the Anascaul Mountains and Dingle Bay and Ross Beigh from the house. The simply furnished rooms are fresh and bright. There is a unique chaise-longue in the hallway. Anascaul is the birthplace of the Antarctic explorer Tom Crean and the well-known sculptor Jerome Connor. Tasty freshly prepared breakfasts are served in the cosy dining room and there is also a comfortable TV lounge. There are plenty of activities for the visitor, including walks, fishing, sandy beaches, mountain climbing and archaeological sites. The house is situated on the Dingle/Tralee Way Walk. Drying facilities available.

OWNER Kathleen & P. J. O'Connor OPEN All year ROOMS 1 double, 2 twin, 1 family; 3 en suite. TERMS €21.50; reduction for children 10%; single supplement €6.50

The 19th Green
Golf Links Road, Ballybunion, Co. Kerry
Tel: 068 27592 Fax: 068 27830
Email: the19thgreen@eircom.net
Website: www.ballybunion19thgreen.com

An immaculate bungalow in a superb location overlooking Ballybunion Golf Course – a two-minute walk to the first tee, and a good seven iron to the club house: a golfer's paradise. The property has recently been upgraded, inside and out. The bedrooms are furnished with rich wood, pretty pastel fabrics and lace curtains. The sitting room is pleasantly furnished and there is a conservatory for guests' use. The guest lounge overlooks the golf course, with a mini bar available. Breakfast is plentiful and is available as early as 6 a.m. for the golfer. Owners Mr and Mrs Beasley are a most accommodating couple, who go out of their way to ensure their guests have everything they need. Tea or coffee is offered upon arrival, and golf storage and a drying room are made available.

Garden furniture is available on fine days. Children are welcome during the month of August; the house is not suitable for children at other times. Breakfast only is served, but there is no shortage of restaurants and pubs for other meals in Ballybunion. Five minutes from sandy beaches, salmon fishing, cliff walks and seaweed baths on the beach. All major credit cards accepted.

OWNER Mrs Mary Beasley OPEN All year except for Christmas ROOMS 2 double, I twin, I family, single, triple; 5 en suite TERMS B&B €25.50–44.50; 25% reduction for children; single supplement €12.50

The Country Haven
Car Ferry Road, Ballybunion, Co. Kerry
Tel: 068 27103
Email: eileenwalsh@eircom.net

This superb Georgian-style house is ideally situated - just 3km from the golf course and a 10-minute drive from the Tarbert car ferry. The driving range with 12 all-weather indoor bays will enable you to practice your golf and enjoy panoramic views of the Atlantic Ocean at the same time. Mrs Eileen Walsh is a friendly lady with a good sense of humour, who takes excellent care of her guests. The house sits on a 65-hectare farm, and there are 7.5 hectares of young forest and a 6.5-km designated walk. The spacious bedrooms are of a very high standard, tastefully decorated with every comfort. There is a ground floor room with a small conservatory. A honeymoon suite is also available. The house has antique furniture throughout and most bedrooms have sea views. Full Irish breakfast is offered with home-made scones, breads and marmalade; early breakfast prepared for golfers. All guests may use the putting green, tennis court and driving range. Guests will be extremely comfortable here, and have easy access to two golf courses and the scenic countryside. Visa accepted.
OWNER Mrs Eileen Walsh OPEN April I – November 31 ROOMS I double, 3 twin, I family; all en suite. TERMS €30–40; reduction for children (50% if sharing); single supplement €6.50

CAHERDANIEL

Moran's Farmhouse
Caherdaniel, Co. Kerry
Tel: 066 9475208
Email: nancymoran@eircom.net

Moran's is a modern bungalow with the most spectacular views, overlooking Derrynane and the Atlantic, and just five minutes' walk to the sea. There are two clean sandy beaches where guests can swim, hike, boat or just relax and enjoy the beautiful scenery. The house is well-maintained, with new carpets, curtains and duvet covers, and has a pleasant, welcoming atmosphere. All bedrooms are on the ground floor. Moran Farm is a working farm of sheep and cows. Home-cooked wholesome evening meals are available by arrangement. Nancy Moran is happy to assist visitors in every way to ensure they have a comfortable stay, and to give advice on what to see and do in the area. Daniel O'Connell's House and Gardens and wonderful walks are close by. 6 miles from Waterville on main ring of Kerry. Farm is sign-posted.

OWNER Nancy Moran OPEN January – November 30 ROOMS 2 double, I twin, I family; all en suite. TERMS €25.50; reduction for children (40% when sharing); single supplement €12.50 MEALS dinner

CAHIRSIVEEN

Cul Draiochta
Points Cross, Cahirsiveen, Co. Kerry
Tel: 066 947 3141 Fax: 066 947 3141
Email: inugent@esatclear.ie

Cul Draiochta means "Magic Nook" in Irish, and this is a magical area of the Ring of Kerry. Situated at the foot of the Bentee Mountains overlooking Valentia Harbour, the house was designed as a bed & breakfast and was built to ensure that guests have every comfort. The well-appointed good-sized bedrooms are light and airy. They have cherrywood furniture, pink candystriped duvets, and are attractively decorated with co-ordinated fabrics; all have orthopaedic beds and overlook the view. All bedrooms have TV, clock radio and hairdryer. Owners Ian and Ann Nugent are from a farming family in North Kerry and are very hos-pitable. They have been in business for more than five years, and have built up a fine reputation for offering very good value accommodation. Tea or coffee is offered upon arrival and other times on request. Excellent breakfasts and table d'hôte dinners are served in the conservatory-style dining room overlooking the view, and packed lunches can be provided upon request. Vegetarian meals are also available with advance notice. The lounge is very comfortable and has multi-channel TV. Smoking in conservatory only. Routes for walkers are provided. This is an ideal spot for nature lovers.

OWNER Ian & Ann Nugent OPEN All year ROOMS 2 twin/ double, 2 family; all en suite. TERMS B&B €38.50; reduction for children; single supplement €12.50 MEALS dinner €17

The Final Furlong
Cahirsiveen, Co. Kerry
Tel: 066 947 3300 Fax: 066 947 2810
Email: finalfurlong@eircom.net

This immaculate, warm bungalow sits in a tranquil location on the banks of the River Fertha estuary, and enjoys lovely views. It is part of a 40-hectare farm with a suckler cow herd and a Sport Horse Enterprise. Approved riding stables offer beach gallops and horseback riding in secluded areas of the Ring of Kerry. Guests can also view the ruins of the old Union Workhouse, and a detailed history is available. The rooms are immaculately maintained and attractively decorated.

Breakfasts and prearranged four-course dinners are served on a large refectory table in the dining room. Kathleen O'Sullivan is an excellent cook (seafood is a speciality) who enjoys chatting with guests and provides information on the area. Smoking is permitted in the lounge only.

Kathleen O'Sullivan's motto is, "You may come as a stranger, but we hope you will leave as a friend". Group rates are available and special offers can be had in May, June and September/October. Deep-sea angling packages as well as trips to Skellig Rock from a nearby pier are offered. Visa, Mastercard, Access, American Express accepted.

OWNER Kathleen O'Sullivan OPEN March 1 – November 1 ROOMS 1 double, 1 twin, triple family, double/single; all en suite TERMS €25.50; reduction for children 20%; single supplement €8.50 MEALS Dinner from €21.50

CARAGH LAKE

Glendalough House
Caragh Lake, Co. Kerry
Tel: 066 976 9156 Fax: 066 976 9156
Email: IrelandJournal@eircom.net
Website: www.kerryweb.ie

Glendalough House is a charming Victorian residence just a short distance from the shores of Caragh Lake. It is a warm country house with mature gardens and views of the lake and Ireland's highest mountain range, the McGillycuddy Reeks. It is furnished with antiques and there are several old paintings. An ideal spot for those looking for peace and tranquillity, the house is approached by a long private gravel drive, bordered with trees, shrubs and wildflowers. There is a garden inhabited by a colourful peacock and peahen. Peace is also maintained by the lack of television. Candlelit dinners featuring Caragh salmon and succulent mountain lamb are served in the elegant dining room. There is a conservatory and also a mews that comprises two double en suite bedrooms with a private living room and south-facing terrace. Smoking is permitted in the conservatory and on the terrace.

Glendalough is truly a house for all seasons: there are several championship golf courses where tee times can be arranged, there is trout and salmon fishing, wonderful walks, and it is an excellent base from which to tour the Ring of Kerry and the Dingle Peninsula. The house is not suitable for children. Visa, Mastercard, American Express accepted.

OWNER Josephine Roder-Bradshaw OPEN March 1 – October 31 ROOMS 4 double, 4 twin; 7 en suite, 1 private bath. TERMS €70; single supplement €19 MEALS dinner

CASTLEISLAND

Beech Grove Farm
Castleisland, Co. Kerry
Tel: 066 7141217 Fax: 066 7142877

Approached along a mature beech tree-lined avenue, Beech Grove Farm has been in the family for four generations. Set on a 200-acre Hereford cattle farm, it is a wonderful place for animal lovers and families who love the outdoors. The hospitality here is outstanding, the ambience warm and friendly. Guests are greeted with tea and home -baked scones. On cool days these are served in the cosy sitting room, with a turf fire burning in the original marble fireplace. The bedrooms are immaculate and comfortable, there are electric blankets, and the rooms are freshly decorated and tastefully furnished. Farm fresh breakfasts are served at separate tables in the inviting dining-room, whose original cornices and ceiling rose have been restored. Breakfast consists of a wide choice of cereals, juice and fruits, followed by a cooked variety with home-made brown bread. Porridge with fresh cream is also on the menu. Evening meals are not served, but there is an restaurant in Castleisland which serves excellent meals at reasonable prices.

The sun lounge overlooks scenic countryside, and offers a wonderful spot to unwind after a busy day of sightseeing. Guests may bring their own wine. There is plenty to see and do in this area, including visits to Crag Cave, trips to the Ring of Kerry and the Dingle Peninsula. So book in for several days, as where better to see them from than Beech Grove Farm, with its warm atmosphere and its own ring fort? Access, Visa accepted.
Three miles west of Castleisland – sign-posted.

OWNER The O'Mahoney family OPEN Easter – September 30 ROOMS 1 double/twin, 1 double/family; all en suite. TERMS €28–31.50; child reduction (50% if sharing); single supplement €6.50

Ard na Greine

Spa Road, Dingle, Co. Kerry
Tel: 066 915 1113 Fax: 066 915 1898
Email: mayhoul@indigo.ie

This warm and inviting bungalow in a quiet location is just a five-minute stroll to the town centre. Mary Houlihan wanted to ensure that her guests had everything they could need, and she has certainly accomplished her goal. All the bedrooms, which are on the ground floor, are equipped with satellite TV, tea-makers, electric blankets, hairdryers, irons and ironing boards, direct dial phones, and bath/shower combinations; the latest additions are refrigerators. The orthopaedic beds have Dorma-designed duvets, and the rooms are bright and attractive. There is a breakfast menu featuring smoked herring, salmon, home-baked breads, Irish cooked breakfast, etc. You certainly won't need lunch. An added bonus is the delightful owner, Mary Houlihan. The house is extremely good value and there is a home-away-from-home atmosphere. The beautiful shamrock/harp tapestry displayed in the dining room was hand-made by Mary's sister. Visa, Mastercard accepted. Third house past the Highgrove Hotel.

OWNER Mary & Michael Houlihan OPEN February 1 – December 15 ROOMS 2 double, 1 twin, 1 family; all en suite TERMS €25.50–31.50; reduction for children; single supplement €6.50

Cill Bhreac

Milltown, Dingle, County Kerry
Tel: 066 513358
Email: cbhreac@iol.ie
Website: www.iol.ie/~cbhreac/index.htm

An attractive spacious residence in a tranquil location, overlooking Dingle Bay and Mount Brandon. The house is immaculate, the rooms are of a good size, and are comfortably furnished. The bedrooms are well equipped, with tea/ coffee-makers, TV, clock radio and hairdryer. All bedrooms have orthopaedic beds and electric blankets. Children are welcome and cots are provided. No smoking in the bedrooms. There is an extensive breakfast menu (special diets can be catered for) prepared fresh daily, juices, cereals, cooked choices, and brown bread; you won't need lunch.
The conservatory also overlooks the bay and is a perfect spot in which to relax after a busy day of sightseeing. Guests may also have use of the garden. The ambience is friendly and Angela McCarthy is very helpful, providing lots of assistance with what

to see and in the area. Close by are facilities for angling, golf, horse riding, sailing, and sandy beaches. Several pubs in the area serve food and have traditional Irish music. Irish is spoken. American Express, Access, Mastercard, Visa, Diners Club accepted. Coming into Dingle on the N86, turn left at first roundabout and left and 2nd roundabout crossing the bridge. Cill Bhreac is the third house on the right.

OWNER Mrs Angela McCarthy OPEN March 1 – November 30 ROOMS 5 double/twin; all en suite. TERMS €25.50–31.50; reduction for children; single supplement €6.50

Devane's Farmhouse
Lispole, Dingle, Co. Kerry
Tel: 066 915 1418

A warm welcome awaits you at this family-run farmhouse, a working dairy farm of 16 hectares nestled at the foot of the mountain with beautiful views all around. The Farmhouse is very popular with walkers and tourists, as it is situated on the Dingle Way Walk. The bedrooms are clean, if a little small, but the owners are so hospitable, offering tea and home-baked bread and cake to guests, that room size seems unimportant. There is an extra cot available.

The sitting room leads out to the conservatory with stunning views of the bay and mountains. Smoking is permitted in conservatory only. Tea and coffee facilities in dining-room, and hairdryers, irons and a trouser press are available on request. Dinner is by advance arrangement only, but there are several establishments for evening meals in Dingle, which is just 5km away. Guests return here year after year, and visitors new to the property sometimes book in for a night and end up staying for a week or more. Guests may have use of the garden, and are welcome to enjoy the daily farm activities, watch the sheep grazing or walk in this beautiful area.

The farmhouse is located on a small side road, but don't give up; just when you think you have passed it, the farm comes into view. Visa, Mastercard accepted.

OWNER Mary Devane OPEN April 1 – November 1 ROOMS 3 double, twin, 1 family; 3 en suite. TERMS €23; reduction for children 25% if sharing (under age 4 free); single supplement €6.50 MEALS dinner

Duinin House

Conor Pass Road, Dingle, Co. Kerry
Tel: 066 915 1335 Fax: 066 915 1335
Email: pandaneligan@eircom.net

Duinin, meaning "little fort," is a friendly ranch-style bungalow with beautiful views of the sea and mountains. There is a large front garden with a manicured lawn and lots of pretty flowers and shrubs. Guests enjoy tea outside on warm days, or in the conservatory that overlooks Dingle Harbour and Valley. The comfortable lounge has a VCR that guests may use, plus an additional lounge for reading or just relaxing after a busy day. This is a non-smoking house. All of the bedrooms are on the ground floor, with modern furnishings, large, fitted wardrobes and chairs. The front bedrooms have lovely views.

The extensive breakfast menu, with fresh baked breads, is served in the sunny dining room over looking the harbour. Golf, fishing, boat trips, beaches, hill walking and excellent pubs and restaurants are close by. Visa, Mastercard, American Express accepted.

OWNER Anne Neligan OPEN February 1 – November 30
ROOMS 3 double, 2 twin; all en suite TERMS €26–29

Greenmount House

Gortonora, Dingle, Co. Kerry
Tel: 066 915 1414 Fax: 066 915 1974
Email: mary@greenmounthouse.com

Greenmount House, also known as Curran's Bed and Breakfast, stands in an elevated site over-looking Dingle town and the harbour. A special feature are the wonderful breakfast feasts: guests help themselves from an enormous buffet choice of fruits, cereals, home-baked bread, muffins, fresh juices, puddings and other delights, followed by tasty omelettes or a traditional Irish breakfast. An added bonus is that it is served in a lovely conservatory/dining room that overlooks the bay. Little wonder the establishment was awarded the Certification of Merit Award. Most of the rooms have been upgraded, and are tastefully decorated with warm autumn colours in Laura Ashley designs. Rooms have refrigerators and direct dial phones in the rooms. There are 7 superior suites and five charming bedrooms. Each suite has a full bathroom, large sitting area, many more extras, and sea views. There are two lounges for guests' use. The house is beautifully maintained by John and Mary Curran, who have been in business for over 25 years. The owners are from local, long established families, and will provide guests with an unlimited amount of knowledge on the area. Plenty of written information is also provided. Local amenities include golf, fishing, horse riding and trips to see Fungi the Dolphin, whom you might even see from your bedroom window. Visa, Mastercard accepted.

OWNER John & Mary Curran OPEN All year ROOMS 12 double/twin/ family; all en suite. TERMS €80–125; reduction for children (from age 8 if sharing)

The Lighthouse
The High Road, Ballinaboula, Dingle, Co. Kerry
Tel: 066 915 1829
Email: lighthousebandb@eircom.net
Website: http://homepage.eircom.net/~murphydenis/

This pleasant two-storey spacious house stands in its own grounds overlooking Dingle Harbour. A galleried landing and a pine staircase lead to the spacious bedrooms, all of which have a bath/shower combination; one is on the ground floor. The bedrooms are bright and fresh; they are furnished with pine and have bright colourful duvets. The lounge and dining room over-look the view. Breakfast only is served, but there are several choices for evening meals in Dingle, which is within walking distance. The Lighthouse offers a high standard of accommoda-tion. Mary Murphy is very helpful indeed, and has information for visitors on what to see and do in this scenic area. To locate drive up main street to town outskirts, the house is on the right.

OWNER Mary Murphy OPEN February 15 – November 15 ROOMS 1 double, 4 double/single; all en suite. TERMS €25.50–29; reduction for children (50% if sharing); single supplement €6.50–10

DINGLE PENINSULA

Barnagh Bridge
Camp, Dingle Peninsula, Co. Kerry
Tel: 066 713 0145 Fax: 066 713 0299
Email: bbguesthouse@eircom.net
Website: www.barnaghbridge.com

Barnagh Bridge stands in eight acres of well-landscaped gardens, an elevated position overlooking Tralee Bay and the Maharee Peninsula. The house was designed by architect Michael Williams and is delightful in every way. Just about everything has been thought of for guests' comfort. The warm attentive hosts offer a house with all the facilities of a hotel at modest prices. The spacious bedrooms, each with an individual wild flower theme, have high standards of décor and furnishings; all have great views. A conservatory has been added, a wonderful spot in which to relax after a busy day. Heather Williams takes great pride in her cooking, which includes a daily breakfast special, featuring tasty dishes such as mushrooms, kippers, smoked trout, French toast, a wide choice of cereals and fruit, yoghurts, fresh squeezed orange juice, home-made jams and marmalade. A traditional Irish breakfast is also on the menu. The lounge leads out to a patio area and the gardens, which guests are welcome to enjoy on fine days. The ambience is warm and informal, and Heather Williams is very helpful and accommodating. This is a perfect combination for folks looking for a taste of luxury in a beautiful "get away from it all" setting. Visa, Access accepted.

OWNER Heather Williams OPEN March 15 – November 7 ROOMS 2 double, 3 twin; all en suite. TERMS €23–35.50; reduction for children; single supplement €6.50–10

GLENBEIGH

Mountain View
Mountain Stage, Glenbeigh, Co. Kerry
Tel: 066 976 8541

This soft green bungalow lives up to its name: the setting is spectacular – it stands in an elevated position with magnificent views all round. The bedrooms are colourful and immaculately maintained; three are on the ground floor. The TV lounge overlooks the view. Breakfast and dinners, if ordered in advance, are served in the bright dining room. Owner Anne O'Riordan is a very helpful, accommodating lady who has been in business for three years. Lassie, the sweet collie, is friendly. Beaches are close by, and there are mountain and hill walks, fishing and horseback riding in the area, and the Kerry Way Walk is close by.

OWNER Mrs Anne O'Riordan OPEN March 15 – October 31 ROOMS 2 double, 2 single; all en suite. TERMS €21.50; reduction for children; single supplement €6.50 MEALS dinner

GLENCAR

Blackstones House
Blackstone Bridge, Glencar, Co. Kerry
Tel: 066 976 0164 Fax: 066 976 0164

This spacious award-winning old-style farmhouse is situated at the foot of Carrantuohill, Ireland's highest mountain, beside Blackstone Bridge, Licken Wood, overlooking the Caragh River. Walkers will be interested to know it is on the Kerry Way Walk. The clean and cosy bedrooms, which have floral fabrics and pine furniture, are in the oldest part of the house. The sitting room has antique pine furniture and comfortable easy chairs. Breakfast and pre-arranged four-course evening meals are served; wild salmon and home-produced lamb are often on the menu. Special dietary requirements may be met if pre-arranged. The house has a wine license. Smoking is allowed in the lounge only. Self-catering is available.

The setting is superb, and kindly Breda Breen makes guests feel immediately at home. She offers a hot drink upon arrival. The perfect spot for nature lovers, outdoor activities include nature walks (guides can be arranged), mountain and hill walking, fishing, rock climbing and canoeing. Also of interest are the ruins of an old smelting works, which can be seen in Blackstone. Visa, Access, Eurocard accepted.

OWNER Mrs Breda Breen OPEN April 1 – October 31 ROOMS 1 double, 2 twin, 2 family, 1 single; 5 en suite. TERMS €25.50; 33% reduction for children; single supplement €8.50 MEALS dinner

KELLS

Glenville Farmhouse
Gleesk, Kells, Co. Kerry
Tel: 066 947 7625 Fax: 066 947 7625

Situated in a delightful position, midway between Glenbeigh and Cahirsiveen on the main Ring of Kerry Road, Glenville is a spacious new country house, with panoramic views of Dingle Bay. The 50 rooms are well-appointed, with an attractive bright décor. There is a comfortable TV lounge. Tasty breakfasts are served in the dining room that overlooks the bay and the moun-tains. For evening meals, the Thatch Tavern very close by serves a good pint of Guinness, and there is dancing and good craic. A restaurant is within a five-minute drive. There is hill walking on the farm, and fishing trips on Skellig Bay can be arranged. The famous 18-hole champion course at Waterville is just 19 km away. Visa, Mastercard, Access, Eurocard accepted.

OWNER Marion O'Grady OPEN April 1 – September 30 ROOMS 1 double, 2 twin, 1 family; 3 en suite. TERMS €21.50; reduction for children; single supplement €6.50

KENMARE

Ardmore House
Killarney Road, Kenmare, Co. Kerry
Tel: 061 41406

This luxurious farmhouse is set in beautiful, scenic countryside overlooking the sea. It is warm and inviting and Kathy Mullen is a delightful and pleasant host. Guests here are assured of true

Irish hospitality. The immaculate bedrooms are well decorated
and have comfortable beds. There are two lounges, one with TV
and an open fire, and one quiet lounge for chatting and/or
reading. Seafood is a speciality for evening meals, and light meals
are also available. Dinners must be ordered in advance. Lake and
deep-sea angling, pony trekking and beautiful walks are all
available in the area: Kenmare golf course is within 1/2 mile of
the house. Scenic farm walks to the cliff and picnic areas can also
be taken. Visa, Access, Mastercard accepted.

OWNER Tom O'Connor OPEN March 1 – November 30
ROOMS 2 double, 1 twin, 3 double/single; all en suite. TERMS
€28; reduction for children (50% if sharing); single supplement
€6.50

Muxnaw Lodge
Kenmare, Co. Kerry
Tel: 064 41252

This interesting eighteenth-century house enjoys a lovely position, set in 1.5 hectares of beautiful landscaped grounds. The
house has an informal, lived-in atmosphere, and is decorated
with Laura Ashley wallpapers, a Waterford Crystal chandelier,
antique furnishings and many items of interest. The comfortable
TV lounge has the original fireplace and window shutters. The
spacious bedrooms are refurbished in keeping with the character
of the house, which has lovely views, original fireplaces and
antique furniture; one bedroom has a brass bed. Telephones are
available on request. The all-weather tennis court is available for
use by guests.

Evening meals are available by arrangement; vegetarians can be
catered for with advance notice. There is no license, but guests
may bring their own wine. A peaceful and relaxing house, this is
a wonderful base for touring this beautiful area. A pleasant
10-minute stroll over the bridge takes you into town.

OWNER Mrs Hannah Boland OPEN All year ROOMS 3 double, 2 twin; all en suite. TERMS €31.50; reduction for children; single supplement from €6.50 MEALS dinner €19

O'Donnells of Ashgrove
Ashgrove, Kenmare, Co. Kerry
Tel: 064 41228 Fax: 064 41228

O'Donnells of Ashgrove is a charming, peaceful house set in tranquil surroundings of pasture and woodland, with a view of the Caha Mountains. Lynne O'Donnell is a friendly lady who welcomes guests into her home as friends. In the evening, guests are welcome to relax in the armchairs in front of the fire, or, if preferred, to join the family in their spacious and elegantly furnished TV lounge. There are many antique pieces around and the house is tastefully furnished. The property is not suitable for children. Breakfasts are served in the Jacobean-style dining room with its exposed beams, stone fireplace and log fire. Smoking is permitted in the lounge only. A range of Lynne O'Donnell's home-made lavender and pot pourri sachets is on display, and available for purchase.

Light snacks are available; tea and coffee can be requested at any time. There is one ground floor room with bath and shower. Of special interest are Kenmare town, the stone circle, sea trips around Kenmare Bay and the Gleninchiquin Amenity Area. Terry O'Donnell loves to fish, and is a local award-winning fisherman. He would be delighted to take small groups up to eight on fishing trips; packed lunches, evening meals and accommodation can be arranged for an inclusive price. The fishing is great and the company friendly. German is spoken. Visa, Mastercard accepted.

OWNER Mrs Lynne O'Donnell OPEN Easter – October 31 ROOMS 2 double en-suite, 1 twin en-suite, 1 standard. TERMS €28; single supplement €8.50

Whispering Pines
Bellheight, Kenmare, Co. Kerry
Tel: 064 41194 Fax: 064 41194
Email: wpines@indigo.ie

Whispering Pines is a delightful place to stay, located a two-minute walk from the town centre, and a five-minute walk from the golf course. This modernised period home with its delightful garden is set back off the road in quiet and peaceful surroundings. The bedrooms are attractively decorated with matching fabrics and duvets. The charming owners John and Mary Fitzgerald make this a wonderful place to stay; fresh baked scones and tea are offered on arrival, and nothing is too much trouble. They are happy to give advice on what to see and do in the area. An ideal location for touring the scenic Ring of Kerry. Pets outside only. Smoking restricted. Private parking. Situated south of town on the N71, five minute walk from the golf course.

OWNER John & Mary Fitzgerald OPEN All year ROOMS 2 double, 2 twin, family; all en suite. TERMS €30.50; reduction for children (under 10 years 50%); single supplement €7.50

KILGARVAN

Sillerdane Lodge
Coolnoohill, Kilgarvan, Co. Kerry
Tel: 064 85359

This inviting bungalow in an "away from it all" spot is surrounded by beautiful scenery. The bedrooms, all on the ground floor, are light and bright; all have a bright pastel décor. Breakfasts are served in the conservatory-style dining room overlooking the view; the lounge has an open fire. This is wonderful walking country and there is a swimming pool (heated in summer) for guests' use. Evening meals are available by arrangement, with everything prepared from fresh produce and local ingredients – special diets may also be catered for. The reputedly highest pub in Ireland is close by.

OWNER Joan McCarthy OPEN May 1 – September 30 ROOMS 2 double, 2 twin, 1 family; all en suite. TERMS €25.50; reduction for children; single supplement €5 MEALS dinner

KILLARNEY

Abbey Lodge
Muckross Lodge, Killarney, County Kerry
Tel: 064 34193 Fax: 064 35877
Email: abbeylodgekly@eircom.net
Website: www.abbey-lodge.com

Abbey Lodge is an attractive building with a stone and brick exterior. It stands in its own grounds a three-minute walk from the town centre. Recently refurbished, the rooms are of a good size, furnished and decorated to a high standard. John King was formerly in the contracting business, and has made creative use of church window supports in two of the bedrooms, most of which have orthopaedic mattresses. Several rooms have a bath/shower combination. There are several antique pieces of furniture; of special interest are the American oak floors. Throughout the house is a mini art gallery, featuring a fine display of prints by the artist William Frandison. This charming property with its attentive host, has all the facilities of a 4-star hotel. Guests would be well advised to leave their car in the parking lot and walk into town. Popular with business people and tourists, this property would be an excellent choice when visiting the Killarney area. Sightseeing tours can be arranged and nearby facilities include golf and horse riding.

OWNER John King OPEN All year ROOMS 5 en-suite TERMS from €44.50; reduction for children (50% if sharing); single supplement €19–25.50

Fair Haven
Lissivigeen, Killarney, Co. Kerry
Tel: 064 32542
Email: fairhavenbb@eircom.net

Fair Haven is a comfortable, warm country house set in half a hectare of land in peaceful, scenic surroundings. The simply furnished bedrooms are spotlessly clean. The lounge has open fires and tea-makers, and guests may help themselves at any time at no extra charge. Smoking is permitted in the guest lounge if other guests have no objection. There is a separate bright dining room where freshly cooked breakfasts are served. Ann Teahan is an extremely friendly lady who has been welcoming visitors since 1984. Fair Haven was named after the hometown of an American who was the first guest. For guests who would enjoy a rest from driving, Ann Teahan can arrange tours of the Ring of Kerry and Dingle Bay at a modest charge. Buses collect guests at the door. Reservations can also be made for the Killarney Manor House Banquet, an excellent evening of food and entertainment which started in 1990. Golf and fishing are nearby. The postal address for Fair Haven is Fair Haven, Lissivigeen (N22), Killarney. A little tricky to find. Situated on the eastern side of Killarney on the N22 heading to Cork. One mile from park roundabout, on the right hand side of the road leaving Killarney.

Guests can be picked up at the property if they would prefer a tour of the Ring Kerry.

OWNER Anne Teahan OPEN May 1 – October 31 ROOMS 2 double, 2 twin, 1 family; all en-suite. TERMS €25.50; reduction for children (25% if sharing); single supplement €6.50

Kathleen's Country House
Tralee Road, Killarney, Co. Kerry
Tel: 064 32810 Fax: 064 32340
Email: info@kathleens.net
Website: www.kathleens.net

Kathleen's Country House is a delightful, family-run guest house where traditional hospitality and courteous personal attention are assured. The house stands in 1.2 hectares of mature gardens, just 1km north of Killarney. It has been completely renovated. Beautifully maintained and very tastefully decorated, improvements to this immaculate property are ongoing. Kathleen's love of art reflects the décor; there is a splendid display of original oil and watercolour paintings, and inspirational verse decorates the walls. The well-appointed bedrooms are elegantly furnished in antique pine with orthopaedic beds. Breakfasts only are served in the spacious dining room at separate tables overlooking the garden. Kathleen's combines the facilities of a 5 star hotel with the comforts and warmth of an Irish home. Wine license. Smoking is not permitted.

The house motto of "Easy to get to, hard to leave" is endorsed by the many repeat visitors who enjoy the traditional hospitality; they may arrive as guests, but they will leave as friends. There are three 18-hole golf courses, plus two 9-hole courses within a five-minute drive, and fishing, lovely country walks, cycling and swimming are all available close by. Special group rates upon request.

OWNER Kathleen O'Regan Sheppard OPEN March 17 – November 2 ROOMS 6 double, 10 twin, 1 family; all en suite TERMS B&B €45–65; reduction for children (50% if sharing with 2 adults); single supplement

Knockcullen
New Road, Killarney, Co. Kerry
Tel: 064 33915
Email: knockcullen@hotmail.com

Knockcullen, which means "hill on top," is an immaculate family home in a private location off the main road, situated two minutes' walk from town and the National Park. Marie O'Brien has been in business for 10 years; she started when the family had grown and she needed to do something to occupy her time and her home. It has become a popular venue; many guests return often for Marie's special hospitality and the warm and welcoming atmosphere. The house is an ideal touring base for this scenic area. Breakfasts only are served, but there are lots of good pubs and restaurants close by. Marie is interested in walking and mountain climbing and is pleased to assist guests with information and/or planned itineraries. Two minutes to town centre and five minutes to bus and railway station.

OWNER Marie O'Brien OPEN March 17 – November 20 ROOMS 2 double with shower, 2 twin, 4 en-suite TERMS €22; 33% reduction for children under 12; single supplement €4.50

Linn Dubh

Aghadoe Heights, Killarney, Co. Kerry
Tel: 064 33828

A dormer bungalow surrounded by scenic countryside, Linn overlooks Killarney's lakes and mountains. The bedrooms are spotlessly clean and nicely decorated; all have pine orthopaedic beds. Tea making facilities are on the landing and hairdryers are available on request. Carmella Sheehy is an enthusiastic lady who decided to open up her home when her children were young; B&B allowed her to stay home with her children and still have the opportunity to meet people.

There is a comfortable lounge with a TV, and a large, furnished patio area and a spacious garden for guests' use. This is a peaceful area and golf, fishing and horseback riding are all available close by. For visitors wanting a rest from driving, local tours can be arranged. Visa, Mastercard accepted.

OWNER Carmella Sheehy OPEN March 1 – November 30
ROOMS 2 double, 1 twin, 2 family; all en suite. TERMS €25.50; reduction for children (50% when sharing with adults); single supplement €6.50–12.50

Lohan's Lodge

Tralee Road, Killarney, Co. Kerry
Tel: 064 33871 Fax: 064 33871

Lohan's Lodge stands back off the road and is surrounded by a beautiful, well tended garden. Two of the nicest things about the Lodge are the owners, Cathy and Mike Lohan; they are a delightful, warm and friendly couple who love what they do – guests are treated more like friends. The bedrooms, all on the ground floor, are average in size and are colour co-ordinated. Most have views of the gardens, which guests are encouraged to enjoy, and the patio is furnished. Electric blankets are provided for cool nights. There is an extensive menu for breakfast, which is served in the dining room at separate tables. The elegant, spacious lounge, which has cathedral ceilings, is warmed by a gas fire. This is a wonderful spot for visiting Killarney, a three-minute drive away, after which guests can return to the tranquillity and comfort of Lohan's Lodge. Non-smoking household. Visa, Mastercard accepted. Situated on the N22 Killarney/Tralee Road, 5 km from Killarney.

OWNER Cathy & Mike Logan OPEN March 5 – November 5
ROOMS 2 double, 1 twin, single, 2 double/single; all en suite.
TERMS €25.50; reduction for children; single supplement €10

The 19th Green

Fossa, Killarney, Co. Kerry
Tel: 064 32868 Fax: 064 32637
Email: 19thgreen@eircom.net
Website: www19thgreen-bb.com

The 19th Green is an immaculate, well maintained property situated in quiet and peaceful countryside, just a five-minute drive from Killorglin and Ring of Kerry Road. High standards prevail here. The house is efficiently run, and the large bedrooms are tastefully decorated with comfortable beds. Smoking is allowed in bedrooms and the TV lounge. The property has been refurbished since the last edition. The spacious lounge has an open fire in a stone fireplace and overlooks the mountains. Situated across the road are Killarney's two 18-hole championship courses, sited in mature woodlands. Tee times can be arranged, part of the service extended by the accommodating owners, Timothy and Bridget Foley. Tours can also be arranged for the Ring of Kerry, Dingle Peninsula, Blarney Castle, etc. Timothy and Bridget are proud of the personal attention guests receive here, and make every effort to ensure that guests feel welcome and comfortable. They are pleased to offer advice on the wide range of restaurants in Killarney. The property is not suitable for children. Visa, Access, Mastercard accepted.

OWNER Timothy & Bridget Foley OPEN March 1 – November 10 ROOMS 5 double, 5 twin, 3 family; all en suite.
TERMS €30–45; single supplement negotiable

Villa Marias

Aghadoe Heights, Killarney, Co. Kerry
Tel: 064 32307
Email: dgcounihan@eircom.net

A dormer bungalow in a peaceful location, five minutes' drive from the scenic Aghadoe Heights area. The house is immaculate, the bedrooms well-appointed and comfortable. There is a separate TV lounge with an open fireplace, over which is displayed a fine Waterford Crystal sword. Smoking is allowed in the TV lounge. Mary Counihan has been established for 14 years, prior to which she was in the catering industry; she went into the B&B business to maintain contact with people. Mary is a wonderful host: her first concern is her guests' comfort, and a warm welcome greets everyone. Guests are greeted with a cup of tea or coffee and biscuits upon arrival, even though there are tea-makers in the bedrooms. Well located and convenient for all local amenities.

OWNER Mary Counihan OPEN April 1 – October 31 ROOMS 3 double, 1 twin; 2 en suite. TERMS €25.50–28; reduction for children; single room €31.50

Grove Lodge

Killorglin, Co. Kerry
Tel: 066 97 61157 Fax: 066 97 62330
Email: info@grovelodge.com
Website: www.grovelodge.com

This gracious country house stands in 1.2 hectares of mature gardens and woodlands on the banks of the River Laune, and has south-facing views of the McGillycuddy Reeks mountains. The rooms are spacious and the reception lounge has a fully restored antique cast-iron fireplace. The luxurious bedrooms are tastefully appointed. They each have co-ordinated floral bedding and curtains (one has a lace-canopied four-poster bed), and four have their own balconies. The Lodge is delightful in every way: there are high ceilings, a galleried landing, a colourful patio area and a conservatory. Breakfasts are excellent: guests can help themselves to yoghurt, cereal, fruit and juices followed by pancakes or a traditional Irish breakfast. Smoking is permitted in the lounge only. A superb place to stay when visiting this beautiful region of Ireland, the location is idyllic, peace and quiet above all, and the welcome is wonderful. Blennerville Windmill Centre, Crag Cave and Killorgan Golf Club are all within driving distance. American Express, Access, Visa and Diners Club accepted.

OWNER Fergus & Delia Foley OPEN All year except for Christmas ROOMS 5 double, 1 twin, 4 family; 6 en suite. TERMS B&B €30–55 per person; reduction for children (50% if sharing); single €32–57

Ceol na h'Abhann

Tralee Road, Listowel, Co. Kerry
Tel: 068 21345 Fax: 068 21345

Ceol na h'Abhann, which means "Music of the River," is aptly named. This charming thatched house stands on the bank of the River Feale, in a lovely garden with a huge chestnut tree. This is an idyllic setting and guests lucky enough to book in here will not be disappointed. Niall and Kathleen Stack, the delightful owners, originally had the house built as a home for their retirement, but missed contact with people, and bed & breakfast seemed a fun thing to do. It was hard work, but enjoyable; successful from the beginning, many guests return for the special hospitality extended here. The immaculately kept bedrooms are individually decorated and have rich, tasteful furniture; they are reached by a staircase with an old cast-iron railing. One bedroom is on the ground floor. Excellent breakfasts are served in the bright dining room, and there is a lounge and sunny conservatory for guests' use. Smoking in sun lounge only. On fine days guests can stroll along the river bank or, for the less energetic, seating is provided. Listowel is within walking distance and there are several venues for evening meals. Visa, Mastercard accepted.

OWNER Kathleen Stack OPEN April 1 – November 1 ROOMS 2 double, 2 twin, 3 family; 3 en suite. TERMS €28.50–31.50; reduction for children 10%; single supplement €12.50

SNEEM

Avonlea House
Sneem, Co. Kerry
Tel: 064 45221
Email: www.sneem.com/avonlea

Avonlea is an immaculate, comfortable home in a secluded spot close to the village. Mrs Hussey began her bed & breakfast business after a friend asked her to take her overflow guests during high season. Mrs Hussey enjoyed the experience so much that she decided to do B&B full time. A most accommodating host, she is assisted by her children during the summer holidays. The modern bedrooms are warm and comfortable. The TV lounge, with a real fire, has a piano that guests may play. The house is situated just two minutes' walk from the village, which has several good restaurants and local pubs with entertainment during the season. Ideal spot for the holiday golfer, walker and fishing enthusiast, as all are available nearby. Advance reservations recommended during high season.

OWNER Mrs Maura Hussey OPEN April 1 – October 31 ROOMS 2 double, 2 twin, 1 family; all en suite. TERMS €24; single supplement €6.50

Derry East Farmhouse
Sneem, Co. Kerry
Tel: 066 45193 Fax: 066 45193
Email: teahans@eircom.net

Derry East is a working beef suckling farm. This is a botanist's paradise, with its wild mountain landscape background. Derry East has its own hard tennis court and a private fish pond stocked with trout. Guests are welcome to use the facilities and to take farm walks. The bedrooms are warm and comfortable, and the bright, colourful dining room offers views from all windows. Dinner, if arranged in advance, is served featuring home-grown vegetables, with vegetarian and special diets catered for. Smoking is permitted in lounge only.

Derry East is an ideal spot for a relaxing holiday. Mrs Teahan is a caring and considerate host, offering guests a truly warm welcome, ably assisted in the summer by her children, who are happy to play Irish music for her guests.

OWNER Mrs Mary Teahan OPEN Easter – October 31 ROOMS 1 double, 2 twin, 1 family; all en suite. TERMS €27; 25% reduction for children; single supplement MEALS dinner from €28

Hillside Haven
Tahilla, Sneem, Co. Kerry
Tel: 064 82065 Fax: 064 82065
Email: hillsidehaven@eircom

This country house stands in an elevated position set in mature gardens with a magnificent view of the sea, mountains and glorious countryside. The bedrooms, all on the ground floor, are spotlessly clean and comfortable. This is very much a family-run establishment with traditional hospitality and friendly, accommo-dating owners. Tasty evening meals are served (if pre-arranged) featuring traditional dishes, Irish stew, bacon and cabbage, home-baked breads and desserts; vegetarians are catered for. Dinner costs from IR£8-15. Breakfasts are served in the dining room, or, if guests prefer, outside in good weather. Smoking is only permit-ted in the lounge. Light snacks are available on request. Walking is one of Helen Foley's hobbies, and she would be pleased to arrange walking holidays for small groups, and to outline local walks for individual walkers. Complimentary tea and coffee is available at any time.

OWNER Helen Foley OPEN April 1 – October 30 ROOMS 2 double, 2 family; all en suite. TERMS €24; 25% reduction for children if sharing; single supplement €7.50 MEALS €10–19 dinner, snacks

Old Convent House
Pier Road, Sneem, Co. Kerry
Tel: 064 45181 Fax: 064 45184

Visitors enjoy the old-world atmosphere of the Old Convent House, set in its own grounds on the estuary of a river. The house was built in the middle of the last century as a convent for the Presentation nuns, who taught in the local school until 1891. Since that time it has been in the hands of the O'Sullivan family, who have been careful to preserve the character of the house while offering modern comforts. There are two lounges – one for reading or chatting with other guests, the other a very

spacious lounge, and a conservatory. Tea, coffee and biscuits are available at all times in the dining-room. Guests are welcome to make use of the large gardens, and there is access to the river. Fishing enthusiasts may take trips out on the Bay from Oysterbed Pier, and Sneem with its gaily painted houses is just a pleasant three-minute stroll away. Alice O'Sullivan is an enthusiastic walker and can provide walking maps and assist guests with walking itineraries.

OWNER Alice O'Sullivan OPEN December 29 – December 22 ROOMS 2 double, 2 twin, 2 family; all en suite. TERMS €25.50; reduction for children (25% if sharing); single supplement €6.50

TRALEE

Brianville
Clogherbrian, Fenit Road, Tralee, Co. Kerry
Tel: 066 712 6645

A luxurious modern bungalow situated in half a hectare of landscaped grounds, Brianville stands back off the road behind a beautiful stone wall entrance, with views of the mountain. The well furnished lounge has a fireplace, TV and piano. The rooms are well maintained, tastefully furnished and have comfortable beds. There is a lovely antique grandfather clock in the hallway. This is very much a family-run establishment and the owners are helpful and provide literature on what to see and do in the area. All rooms are on the ground floor. There are some excellent seafood restaurants nearby, and golf, fishing, windsurfing and sailing are also within easy reach.

OWNER Mrs Joan Smith OPEN All year ROOMS 2 double, 1 twin, 1 family, 1 single, triple; 4 en suite. TERMS €21.50, reduction for children; single supplement €6.50

Castlemorris House

Ballymullen, Tralee, Co. Kerry
Tel: 066 718 0060 Fax: 066 712 8007
Email: castlemorris@eircom.net

Castlemorris House, a beautiful ivy-clad Victorian house, stands in its own grounds on the edge of town. It was built in 1870 by the local regiment of the British Army and used by the commanding officer as his private residence. The house was purchased by the charming owners, Paddy and Mary Barry, in 1997. They have lovingly restored the residence, carefully combining old-world charm with modern comforts. Many original features remain, such as stained-glass windows and casement shutters. The coving and fireplaces were removed and reinserted after restoration. A warm and simple elegance pervades, the ambience is unpretentious, and the Barrys are fine hosts. The spacious bedrooms, three with original fireplaces, have king-size beds and are furnished in keeping with the character of the house; two have sloping ceilings and beams, and there several interesting antique pieces about. The peaceful drawing room has an open fire, which is lit at the first sign of a chill in the air. Mary is a trained chef and takes pride in her cooking. Imaginative breakfasts and candlelit dinners are served at separate tables in the dining room. There is a wine license. Meals must be ordered in advance: evening meals must be booked before noon. Vegetarian and special diets are catered for. There is plenty to interest the visitor, including Siamsa Tíre (the National Folk Theatre), and Irish music can be heard at local pubs. An Equine Centre is within walking distance of the house. Visa, Mastercard, American Express accepted. The house is a little tricky to find. Take N21 from Limerick, take left off roundabout, signed Dingle/Killorglin, 1/4 mile to T-junction, take a right, the house is immediately on right.

OWNER Mary & Paddy Barry OPEN All year ROOMS 3 double, 3 twin; all en suite. TERMS €38–44.50; single supplement €6.50–12.50 MEALS dinner €25.50

The Fairways

The Kerries, Fenit Road, Tralee, Co. Kerry
Tel: 066 712 7691 Fax: 066 712 7691

The Fairways is in a tranquil spot with beautiful views of Tralee Bay and the Slieve Mish Mountains and overlooks cattle grazing pastures and a 9-hole golf course. The light and airy modern country house is impeccably maintained and well-appointed. The bedrooms are large and tastefully decorated, two are on the ground floor. There is an excellent choice for breakfast: guests can have just about anything they want, including yoghurts, fruits, cereals, home-made brown bread and/or a traditional cooked breakfast. Evening meals are not available, but there are some excellent restaurants in Tralee. An ideal spot for golfers and tourists, fishing, sailing and beaches are all close by. Visa, Mastercard, Eurocard accepted.

OWNER Marion Barry OPEN March 1 – October 31 ROOMS 2 double, 1 twin, 1 family; all en suite. TERMS €25.50; reduction for children (50% when sharing); single supplement €12.50

WATERVILLE

Seaview
Toor, Waterville, Co. Kerry
Tel: 066 947 4297 Email: jfcurran@eircom.net

Seaview is situated in a "top of the world" location and has panoramic views of Ballinskelligs Bay, the Ballinskelligs Mountains and Hogs Head. The house is clean and modestly furnished, and the family suite is ideal for a family or friends travelling together. All bedrooms have new carpets and curtains and TV, as well as showers. The hallway now has an attractive wooden floor, the dining room has been redecorated. Very tastefully refurbished, Seaview is maintained to a high standard. This is a friendly, informal house, the welcome is warm, and the owners are very happy to sit and chat with guests. Complimentary tea or coffee is offered on arrival. There is a cosy conservatory which overlooks the view, and there is a good supply of games and books around. Guests are also welcome to share the family lounge. Breakfast only is served, but Margaret Curran is happy to give advice on local places serving evening meals. No smoking.

OWNER Margaret Curran OPEN February 1 – November 31 ROOMS 1 double, 1 twin, 1 family; all en suite. TERMS €25.50; reduction for children (25% if sharing); single supplement €6.50

Sunset House
Waterville, Co. Kerry
Tel: 066 947 4258

This attractive bungalow overlooks Ballinskelligs Bay on the edge of town. The house is clean and pleasantly furnished with a spacious dining room and a lounge with TV and piano. There is a pretty furnished patio for guests' use. Mrs Fitzgerald began offering bed & breakfast over 16 years ago, adding more rooms for the many guests looking for accommodation. However, she still has to turn people away, advance reservations are recommended, particularly during high season. Evening meals are not available, but the accommodating Mrs Fitzgerald would be happy to recommend local eating places serving good food at reasonable prices. Horseback riding and the beach are close by. The world-famous Waterville golf course is only 1 mile from the house.

OWNER Mrs Patricia Fitzgerald OPEN All year ROOMS 1 double, 7 twin; 4 en suite. TERMS €24–28; reduction for children (25% if sharing); single supplement €5

COUNTY WATERFORD

Waterford is probably best known for its crystal factory, which has regular hours for visits. Situated in the southeast of the country, it is reputedly one of the sunniest spots in Ireland. Waterford has a pretty coastline and a more rugged interior, with good farmland. The Nire Valley is good for walking and pony trekking, and has wonderful views.

Waterford city has much of interest to visit. Reginald's Tower, a massive circular fortress, is now the civic museum. Christ Church Cathedral, built in 1779; the French church; the Chamber of Commerce, a lovely Georgian building; and the City Hall, which houses two old theatres, are all worth seeing. The International Festival of Light Opera is held in Waterford in September.

Dunmore East, Tramore, Annestown and Dungarvan are all pleasant seaside spots, particularly Dunmore East, which resembles a Devon fishing village. Farther south is the Irish-speaking village of Ring, where Irish scholars go to study. St Declan's Oratory, built in the ninth century, and St Declan's Well and Temple Disert, can be found at Ardmore. The cathedral, which dates back to the twelfth century, is known for its sculptured figures.

Seven kilometres from Cappoquin is the Cistercian Abbey of Mount Melleray. The Abbey maintains the tradition of monastic hospitality, so it is quite in order to accept a meal if it is offered to you.

Lismore, which was at one time a great centre of learning, was built by King John in 1185 and once belonged to Sir Walter Raleigh. The gardens are open to the public. The medieval Cathedral of St Cathach is most attractive, and was restored in 1633.

ANNESTOWN

Annestown House
Annestown, Co. Waterford
Tel: 051 396160 Fax: 051 396474
Email: relax@annestown.com
Website: homepage.tinet.ie/~annestown

Annestown House has been in the Galloway family since 1830. The grounds stretch down to a wonderful sandy beach, and there are lovely sea and river views. It is a wonderful, old, long narrow house that was originally three or four houses. One end of the building at one time was the curate's house and the other end housed the village shop. The interior of this lived-in family home, with old family portraits and lots of prints, is on many different levels. It rambles from the billiard room, lined with old books and an open fire, to the small, cosy sitting room and comfortable drawing room. At one time there used to be a restaurant in the house and evening meals, served either at one big table or separate tables, are still available if arranged in advance. The bedrooms, four of which have sea views, all have telephones and tea- and coffee-making facilities. John and Pippa are a delightful, easygoing and interesting couple, and are happy to suggest activities ranging from golf to hill walking to just exploring the beautiful rugged coastline. Close at hand, Annestown has both a croquet lawn and a grass tennis court. Pets in cars only. No smoking in the bedrooms. Mastercard, Visa and American Express accepted. The house is in the centre of the village.

OWNER John & Pippa Galloway OPEN I March – 31 October ROOMS 5 double/twin; all en suite TERMS €55; single supplement €15 MEALS dinner €30

BALLYMACARBRY

Cnoc-na-Ri
Nire Valley, Ballymacarbry, Co. Waterford
Tel: 052 36239 or 087 9477143 Fax:
Email: nharte@ireland.com
Website: homepage.eircom.net/~cnocnari/

Cnoc-na-Ri, meaning "hill of the kings", is a small country home set in a peaceful, quiet spot in the Comeraghs in the heart of the Nire Valley. It has a welcoming, friendly atmosphere and lovely views. Richard and Nora added a wing to their house especially to cater for visitors. The rooms are very comfortable and well equipped with hairdryers, TV and tea- and coffee-making facilities, and two have views. One bedroom has a jacuzzi bath. Nora, an excellent cook, provides a wide menu for breakfast, and evening meals are served, with advance notice, at separate tables in the dining room, which overlooks the nicely landscaped garden and patio. The patio is a lovely place to sit and absorb the peace that surrounds Cnoc-na-Ri. Richard and Nora can provide walking maps and packed lunches, and if needed a local guide is available. Golf, riding and fishing are also popular pastimes in this area, and traditional music and dance is usually to be found in one of the local pubs. Pets in cars only, smoking is permitted in the sitting room. Visa, Mastercard, Access and Eurocard accepted. The house is five kilometres from Ballymacarbry.

OWNER Richard & Nora Harte OPEN January 1 – December 14
ROOMS 1 double, 2 triple, 2 twin; all en suite TERMS €28–31.50;
single supplement €7.50 reductions for children MEALS dinner €25.50

Hanora's Cottage
Nire Valley, Ballymacarbry, Co. Waterford
Tel: 052 36134 Fax: 052 36540
Email: hanorascottage@eircom.net

An absolute haven of peace and tranquillity, Hanora's Cottage
nestles at the foot of the Comeragh Mountains, beside the Nire
Church and the old schoolhouse, with the Nire River running
alongside. The little cottage was built for Seamus' great grandparents in the late 1800s, and Seamus and Mary, the fourth generation of the family, bought it in 1967 as a two bedroom cottage.
It has come a long way since then, and it seems the Walls are
always adding on and making improvements! Currently the
house has eleven spacious, very comfortable bedrooms with
every possible amenity. Some have jacuzzi baths and king-size
beds, and they all have hairdryers, telephones, TV and tea- and
coffee-making facilities. Breakfasts at Hanora's are quite a feast.
Before leaving for work, Seamus bakes all the bread, which
includes a variety of loaves as well as rolls, scones, etc. There is
an exotic array of fruits and Mary's special porridge, local
cheeses, smoked salmon and a choice of cooked breakfasts.
There are a variety of activities for guests - guided or do it
yourself walks both strenuous and gentle in the Comeragh
Mountains; golf (Seamus is past Captain of Clonmel Golf Club,
and held the course record for 11 years); and riding and
bicycling. Having worked off breakfast, there's Eoin and Judith
Wall's dinner to look forward to. Eoin, Seamus and Mary's son,
trained at Ballymaloe Cookery School and has worked in some
renowned restaurants. Later in the evening join the locals at one
of the pubs for traditional music, singing and dancing. Pets in car
only. Smoking only in the lounge. Visa and Mastercard accepted.
The house is sign-posted at Ballymacarbry, and is beside the Nire
Church by the river.

OWNER Seamus & Mary Wall OPEN All year except for
Christmas ROOMS 7 double, 4 twin; all en suite TERMS
€63.50–76; single supplement €25.50 not suitable for children
MEALS dinner a la carte

Aglish House

Aglish, Cappoquin, Co. Waterford
Tel: 024 96191 Fax: 024 96482
Email: aglishhouse@eircom.net
Website: www.aglishhouse.com

This seventeenth century house is on a working dairy farm in
the Blackwater Valley, lying between the Knockmealdown
Mountains and the sea. Aglish House is very much a family home,
with six children and five dogs, and has a relaxed, informal
atmosphere and friendly hosts. Families are particularly welcome.
The bedrooms have telephones and TV, and dinner, by arrangement, is served in the dining room. The house has a wine licence.
Golf, deep-sea fishing, pony trekking and bike hire can be
arranged locally. Smoking is permitted in the sitting room. Visa
and Mastercard accepted. Aglish House can be accessed off the
N25 or N72.

OWNER Tom & Terry Moore OPEN All year ROOMS 1 double, 1
twin, 2 family; 3 en suite, 1 private bathroom TERMS €38; single
supplement €12.50 reductions for children MEALS dinner

Richmond House

Cappoquin, Co. Waterford
Tel: 058 54278 Fax: 058 54988
Email: info@richmondhouse.net
Website: www.richmondhouse.net

This substantial house was built in 1704 by the Earl of Cork and
Burlington and stands in well maintained parkland. It is a peaceful, comfortable country house, beautifully furnished and decorated with spacious, bright rooms. Paul Deevy trained as a chef
at Ballymaloe, and the restaurant at Richmond House has won
several awards for the excellence of its cuisine. Dinner is served
in two elegant dining rooms, which are also open to non residents, and there is a full bar licence. Guests have use of two sitting rooms and a conservatory overlooking the garden. The
comfortable bedrooms are furnished in keeping with the style of
the house and have telephones, TV, trouser presses, hairdryers
and tea- and coffee-making facilities. Arrangements can be made
for salmon fishing on the Blackwater, and trout fishing on the
Blackwater, Suir and the Bride. Deep-sea and coarse fishing are
also available. Other amenities nearby include pony trekking,
walking, mountain rambling and golf. No pets, smoking only in
the lounge. All major credit cards accepted. Richmond House is
half a mile outside Cappoquin on the N72.

OWNER The Deevy Family OPEN Mid-January – 23 December
ROOMS 5 double, 3 twin, 1 single; all en suite TERMS
€57–101.50; reductions for children single supplement €12.50
MEALS Dinner €40.50

Ballyquiry Farm
Dungarvan, Co. Waterford
Tel: 058 41194 Fax: 058 41194
Email: katkiely@eircom.net

Ballyquiry Farm is a 300-year-old building, with a front façade
dating from the Georgian period, and it stands in a wonderful
spot with superb views. It is part of a mixed farm, with the farm
buildings to the rear of the property. In 1940 it was bought by
the Kiely family for IR£1,200. The accommodation is simple, and
is especially suited to families. Two of the rooms each have two
bedrooms, and most have TV and hairdryers. The house is
immaculately kept, the reception rooms have had reproduction
plasterwork installed. Dinner is available if arranged in advance.
No pets. No smoking. Visa and Mastercard accepted. The farm is
sign-posted off the N25 to the south of Dungarvan.

OWNER Kathleen Kiely OPEN April 1 – October 31 ROOMS 2
family, 1 double, 1 single, 1 twin; 4 en suite, 1 public bathroom
TERMS €31.50; single supplement €7.50; reductions for children;
MEALS dinner €16

Powersfield House
Ballinamuck West, Dungarvan, Co. Waterford
Tel: 058 45594 Fax: 058 45550

Enice Power trained in the hotel business in Switzerland, came
home and married a farmer. With two small children she and
Edmund needed to build a house - so decided to incorporate a
family home with a guesthouse and restaurant. The home they
built, finished in 2001, is a classical looking building in the
Georgian style, standing about a mile from Dungarvan, just off
the Clonmel road. Some land surrounds the house, but most of
the dairy and beef farm is a short distance away. Eunice has a
bundle of energy and a love for what she's doing. She's a first
class cook, and the small restaurant is open to the public and
residents alike. The house is attractively furnished, the decor
bright and simple, and the walls adorned with pictures of local
artists. The ground floor bedroom is suitable for wheel chair
access. The bedrooms have TV and telephones, and tea and
coffee can be ordered when required. No pets. No smoking in
bedrooms. Major credit cards accepted.

OWNER Eunice & Edmund Power OPEN All year ROOMS 5
twins/doubles; all en suite. TERMS €38; single supplement
€6.50–11.50 reductions for children MEALS dinner €34.50

Gortnadiha House

Gortnadiha, Ring, Dungarvan, Co. Waterford
Tel: 058 46142 Fax: 058 46538
Email: ringcheese@tinet.ie

Guests will appreciate old-fashioned hospitality at Gortnadiha House, which has been in the Harty family for several generations. The original farmhouse was a long, low thatched building (now the chicken house) and was replaced by the existing farmhouse in 1925 - a good solid house in a most beautiful position. It is surrounded by lovely gardens and every room has a sea, garden or farm view. The house, where Eileen Harty has been welcoming guests for the last four years, is traditionally and comfortably furnished. The sitting room has a TV and tea- and coffee-making facilities. The soaps provided are locally made, and until recently this 300 acre dairy farm made Irish farmhouse cheese. Gortnadiha House is only 3 kilometres from Dungarvan and is sign-posted off the main N25 between Dungarvan and Youghal. Pets can be put up in the stables. No smoking. Major credit cards accepted.

OWNER Eileen & Thomas Harty OPEN March – November
ROOMS 2 doubles en suite, 1 twin with private bath. TERMS €38;
single supplement €6.50; reductions for children

The Castle Farm

Cappagh, Dungarvan, Co. Waterford
Tel: 058 68049 Fax: 058 68099
Email: castlefm@iol.ie
Website: www.waterfordfarms.com/castlefarm/

Mountain Castle was the principal seat of the McGraths of Sliabh gCua, one of the two Gaelic families that owned land in this country before the arrival of Cromwell. The accommodation is in a restored wing of the fifteenth century castle, which stands in lovely countryside with fine views. The oldest section, with the original archway, contains the attractive, long, narrow dining room with its 1.25 metre thick stone walls. Joan Nugent is a very friendly, welcoming lady who has recently refurbished the house with tasteful décor and furniture. It is very comfortable and has a welcoming sitting room where tea and scones are served on arrival. The bedrooms have TV, hairdryers and tea making facilities. Dinner, or lighter meals are available on request, featuring fruit, vegetables, herbs and meats from the family farm, and at breakfast guests are served farm milk and home-made jam. Guests can help themselves to tea or coffee in the kitchen. There is a hard tennis court, garden walks through the acre and a half of gardens, and fishing on the River Finisk, which flows through the farm. The farmhouse is set on 49 hectares of dairy land, and organised farm groups are accepted. Small dogs by arrangement. Smoking in the TV lounge. Visa and Mastercard are accepted. Castle Farm is sign-posted at the N72 and R671.

OWNER Joan & Emmett Nugent OPEN March 17 – November 1 ROOMS 5 doubles/twins; all en suite. TERMS €31.50–38; single supplement ; reductions for children; MEALS dinner €24 light meals €15

DUNMORE EAST

Church Villa
Dunmore East, Co. Waterford
Tel: 051 383390 Fax: 051 383023
Email: churchvilla@eircom.net
Website: homepage.eircom.net/~churchvilla/

This whitewashed period house, one of a row of cottages opposite the Church of Ireland church and adjacent to the Ship Bar and Restaurant, is right in the centre of the attractive village of Dunmore East. The bright bedrooms have been enlarged and redecorated, some retaining their original fireplaces, and they all have TV, hairdryers and tea- and coffee-making facilities. There is a guest lounge with TV, and breakfast is served in the conservatory. There are plenty of eating places in Dunmore East, including the restaurant next door. Church Villa is ten minutes from the beach and fishing harbour and close to the park where there are caves to explore. There are bicycles for guests' use, and free email access. Pets in car only. No smoking.

OWNER Phyllis & Ed Lannon OPEN All year except for Christmas ROOMS 1 triple, 2 twin/double, 2 double, 1 single; all en suite TERMS €25.50–28; single supplement €6.50–9 reductions for children

GLENCAIRN

Buggy's Glencairn Inn
Glencairn, Co. Waterford
Tel: 068 56232 Fax:
Email: buggysglencairninn@eircom.net
Website: www.welcome.to/buggys

This delightful old inn was acquired by the Buggys when they decided to leave Kinsale for a quieter life. It has stood at the crossroads in the tiny hamlet of Glencairn since 1720 and has never lost its licence to be a pub. Seven years ago when Ken and Cathleen moved here it needed a lot of work, and they have transformed it more into a charming restaurant and bar with rooms, than a local pub. It's quaint, cosy and comfortable, decorated with all kinds of knick-knacks, pots and pictures, including a collection of Ken's drawings and cartoons which decorated the walls. The stone floored bar is mostly taken up as a dining room with individual tables. On occasion the table in the old kitchen is used for dinner guests, and breakfast is served in another atmospheric room. The upstairs bedrooms have a lot of character, with brass beds and each of the doubles has a claw foot bath in their en suite bathrooms - the twin has an en suite shower. They all have TV, tea- and coffee-making facilities and hairdryers. Not suitable for children. No smoking in the bedrooms. No pets. All major credit cards accepted.

OWNER Ken & Cathleen Buggy OPEN All year except for Christmas ROOMS 3 doubles, I twin; all en suite. TERMS €45.50; single supplement €12.50 MEALS dinner from €30.50

STRADBALLY

Park House
Stradbally, Co. Waterford
Tel: 051 293185 Fax: 051 293185

Just a kilometre from the charming little village of Stradbally Park House is approached up a long driveway through its 300 acres of farmland. A most colourful and beautifully kept garden lies to the front of the house, which although having the appearance of a more modern building actually dates from the 1800s. Peg Connors has a good sense of humour and likes to keep a well orderly and immaculate home. A long cheerful dining room, where breakfast only is served, lies to one side of the hall way, and a matching size sitting room on the other side. The bedrooms are attractively and simply furnished, mostly in pine with bright, fresh colours. Park House is a peaceful place, and beaches and good restaurants are nearby. Not suitable for children. No smoking. Pets in stables by arrangement.

OWNER Mrs. P. Connors OPEN March I – November I ROOMS 3 twin/double, I single, I family, 2 en suite. TERMS €25.50; single supplement €6.50

TRAMORE

Cliff House
Cliff Road, Tramore, Co. Waterford
Tel: 051 381497 or 391296 Fax: 051 381497
Email: hilary@cliffhouse.ie
Website: www.cliffhouse.ie

Cliff House, built by its owners, stands in landscaped gardens overlooking the sea. Pat and Hilary are friendly and welcoming and run the guest house in a professional manner. There are now two family suites each consisting of two rooms with en suite bathrooms, and the remaining rooms are well appointed, most having sea views and two are on the ground floor. The bedrooms have TV and hairdryers. The large conservatory overlooks Tramore Bay and is a popular place to relax and have a cup of tea or coffee. The extensive breakfast menu has some interesting options. Cliff House is within walking distance of Tramore Golf Club and the town centre and adjacent to the new leisure centre. It is a 10 minute drive from the Waterford Glass Factory. No pets. No smoking. Visa, Access and Mastercard accepted. The house is off the R675 as you exit from Tramore to Dungarvan.

OWNER Pat & Hilary O'Sullivan OPEN 1 February – 15 December ROOMS 8 double/twin/single/family; all en suite. TERMS €30.50; single supplement €5–14; reductions for children

Glenorney
Newtown Hill, Tramore, Co. Waterford
Tel: 051 381056 Fax: 051 381103
Email: glenorney@iol.ie
Website: www.glenorney.com

This attractive looking house on the edge of Tramore was built eight years ago and has a nice front garden. It is very well cared for and has good furniture and decorations. The spacious bedrooms are clean and bright and most have a sea view, and they each have hairdryer, trouser press, telephone, TV and tea- and coffee-making facilities. The nice, bright sitting room has a TV, open fire, piano and sea views. Double doors lead into the breakfast room, which has separate tables with linen cloths. The sun room, garden and patio area are great places to sit and admire the view over Tramore Bay. Pets in cars only. No smoking. Glenorney is on the edge of Tramore and within walking distance of the Golf Club and beaches.

OWNER Marie Murphy OPEN All year except for Christmas ROOMS 2 doubles, 2 twins, 2 family; all en suite. TERMS €42–48.50; single occupancy €6.50; reductions for children

WATERFORD

Blenheim House
Blenheim Heights, Waterford, Co. Waterford
Tel: 051 874115 Fax:
Email: blenheim@eircom.net

Blenheim House was built in 1763 and stands in 1.5 hectares of grounds, including a deer park and a children's play area. Most of the bedrooms have the original Georgian fireplaces and they have tea- and coffee-making facilities. The large lounge with an open fire overlooks the grounds. The Waterford Glass Factory is close by, and other local activities include swimming, riding, golf and fishing. No smoking in the dining room. Pets negotiable. Blenheim House is 5.5 km from the centre of Waterford on the Passage East Road, just a seven-minute drive from the ferry.

OWNER Margaret Fitzmaurice OPEN All year ROOMS 6 twin/double; all en suite. TERMS from €26; reductions for children

Brown's Town House
29 South Parade, Waterford, Co. Waterford
Tel: 051 870594 Fax: 051 871923
Email: info@brownstownhouse.com
Website: www.brownstownhouse.com

This modest looking, brick built Victorian town house is on a residential street, only a few minutes' walk into the centre. It is run by genial Les Brown; his wife, Barbara, is an accountant and financial controller for the Port of Waterford. The house was renovated some three years ago and then added on to in 1998, now providing spacious, attractive accommodation with every possible amenity. The en suite bedrooms each have hairdryer, trouser press, telephone, TV, tea- and coffee-making facilities and mineral water. One double room has a rooftop garden, and one is a suite. There is a small sitting room for guests' use and a dining room where excellent breakfasts are served at one table. Waterford's restaurants are within a five-minute walk, as is the Waterford Show. No pets, smoking is permitted in the lounge. Visa and Mastercard accepted.

OWNER Leslie Brown OPEN 1 February – 15 December ROOMS 1 suite/double, 2 twins, 2 doubles, 1 family; all en suite TERMS €44.50; single supplement €12.50

Foxmount Country House
Passage East Road, Waterford, Co. Waterford
Tel: 051 874308 Fax: 051 854906
Email: foxmount@iol.ie
Website: www.iol.ie/tipp/foxmount.htm

This lovely seventeenth century house is set in attractive countryside surrounded by its 100 hectare farm, run by David Kent and one of his sons. The Kents are a most welcoming, friendly couple, and have been many years in the bed & breakfast business. The drawing room is very attractive with an open fireplace, and is a nice spot to unwind over tea or a pre-dinner drink in front of a warming log fire. The dining room, where excellent

home cooked meals using the farm's own produce - beef, lamb, wild salmon, fresh vegetables and free-range eggs - are served in a party-like atmosphere, has separate tables and a piano. After dinner it is a pleasant stroll to the atmospheric pub under the bridge. Margaret is continuously updating the furnishings and décor, and most recently has created a lovely twin bedded room overlooking the herb garden. All rooms have hairdryers. Guests are welcome to use the hard tennis court and to play table tennis. No pets. Smoking only in the drawing room. To reach Foxmount from Waterford take the Dunmore East Road and after three miles take the Passage East Road.

OWNER David & Margaret Kent OPEN March 10 – November 1 ROOMS 4 double/twin, 1 family; all en suite or with private bathroom. TERMS €44.50; single supplement €12.50; reductions for children MEALS dinner €25.50

Lakefield House
Rossduff, Dunmore Road, Waterford, Co. Waterford
Tel: 051 382582 Fax: 051 382582

This large, modern house is set in its own grounds overlooking Bellake, just below the house, and there are views to the coast at Woodstown beach about three kilometres away. The surrounding farmland is mostly tillage. Mrs. Carney is a friendly lady who was previously in the hotel and restaurant management business. The house has pleasant, well furnished, comfortable rooms. Most of the bedrooms have views, two are on the ground floor, and they all have TV and hairdryers. There is a patio outside the drawing room, and breakfast is served in the dining room. Smoking is allowed in designated bedrooms. All major credit cards accepted. Lakefield House is about 8 km from Waterford and is sign-posted on the R684 Dunmore East road.

OWNER Cally Carney OPEN March 1 – November 1 ROOMS 7 double/twin/family; all en suite. TERMS €25.50–28; single supplement €12.50; reductions for children

Sion Hill House & Gardens

Ferrybank, Waterford, Co. Waterford
Tel: 051 851558 Fax: 051 851678
Email: sionhill@tinet.ie

This house has a fascinating history and a wonderful, charming
atmosphere. It stands high above the river Suir overlooking the
city of Waterford and was built about 1730 for the founder of
the famous Pope (shipping) family. The present owners, George
and Antoinette Kavanagh, are most delightful and attentive hosts
and enjoy relating interesting stories of the house and gardens.
Sion House is full of books and pictures and has a grand piano in
the lived in drawing room, and a beautiful grandfather clock
dating from 1750 in the hall. The Kavanaghs, who are avid
gardeners, were lucky enough to have not only the old plans of
the gardens, dating from 1763, but also to inherit the old
gardener, now in his 80s. Through these two sources they have
been able to restore the lovely garden, which is full of rare and
interesting plants, trees and ferns, and which is open to the
public. A great iron bell made locally and hanging at the side of
the house is sounded on New Year's Eve. The pleasant, comfortable bedrooms overlook the gardens or river, and have TV and
tea- and coffee-making facilities. No smoking. Pets outside only.
Visa and Mastercard accepted.

OWNER George Kavanagh OPEN All year except for Christmas
ROOMS 4 double/twin; all en suite. TERMS €44.50; single supplement €6.50–12.50

COUNTY WEXFORD

The most southerly county and one of the main gateways,
through the port of Rosslare, Wexford is also the warmest part
of the whole country, an area of gentle hills, fertile farmland and
a coastline of sandy beaches. Much of Wexford history is associated with the Norman invasion and the 1798 rebellion.

The Wexford Opera Festival, which takes place in
October, is world-renowned and features top international
singers. The town throbs with an influx of opera lovers, and
many fringe events take place during the festival. It is an
attractive town, with narrow, winding streets, and the Maritime
Museum and the twelfth-century ruins of Selskar Abbey are of
particular interest.

The castle at the attractive market town of Enniscorthy
now houses the county museum, with an interesting folk section.
Worth a visit are the thirteenth-century castle at Ferns, the old
town of New Ross, and Dunrody Abbey, dating from 1182, near
Campile. Nearby at Dunganstown is the Kennedy ancestral
home.

Glendine Country House

Arthurstown, Co. Wexford
Tel: 051 389258 Fax: 051 389677
Email: glendinehouse@eircom.net
Website: www.glendinehouse.com

Built in 1830 as the dower house to Dunbrody, Glendine stands above the village of Arthurstown, where the ferry runs to Passage East It is surrounded by 50 acres of farmland and has lovely views over the estuary. Ann Crosbie, who is a lovely, friendly, cheerful young mother of three sons, inherited the house from her grandparents. The Crosbies did a lot of renovation when they took over the house and have managed to preserve many original features. These include the pine floors, wide back passageway which runs the length of the house, and the old shutters. It has the feel of a family home and is simply decorated and furnished. Ann grows all her own herbs, strives to serve organic food, and runs a coffee shop in the dining room during July and August. Apart from the 50 acres surrounding the house Tom works another farm five miles away and has horses, sheep and cattle. There are 2 self catering units in the converted stables. No smoking. One dog allowed per party - otherwise pets have to be outside. All major credit cards accepted.

OWNER Tom & Ann Crosbie OPEN All year except for Christmas ROOMS 5 doubles/twins, all en suite. TERMS from €31.50; single supplement €12.50; reductions for children MEALS dinner by arrangement

Kilmokea House

Great Island, Campile, Co. Wexford
Tel: 051 388109 Fax: 051 388776
Email: kilmokea@indigo.ie
Website: www.kilmokea.com

Kilmokea was built in 1794 as a Church of Ireland rectory, and it was eventually acquired by David Price in 1947, who was responsible for creating the seven acres of gardens. In 1997 Mark and Emma Hewlett bought the property and spent an enormous amount of energy renovating and restoring it back to its original charm. They have succeeded in creating a peaceful and elegant retreat. Each room has its own character and theme and offers, to a lesser or greater extent, vistas and glimpses of the magnificent gardens. The downstairs loo, which was formerly a bathroom, has been decorated and equipped with pictures, photographs and literature, encouraging a long visit! Kilmokea Gardens, which include a formal walled garden full of rare species from all over the world, and a woodland garden with exotic plants, are open March to October, with the exception of Mondays. The craft shop and tea room serve both teas and light lunches. Visa, Mastercard and Laser and accepted. From New Ross take the R733 to Campile and follow the signs to Kilmokea Gardens.

OWNER Mark & Emma Hewlett OPEN February 1 – November 4 ROOMS 6 double/twin, 5 en suite, 1 with private bathroom. TERMS €57–102; single supplement €19 MEALS dinner €36

ENNISCORTHY

Ballinkeele House

Ballymurn, Enniscorthy, Co. Wexford
Tel: 053 38105 Fax: 053 38468
Email: info@ballinkeele.com
Website: www.ballinkeele.com

Built in 1840, this impressive country house still belongs to the Maher family four generations later. It is approached up a sweeping avenue through game filled parkland, and is set in 140 hectares of farmland. Apart from the addition of such modern conveniences as bathrooms and heating, it remains much as it was built, with a distinctively Victorian flavour. The master bedroom, which has a four poster bed, is the same shape as the drawing room below. The rooms are furnished and decorated to a high standard, and they all have hairdryers, as well as bottled water and a glass of sherry. The Mahers are a friendly, welcoming couple, and Margaret produces delicious dinners (if booked in advance), which include produce from the farm and garden and fresh local ingredients. Meals are served by candlelight in the elegant dining room, and the house does have a wine licence.

Breakfast, which is organised by John, can include hot pancakes and homemade jams. The former billiard room has reverted to the big drawing room again, and has a TV. It is the only place where guests can smoke. Visitors are welcome to walk around the farm, old walled garden and grounds, and Wellington boots can be supplied if it is muddy. There is also a croquet lawn. Pets must stay in owners' cars, Visa and Mastercard accepted. To reach Ballinkeele from the N11, turn in Oilgate at the signpost.

OWNER John & Margaret Maher OPEN 1 March – 6 November ROOMS 3 double, 2 twin/double, all en suite TERMS €58–77; single supplement €16 MEALS dinner €33

Clone House
Ferns, Enniscorthy, Co. Wexford
Tel: 054 66113 or 087 2670164 Fax: 054 66113
Email: breentom@hotmail.com

This attractive, creeper-covered, 300 year old farm house is in a quiet location on nearly 120 hectares of mixed farmland. Guests can fish on the Bann River, which runs through the property, feed the lambs, see calves born or just go for wonderful walks. The Breens bought the property about 40 years ago, and gradually did it up. Betty is partiuclarly gifted at landscaping and has created a lovely garden. Guests are treated as friends and enjoy such luxuries as breakfast in bed, served at any time, using home-grown or reared produce. The house is very comfortable and has been attractively furnished. Two of the rooms have balconies, which are very popular with guests, and they have hairdryers and most have TVs. There is a comfortable sitting room and dining room, baby-sitting is available, and there is a pony for children to ride. Many guests come to buy horses, others to visit a local herbalist, other to hunt, or just to relax. Pets by arrangement. Smoking is permitted in the living room and on the bedroom balconies. Clone House is signposted on the N11 at Ferns, three kilometres away.

OWNER Mrs. Betty Breen OPEN March – October ROOMS I twin, 2 family, 2 double/twin, 3 en suite, 2 private bathrooms TERMS €35; single supplement €9; reductions for children

Salville House
Enniscorthy, Co. Wexford
Tel: 054 35252 Fax: 054 35252
Email: salvillehouse@eircom.net

This lovely old house, built in the mid nineteenth century, stands in its own grounds overlooking the River Slaney and the Blackstairs Mountains. The interior is light and bright with spacious, simply furnished rooms and wooden floorboards. The bedrooms have hairdryers and tea- and coffee-making facilities. Salville House has a good reputation for its food, and dinner, by arrangement, is served at one long table in the dining room. Guests are welcome to bring their own wine, and they have use of a comfortable drawing room. The house is located just outside the cathedral town of Enniscorthy, noted for is thirteenth century castle. There are a number of golf courses in the area, good hill walking on the Blackstairs Mountains and fine beaches along the Wexford coastline. There is also a self catering unit available. Pets by arrangement, no smoking in bedrooms. To find Salville House from Enniscorthy take the N11 towards Wexford, after a mile take the first left after the hospital, go up the hill and turn left. The house is the third on the left.

OWNER Gordon & Jane Parker OPEN All year ROOMS 3 doubles, 1 2-bedroom suite, 2 en suite, 2 private bathrooms TERMS €35–38; single supplement €6.50–12.50; reductions for children MEALS dinner €28.50

The Old Deanery
Ferns, Enniscorthy, Co. Wexford
Tel: 054 66474 Fax: 054 66123
Email: deanery@indigo.ie
Website: indigo.ie/-deanery

The Sinnotts bought this lovely old house in 1996, primarily because their daughter wanted to run the Garden Centre at the end of the driveway. Originally built in 1735, the house was extended in 1812 to accommodate the then incumbent's 11 children, and the front door was moved to the side of the house. There is a lovely central hall both on the ground floor and the upper floor, off which are the spacious, beautifully furnished, comfortable bedrooms. In spite of all the work to the house itself, Valerie is most proud, and justifiably so, of the five delightful self catering coach houses, which have been beautifully designed and equipped, and are excellent value. The rate per person includes a continental breakfast tray. The old gate lodge is now the flower shop, which compliments the garden centre, and there are lovely gardens surrounding the house. At night the floodlit abbey and cathedral are particularly picturesque. Not suitable for children except in self-catering accommodation. No smoking. Most credit cards accepted.

OWNER Lorcan & Valerie Sinnott OPEN March – November ROOMS 4 double/twin all en suite. TERMS €75; €37.50 per person in cottages

Woodbrook
Killann, Enniscorthy, Co. Wexford
Tel: 054 55114 Fax: 054 55671

Woodbrook is a lovely, large, Georgian house, first built in the 1770s, but damaged in the rebellion of 1798. Giles and Alexandra FitzHerbert, who both have ties to South America, have lived here with their four children since 1998, and have worked on improvements to the house. The rooms are spectacularly large, and the first floor central corridor is particularly impressive, with the two outstanding features of the house being the 'flying staircase' and the enormous drawing room. Woodbrook is set in lovely parklands, gardens and woods and is part of a farm that provides a house cow and a small herd of pure bred Hereford cattle. The FitzHerberts on occasion arrange opera performances in the grounds, there is a grass tennis court, and the walled garden produces organic fruit and vegetables for sale, and for home consumption. Good home cooked dinners are available if booked in advance, and the house carries a selection of wines. There are lovely walks on the nearby Blackstairs Mountains, and riding, fishing and golf are all available in the area. Major credit cards are accepted. Woodbrook is 2 miles from Kiltealy and 2 miles from Killann, off the R730.

OWNER Giles & Alexandra FitzHerbert OPEN June – September, and for Wexford Festival ROOMS 4 double/twin; 3 en suite, 1 private bathroom. TERMS €63.50; single supplement €12.50; reductions for children MEALS dinner

FOULKSMILLS

Farmhouse
Foulksmills, Co. Wexford
Tel: 051 565616

Records of this old building, originally a thatched house, go back to 1614. The Farmhouse is from a bygone era, and is part of a 60 hectare mixed farm, run by one of Mrs. Crosbie's sons. She is a friendly, welcoming older lady, who was one of the founding members of the Farmhouse Assocation. When she started doing bed & breakfast 35 years ago she charged sixpence a night and six shillings for a week's full board. The accommodation is old fashioned and comfortable, with compact bedrooms, some of them attic shaped. The reading room has lots of bookcases around the room and a large dining room table, and there is an attractive sitting room. The dining room with separate tables is an enormous room with a high ceiling, and was originally a farm building. Pets outside only. Smoking permitted in the sun room. The Farmhouse provides old fashioned basic accommodation with none of the modern day extras. The house can be found 12 miles from Wexford off the N25.

OWNER Joan Crosbie OPEN April – November ROOMS 4 doubles, 3 twins, 2 singles, 1 family; 3 public bathrooms. TERMS €23; no single supplement; reductions for children

Horetown House
Foulksmills, Co. Wexford
Tel: 051 565771 Fax: 051 565633
Email: poloxirl@iol.ie

Horetown House is a lovely, seventeenth century Georgian manor house situated in beautiful parklands and tranquil countryside, amidst 100 hectares of mixed farming. The process of renovating the house is gradual, and more recent improvements include the addition of en suite bedrooms and a wine bar, which is open for light meals and snacks. The entrance hall is lined with the heads of deer and other animals, and the rooms have old fashioned functional furnishings. The bedroomss are spacious and comfortable, and guests can relax in the drawing room in front of the log fire. There's a separate TV room and also the Cellar Restaurant - open to the public - which has a good reputation. Lawn croquet and table tennis are available, and small conferences and business lunches can be catered for. The equestrian centre covers dressage instruction, polocrosse, escorted rideouts and instruction for beginners, and it has two large all weather indoor arenas. No pets, no smoking in the dinring room. Visa and Mastercard accepted. To find Horetown House, take the right fork at the bottom ol Foulksmills for approximately one and a half kilometres, pass a country pub and sharp bend and it is the next turn left.

OWNER Ivor Young OPEN March 1 – October 31 ROOMS 10 doubles/twins, 2 triples; 10 en suite, 2 public bathrooms. TERMS €38–44.50; single supplement €15; reductions for children MEALS lunchtime snacks, dinner from €21–28.50

Perrymount House
Gorey, Inch, Co. Wexford
Tel: 0402 37387

Built by Colonel Perry in 1798, Perrymount has been in Peter's family for the last 100 years. The Donnellys' offer delightful hospitality with both comfortable en suite bedrooms in the house and very pretty self-contained cottages in the courtyard. Peter runs the most picturesque dairy farm, sometimes with the help of their three young sons. This place is a paradise for children. They are made very welcome and there are all sorts of safe play areas for them. They can ride a pony and play with all sorts of pets. There is a lovely view over the hills and walks down to a large pond full of ducks and geese. Anne is an enthusiastic and very successful gardener, and provides delicious food which is traditionally Irish, and mostly home produced. Pets and smoking outside only. Visa and Mastercard accepted. The self catering units are open all year

OWNER Peter & Anne Donnelly OPEN March 1 – December 1 ROOMS 4 doubles/twins all en suite. TERMS €25.50; reductions for children MEALS dinner €12.50–18

Healthfield Manor
Killiuin, Co. Wexford
Tel: 053 28253 Fax: 053 28253

The story runs that back in the 1400-1500s there was a plague in Wexford, and consequently the water was undrinkable. Healthfield, which has its own well, was the nearest place to the city with good water - hence the name. Built in 1820, this country house is reached up a long driveway through its 40 hectares of farmland, which supports organically reared sheep, and is bordered by mature shrubs and wonderful rhododendrons. At the top there are spectacular views over the river Slaney. The entrance to the house is through a small conservatory, and beyond is the very large drawing room. The bedrooms are incredibly spacious, some have their own sitting rooms - such as the "Five Acre Suite" - and the top floor suite has furniture made from an elm from the property, including a four poster bed. They all have hairdryers and all but one room has the lovely front view over the grounds to the river. Packed lunches can be prepared with notice, and pets can be accommodated in the stables. Smoking is permitted in the drawing room. Healthfield is eight kilometres from Wexford, and is signposted on the Killurin road.

OWNER Mayler & Lorette Colloton OPEN All year except for
Christmas ROOMS 3 double or twin, 1 family; 1 en suite, 3 private
bathrooms. TERMS €31.50; single supplement €12.50; reductions
for children MEALS packed lunches

KILMORE

Ballyhealy House
Ballyhealy Beach, Kilmore, Co. Wexford
Tel: 053 35035 Fax: 053 35038
Email: bhh@gofree.indigo.ie

Once the seat of Wexford's High Sherriff, it is very close to the
sea and a pleasant beach. The present owner, Betty Maher-
Caulfield, acquired the then ruined eighteenth century house
four years ago, and has created the sort of holiday house of
childhood dreams. There are horses and ponies to ride (there is
a certified riding school), swimming and sea fishing, and a feeling
of freedom and happiness for people of all ages. The three bedrooms are very spacious, some with enough beds for a family of
four or five, and all have a sea or castle view. Dinner served at 8
p.m. needs to be booked in advance. Children and pets especially
welcome. No smoking in bedrooms. Major credit cards accepted.

OWNER Betty Maher-Caulfield OPEN All year ROOMS 3
double/twin/family all en suite. TERMS €28–34.50; single supplement €16.50; reductions for children MEALS dinner €31.50

NEW ROSS

Creacon
New Ross, Co. Wexford
Tel: 051 421897 Fax: 051 422560
Email: info@creaconlodge.com

This charming, long, low whitewashed house, built in the 1840s,
is covered with climbing plants and is set in a very pretty, sheltered garden. Some of the attractive bedrooms are in the main
house, tucked under the roof, three are in the old byre and two
in the former greenhouse. All rooms have hairdryer, telephone
and TV. The drawing room is full of comfortable chairs and sofas
and has a log fire to relax in front of with a drink before or after
dinner. The very popular restaurant serves wonderful food, and
there is a large bar for both residents and non-residents.
Josephine Flood is a most imaginative and attentive host, and her
slogan "Well worth the trouble of finding us' is true. The John F.
Kennedy Memorial Park is a ten minute drive away, and nearby is
the Hook Peninsula, with secluded beaches and coves and the
oldest lighthouse in Europe. No pets. Smoking allowed in the

drawing room. Visa and Mastercard accepted. To find Creacon, take the R733 signposted to John F. Kennedy Park and after five kilometres turn left for the house.

OWNER Mrs Josephine Flood OPEN All year ROOMS 9 double/twin, all en suite. TERMS €38–44.50; single supplement; reductions for children MEALS dinner €22

Dunbrody Country House Hotel

Arthurstown, New Ross, Co. Wexford
Tel: 051 389 600 Fax: 051 389 601
Email: info@dunbrodyhouse.com
Website: www.dunbrodyhouse.com

This beautiful Georgian house in a wonderful park like setting opened as a country house hotel and restaurant in the summer of 1997. It was built in 1830 for Lord Spencer Chichester, and remained in the family until recently. Kevin and Catherine Dundon have done an outstanding job renovating the house and transforming it into an elegant and comfortable small hotel, where guests can sample the best of Irish hospitality. Kevin, a master chef, specialises in contemporary Irish cuisine. Beautifully presented dishes are served in the enormous dining room, which has well spaced out tables, and was previously both the drawing and dining rooms. There is an attractive bar, and a wonderful entrance hall. The lovely bedrooms are large and all have splendid views. For those wanting a lazy morning, breakfast can be served in bed. The land around the house runs down to the river; there are horses, a nursery garden and well tended gardens containing many unusual plants and flowers. Any number of special packages can be arranged, as well as conferences and weddings. Pets can be accommodated in the stables, and smoking is permitted in specific areas. Visa, American Express and Mastercard are accepted. Dunbrody is on the R733, 11 kilometres from Waterford via the Passage East car ferry and 19 kilometres south of New Ross.

OWNER Catherine & Kevin Dundon OPEN All year except for Christmas ROOMS 20 doubles/twins/suites; all en suite. TERMS €89; single supplement; reductions for children MEALS lunch €25.50, dinner €38

Oakwood House

Ring Road, Mountgarrett, New Ross, Co. Wexford
Tel: 051 425494 Fax: 051 425494
Email: susan@oakwoodhouse.net
Website: www.oakwoodhouse.net

Susan Halpin and her husband built Oakwood House as a guest

house some five years ago. It is neat and immaculately kept, enjoys lovely views of the Barrow Valley and is located on the ring road (N 30) above New Ross. The accommodation offers a small, comfortable sitting room, and an extensive, sunny breakfast room which has the view. The bedrooms are simply furnished in pine and have TVs, hairdryers and tea- and coffee-making facilities. It is a 15 minute walk into town - somewhat longer on the way back up the hill, and a close by pub offers evening meals, snacks and Irish music at the weekend. No smoking. No pets. Major credit cards accepted.

OWNER Susan Halpin OPEN March 1 – November 1 ROOMS 4 double/twin; all en suite. TERMS €28–31.50; single supplement €4–6.50

Riversdale House
Lower William Street, New Ross, Co. Wexford
Tel: 051 422515 Fax: 051 422800
Email: riversdalehse@eircom.net

This large, modern house is just three minutes from the town centre. It was built by the Foleys eight years ago and is surrounded by half a hectare of gardens. The pretty, walled rear garden originally belonged to the nearby convent. Riversdale has lovely views over the town and the River Barrow, and from the back it is particularly attractive at night, when the church is floodlit. This is a comfortable house with an upstairs lounge; the dining room and recently added conservatory are on the ground floor. The bedrooms have hairdryers, TVs and tea- and coffee-making facilities. Ann Foley is a friendly, chatty lady who teaches cookery classes. Pets in owners cars, no smoking. Visa and Mastercard accepted. The house is signposted from the quayside.

OWNER Ann Foley OPEN February 1 – November 1 ROOMS 4 double/twin/family, all en suite. TERMS €25.50–28; single supplement €12.50

ROSSLARE

Churchtown House
Tagoat, Rosslare, Co. Wexford
Tel: 053 32555 Fax: 053 32577
Email: churchtown.rosslare@indigo.ie
Website: www.churchtown~rosslare.com

Set in 3.25 hectares of park like grounds, this attractive house dates from 1703. Patricia and Austin Cody have worked miracles in transforming Churchtown House to what it is today. When they bought it, it had been inhabited by one old man, who used a kitchen with stairs up through a cupboard to one room above. The spacious rooms have been tastefully decorated and furnished, and a bedroom on the ground floor is suitable for wheelchairs. All have telephones, TVs and hairdryers. There are two comfortable drawing rooms and three dining rooms, one of which is a conservatory like room with windows all around looking out over the garden. Good old fashioned cooking and local ingredients are what make dinners at Churchtown House memorable. These need to be booked in advance, and there is a wine licence. Activities such as bird watching, golf, fishing, swimming, walking and riding are available locally. No pets, smoking in the garden lounge only. Most major credit cards accepted. Churchtown is on the R736.

OWNER Patricia & Austin Cody OPEN March – November
ROOMS 5 double, 5 twin, 1 suite, 1 single; all en suite
TERMS from €76; single supplement €25.50 MEALS dinner €35

ROSSLARE HARBOUR

Laurel Lodge
Rosslare Harbour, Co. Wexford
Tel: 053 33291

This attractive, low, modern house is down a quiet country lane in the village of Kilrane. The bedrooms are clean, simply furnished and have TVs and tea- and coffee-making facilities. There is a guest lounge, and the dining room, where breakfast is served, overlooks a small patio at the back of the house. There are four hotels and two pubs within walking distance. No smoking and no pets. Mastercard, Visa and Access are accepted. Laurel Lodge is signposted off the main road and also in the village.

OWNER Mr. & Mrs. O'Donoghue OPEN March 1 – October 31
ROOMS 1 double, 2 twins, 1 double/twin, all en suite. TERMS
€24; single supplement €8.50; reductions for children

WEXFORD

Broom Cottage
Rosslare Road, Drinagh, Wexford, Co. Wexford
Tel: 053 44434

This attractive, creeper-clad, eighteenth century farmhouse is set back a little from the main road, and is part of a 56 hectare beef, sheep and tillage farm. Eleven hectares of the land lie around the house, which is three kilometres from the centre of Wexford on the Rosslare road. Broom Cottage has been in the same family for the last 200 years and an extension was built on 25 years ago. It offers comfortable, clean, well equipped bedrooms, and guests have use of a TV lounge and conservatory. Breakfast only is served in the dining room. No pets. No smoking in the bedrooms. The accommodation is good value and it is convenient for the Rosslare car ferry.

OWNER John & Theresa Devereux OPEN May – September 30 ROOMS 4 double/twin; all en suite. TERMS €25.50; single supplement; reductions for children

Clonard House
Wexford, Co. Wexford
Tel: 053 43141 Fax: 053 43141
Email: clonardhouse@indigo.ie

This elegant Georgian farmhouse, part of a 48 hectare dairy farm, is set in idyllic surroundings with a clear view of Wexford harbour. Clonard House was completely renovated and retains many of its original features, such as cornices, ceiling roses and the dining room fireplace. Since then there has been a continuous programme of updating and refurbishing to maintain its already high standard. The bedrooms are extremely attractive, with traditional and antique furnishings, and they have TVs, hairdryers, tea- and coffee-making facilities, and some have four poster beds. The lounge has plenty of room to relax in after a busy day's sightseeing. There is a games room in the basement for guests. This is a lovely, peaceful house with a lot of character (and a stairway to nowhere!). Pets only in car, and smoking is permitted in one reception room. It is signposted off the N11 ring road, one kilometre away.

OWNER Kathleen Hayes OPEN March 1 – November 1 ROOMS 4 double/twin, 3 triples, 1 family; all en suite TERMS €28–31.50; single supplement €6.50; reductions for children

Darral House

Spawell Road, Wexford, Co. Wexford
Tel: 053 24264 Fax: 053 24284

This attractive looking town house was built in 1803 and is set
back a little from the road. The Nolans, who are a welcoming
couple, renovated the building in 1994, making it warm and
comfortable and retaining the elegance of the period. It has very
spacious rooms with high ceilings in the dining room and lounge.
The bedrooms are very comfortable and thoughtfully equipped
and all have hairdryers, TVs and tea- and coffee-making facilities.
Darral House has plenty of parking and a pleasant back garden,
which guests are welcome to use. No pets, smoking permitted in
the lounge. Visa and Access acepted. The house is a few minutes
walk to the centre, and offers good value.

OWNER Sean & Kathleen Nolan OPEN All year except for
Christmas ROOMS 1 double, 3 family; all en suite. TERMS €35;
single supplement €12.50; reductions for children

Killiane Castle

Drinagh, Wexford, Co. Wexford
Tel: 053 58885 Fax: 053 58885
Email: killianecastle@yahoo.com
Website: www.killianecastle.com

This eighteenth century house is attached to the tower of a
fourteenth century castle and is part of a dairy farm. Killiane
Castle is down a quiet country lane and is very handy to the
Rosslare ferry, which is only a ten minute drive away. The
Mernaghs are constantly striving to keep up standards, and
regularly redecorate the house, which is attractively furnished.
The first floor bedrooms are particularly large and they all have
TVs, hairdryers and tea- and coffee-making facilities. Coffee or
tea are available in a small ground floor lounge, and another sit-
ting room is a nice place to relax in. For those catching early
morning ferries, breakfast is provided. There is a hard tennis
court and four self-catering apartments at the back of the house.
No pets, and smoking is allowed only in one lounge. Visa and
Mastercard are accepted. Killiane Castle is signposted on the
N25 between Wexford and Rosslare.

OWNER Jack & Kathleen Mernagh OPEN March 17 – October
17 ROOMS 3 double, 3 twin, 2 family; all en suite. TERMS €31.50;
single supplement €12.50; reductions for children MEALS light
meals

COUNTY CLARE

Two hundred castles and 2,300 stone forts going back to pre-Celtic times testify to County Clare's turbulent past. Although Shannon Airport lies on the southern border, most of the county is underpopulated by tourists. The scenery varies from the barren terrain of the Burren, which in spring is covered in a profusion of northern and southern plants, to the scenic lakes and hills of Slieve Bernagh, wonderful walking country, and the towering Cliffs of Moher. Water plays an important role, the sea bordering the west, and the Shannon Estuary the south and east. The Franciscan Ennis Friary, noted for its sculptures and decorated tombs, is one of the principal sights of the county capital Ennis, which is situated on a bend of the River Fergus.

A bridge crosses the Shannon at Killaloe. Nearby is a twelfth-century cathedral built on the site of an earlier church. It has a magnificent door and the views from the top of the square tower are splendid. Across the Shannon lies Bunratty Castle, well known for its medieval banquets. It dates from 1460 and was at one time occupied by Admiral Penn, the father of William Penn, founder of Pennsylvania. There is a Folk Park in the castle grounds, with examples of houses from the Shannon area. The island of Iniscealta on Lough Derg can be reached by boat from the attractive village of Mountshannon. There are five old churches, a round tower, saints' graveyard, hermit's cell and a holy well.

Moohaun Fort, one of the largest Iron Age forts in Europe, is to be found at Newmarket on Fergus. Knappogue Castle, another venue for medieval banquets, and Quinn Abbey are close to Craggaunowen.

Of special interest to both botanists and historians is the Burren. Once densely populated, this savagely rocky area is rich in prehistoric and historic monuments. Look closely at its limestone and discover a wealth of exquisite, delicate plant life thriving in a myriad of tiny crevices. The Burren Display Centre explains the fauna and flora of the 500 square kilometres of the Burren and its remains of ancient civilisation. The ruined Leamaneh Castle is near Kilfenora, which is on the edge of the Burren. Between Kilfenora and Ballyvaughan is Ballkkinvarra, one of Ireland's finest stone forts, and southeast of Ballyvaughan is Aillwee Cave, which dates back to 2 million B.C.

The road from Lisdoonvarna, Ireland's foremost spa town, leads to the impressive Cliffs of Moher, which stretches for nearly 8 km. Liscannor is famous for the Holy Well of St Brigid, which is an important place of pilgrimage.

Lahinch, a small seaside resort, is best known for its championship golf course, and to the south is Spanish Point, where many ships of the Spanish Armada were wrecked.

Around the village of Quilty, seaweed can be seen drying on the stone walls. The coast south of Kilkee is every bit as spectacular as the Cliffs of Moher, with caverns and strange rock formations.

BALLINA

Carramore Lodge
Oolagh, Ballina, Co. Clare
Tel: 061 376704

This spacious country house stands in one and a half acres of landscaped grounds, overlooking Lough Derg. The good sized, bright and fresh bedrooms are, luxuriously furnished, immaculately maintained, and have either a mountain or lake views. All rooms have en-suite facilities, TV and tea making facilities. Carramore House is popular with tourists and outdoor enthusiasts, there are lovely walks close by, and is convenient to golf, horse riding, and fishing. Evening meals are not served, but there are several restaurants, and pubs, in Killaloe, which is with walking distance. Imaginative tasty breakfasts are served, at separate tables, in the dining/room/lounge, and include smoked salmon, home baked brown bread, fruit, a good choice of cooked items and plenty of tea and coffee. Eileen Brennan, loves her business, and is a thoughtful and considerate host. This is a non-smoking property. Visa, Mastercard accepted. Situated 30 minutes from Shannon airport, and easily located on the Limerick to Ballina Road, just before the village.

OWNER Eileen Brennan OPEN March 1 – October 31 ROOMS 4 double/twin/family; all en suite. TERMS €25.50; reduction for children; single supplement €9

BALLYVAUGHAN

Dolmen Lodge
Tonarussa, Ballyvaughan, Co. Clare
Tel: 065 707 7202 Fax: 065 707 7202

This elegant, modern farmhouse stands in open scenic countryside and has stunning views of the Burren and Galway Bay. It is part of a working cattle farm, and there are some interesting rock formations on the land. The bedrooms are large and have dainty duvets and a light pastel décor. The dining room, where breakfasts are served at separate tables, has lace tablecloths; this room overlooks the view, as does the lounge. This is a non-smoking establishment. There are some interesting antiques about, including a grandmother clock in the hallway. Dolmen Lodge offers luxurious, high-quality accommodation at modest prices. It is a superb choice for guests touring this beautiful area. Breakfast only is served, but Ballyvaughan is only 1 km away and Philip and Mary Kyne will be happy to assist with choosing venues for evening meals, and also to give advice on what to see and do in the area. Sign-posted on N67 Ballyvaughan-Galway Road.

OWNER Philip & Mary Kyne OPEN March 17 – October 10 ROOMS 2 double, 2 twin; all en suite. TERMS €25.50–28; reduction for children; single supplement (seasonal)

BUNRATTY

Bunratty View
Cratloe, nr. Bunratty, Co. Clare
Tel: 061 357352 Fax: 061 356491

Bunratty View was designed and built as a purpose built bed and breakfast, and stands on 20 acres of open farmland. The bedrooms are large, have orthopaedic beds, dressing tables, TV, tea-makers and direct dial telephones. Breakfasts are served in the bright dining room, which has a conservatory effect, due to the large windows that overlook scenic countryside. The house is well maintained; all of the rooms are on the ground floor, one of which is suitable for wheelchair access. There are several interesting pieces of furniture about, including two antique sideboards.

There is a guest lounge, where smoking is permitted, and a conservatory, which provides a peaceful spot in which to relax after a busy day. Evening meals are not served, but there are establishments for food within walking distance.

There are views of floodlit Bunratty Castle at night; free transportation to the castle is arranged, and reservations for the banquet can also be organised. Bunratty View is in a peaceful location, just less than a mile from the castle. Cratloe Church is worth a visit: built over 200 years ago, it is one of the last of the three Barn Churches remaining in the country. Shannon Airport is a ten-minute drive. Visa, Mastercard accepted.

OWNER Joe & Maura Brodie OPEN All year ROOMS 7 double/twin/family; all en suite. TERMS €25.50–33; reduction for children; single supplement €9

Tudor Lodge
Hill Road, Bunratty, Co. Clare
Tel: 061 362248 Fax: 061 362569
Email: tudorlodge@esatclear.ie

This gracious and elegant home stands in a secluded, peaceful, wooded setting where guests awaken to the sound of birds singing. The house was in a derelict condition when it was purchased seven years ago. It has been beautifully restored into a comfortable and quite luxurious home. The tiled entryway is full of plants and the bedrooms are furnished and decorated to a high standard. The bathrooms are large and have powerful showers. There is a very comfortable lounge, with blue leather furniture, which leads out to a conservatory overlooking the well tended garden. An added bonus are the accommodating and helpful owners, Carmel and Michael Dennehey, both local people who provide lots of information for guests on what to see and do in the area. Reservations can be made for the medieval banquet at Bunratty Castle, which is within walking distance, as is Durty Nellie's pub, which serves lunch and dinner. Shannon Airport is a 15-minute drive from the house. Visa, Mastercard accepted. Situated in Bunratty, 500 m up the hill on the right.

OWNER Mr & Mrs Carmel & Michael Dennehy OPEN Mid-February – November 31 ROOMS 2 double, 2 twin, 1 triple; all en suite. TERMS €28; single supplement €16.50

KILRUSH

Old Parochial House
Cooraclare, Kilrush, Co. Clare
Tel: 065 905 9059 Fax: 065 905 9059
Email: oldparochailhouse@eircom.net
Website: www.oldparochialhouse.com

Old Parochial House, built in 1871, was formerly the parish priest's residence, and stands in 1.25 hectares of grounds in an unspoiled area ideal for walking. The house has been tastefully restored, and is non-smoking.

It has great views and all-modern comforts, yet retains the character and ambience of a bygone era. There are high ceilings, polished wood floors, original fireplaces and stripped pine doors; the house is furnished in keeping with its character, and is well maintained by Alyson O'Neill, who made all the curtains. She is an informal, congenial lady who takes excellent care of her guests.

The bedrooms are large, and one of the public bathrooms has an original Victorian bath. The spacious sitting room has a bay window overlooking the view, and the dining room, where a varied breakfast is served, has an original black marble fireplace. A field on the property has been converted to a 9-hole pitch and putt course, and there is a snooker room, play room and play area, as well as a fish tackle room for lake fishing. There are also local bog walks, ring forts, ancient prayer sites and an old church close by. There are pubs and restaurants in the immediate area for meals. The stables have been converted to provide comfortable self-catering accommodation. Visa, Mastercard accepted. 200 m from Cooraclare and on the car ferry route.

OWNER Alyson & Sean O'Neill OPEN April 1 – October 31 ROOMS 1 double, 1 twin, 2 family; 3 en suite, 1 with own bathroom. TERMS B&B €32–40; reduction for children under 12 years; single supplement €12

LISDOONVARNA

Fermona House
Bog Road, Lisdoonvarna, Co. Clare
Tel: 065 707 4243
Email: fermona@eircom.net

This pleasant cream and green bungalow is set back off the road in a quiet location close to Spa Wells. It is just a five-minute walk from town. The bedrooms and en suite facilities are quite spacious, and are individually decorated in soft colours of blue and peach. There is a small, cosy TV lounge with a stereo which guests may use. The house is exceptionally well maintained and everything is spotlessly clean. Breakfasts are served at separate tables and there are several establishments in town for evening meals. Vera Fitzpatrick is an excellent host and is happy to provide information on sightseeing. Doolin, the Cliffs of Moher and the Burren, golfing, pony trekking and hill walking are all nearby. Visa, Mastercard accepted.

OWNER Vera Fitzpatrick OPEN April 1 – October 1 ROOMS 2 double, 2 twin, 1 family; all en suite. TERMS €28–31.50; reduction for children; single supplement €6.50

LAHINCH

Edenladia
School Road, Lahinch, Co. Clare
Tel: 065 708 1361 Fax: 065 7081361
Email: xbarrett@iol.ie

This cosy bungalow has a warm and inviting ambience, and is great spot for golfers. Martin Barrett was Captain of the Lahinch Golf Course and he is happy to arrange tee times for players. The bedrooms are immaculate, have modern furnishings, comfortable beds, and electric blankets, as well as TV and hairdryer. Joanne is a warm and friendly lady, guests immediately feel at home, some guests commenting they "arrived as guests, but departed as friends". Smoking is allowed in the dining room. A tasty breakfast is served, and although evening meals are not available, there are plenty of establishments in Lahinch that serve good food. Joanne would be happy to make recommendations and/or make reservations.

OWNER Joanne Bennett OPEN All year ROOMS 3 double, 1 twin, 1 family; all en suite. TERMS from €25.50; reduction for children; single supplement €12.50

Moy House
Lahinch, Co. Clare
Tel: 065 7082800 Fax: 065 7082500
Email: moyhouse@tinet.ie

A classic country house, with views of beautiful Lahinch Bay, approached up a long drive, peacefully set in 15 acres of park like grounds, and mature woodland. It was built in the 18th century as home to Sir Augustine Fitzgerald and overlooks beautiful Lahinch Bay. Before the restoration, which took place over a three year period, the house had stood empty for ten years, and was totally derelict.

Antoin O'Looney, purchased the house and undertook the daunting job of restoration. The results are stunning, the original oak floors were used, and part of the stone stable wall can be seen. The bedrooms are luxurious and individually designed, using a combination of styles from past and present. All have TV, tea makers and hairdryer. All bedrooms are furnished and decorated with beautiful fabrics, most have working log burning fireplaces, and all but two have sea views. The bathrooms, are equipped with toiletries, dressing gowns, large fluffy towels, and most have shower/bath combination. One bedroom features the original well, from which the water was drawn. The house is not suitable for children under 12 years.

Gourmet candlelit dinners are served in the elegant dining-room which overlooks the bay. Everything is prepared with fresh local produce, fish meats, mouth watering home-made desserts, presented with flair and style. The gracious drawing room, has a real fire, where guests can enjoy a pre- or after-dinner drink. Moy House pampers and spoils her guests, Bernadette is the perfect host, who has thought of everything possible to ensure guest's comfort and satisfaction. Situated on the coast road, one and half miles from Lahinch Golf Course. Smoking is permitted in the drawing room.

OPEN All year except Christmas ROOMS 8 Twin/double/family; all en suite. TERMS €95 120.50; single supplement €31.50–57 MEALS Dinner

The Greenbrier Inn
Ennistymon Road, Lahinch, Co. Clare
Tel: 065 7081242 Fax: 065 708 11247
Email: gbrier@indigo.ie
Website: www.greenbrierinn.com

This impressive five year old property offers first class accommodation. Situated on the main road, it has views of the Atlantic Ocean and the Golf Course. The spacious, tastefully decorated bedrooms have pine furniture, white cotton sheets and bedspreads, multi channel TV and direct dial phones. Guests have use of a large sitting room, a comfortable place from which to plan your daily activities, and unwind after a busy day. The Inn is non-smoking. Special diets can be accommodated at breakfast. Evening meals are not served, but there are plenty of venues for evening meals within walking distance. The Burren and Cliffs of Moher are within driving distance. Visa, Mastercard accepted.

OWNER Margaret & Victor Mulcahy OPEN March 1 – New Year ROOMS 14 double/twins/family; all en suite TERMS from €35.50; reduction for children; single supplement €15–19

COUNTY DONEGAL

County Donegal is a large county with a spectacular variety of scenery and an indented coastline of bays, beaches, cliffs and peninsulas set against a backdrop of mountains, moors and lakes. It has many archaeological sites and much evidence of the old Irish culture and traditions. The Irish language is still spoken in areas north and west of Killybegs, an important fishing port. Donegal takes its name from the fort the Vikings established: Dún na nGall, the Fort of the Foreigners. The town built by Sir Basil Brooke is on the estuary of the River Eske, a busy place that is good for buying tweeds. The castle with its great square tower, once the stronghold of the O'Donnells, was refurbished by Brooke in 1610.

Bundoran is one of Ireland's best-known seaside resorts with a good golf course and famous beaches. Farther north is Ballyshannon, long a centre of importance because of its river; the town winds up a steep hill above the River Erne. Rossnowlagh's beach stretches for some 4 km.

Beyond Killybegs, the coastal scenery becomes wild and spectacular. Kilcar is a centre for the hand-woven tweed industry, as is Ardara. The scenery at Glencolumbkille is magnificent, with its blend of hills and sea. Here, the late Father MacDyer organised a cooperative movement to try to keep young people from emigrating, and also established a folk museum. Portnoo and Narin are other popular seaside towns for holidaymakers. Letterkenny is the largest town in Donegal, dominated by

St Eunan's Cathedral, built in the modern Gothic style between 1890 and 1900. The winding road approaching Doocharry from Fintown is known as the "corkscrew" and brings you through the Gweebarra Glen to the sea. Aranmore Island is the most populated and largest of a series of islands. It can be reached by ferry from Burtonport, an attractive, unspoilt fishing port. Gweedore, situated in the spectacularly wild country, is a major holiday centre. From here, there is a road of remarkable scenic beauty by Loughs Nacung and Dunlewy into the Derryveagh Mountains.

Gortahork and Falcarragh are Irish-speaking areas, and are good places from which to start a climb of Muckish Mountain. Dunfanaghy has a fine beach and is a good place to explore the granite promontory of Horn Head. Between Creeslough, attractively situated on Sheephaven Bay, and Carrigart is the romantic Doe Castle, almost surrounded by the sea. Rosapenna, a resort town with a good golf course, is on the way to the beautiful Rosguill Peninsula, with wonderful views of Melmore Head, Horn Head and Muckish Mountain. Milford is a pretty town from where the Fanad Peninsula with its sandy beaches can be explored. The tranquil village of Rathmullan is beautifully situated with a sandy beach and is famous for its historical associations. The road between here and Ramelton is also in a lovely location and is a planned Planter's town, begun in the early seventeenth-century.

The Inishowen Peninsula, which lies between the waters of Lough Foyle and Lough Swilly, is quite different from the rest of Donegal. The centre is very hilly, Slieve Snaght at 615 m being the highest point. From the Buncrana to Clonmany and Cardonagh road, there are fine views of sea and mountains, and a road runs right to the tip of the peninsula at Malin Head. One of the best views to be had of this part of Donegal is from the Grianan of Aileach. It is 250 m high and consists of a cashel, or stone fort, enclosed within three earthen banks. Cardonagh's chief glory is St Patrick's Cross, which dates from the seventh century, making it one of the very important Christian crosses. Glenveagh lies in a deep gorge and is the setting for a fairytale castle, as well as wonderful gardens that were developed by Henry McIlhenny. The garden and the estate are now a national park, and Mr McIlhenny had bequeathed the castle to the nation. Gartan, Kilmacrenan and Raphoe, which has a fine old cathedral, are all associated with St Columba.

ARDARA

Rose Wood House
Edergole, Killybegs Road, Ardara, Co. Donegal
Tel: 075 41168 Fax: 075 41168

Guests continue to enjoy this two-storey house situated on the edge of Ardara. It is run in a friendly manner by Susan

McConnell, who lived in New York for 11 years. Formerly a bungalow, a second storey was added in 1990; the very large lounge/dining room is in this part of the house, and has lovely views of the river. Susan McConnell is an excellent host; nothing is too much trouble for her guests' comfort, and a hot drink is offered to guests upon arrival. Breakfast only is served, but there are good choices in Ardara, and Susan would be happy to make recommendations. Visa, Mastercard, Eurocard accepted.

OWNER Susan & Vincent McConnell OPEN January 1 – December 20 ROOMS 4 double, 2 twin; all en suite. TERMS €21.50; reduction for children

Woodhill House
Ardara, Co. Donegal
Tel: 075 41112 Fax: 075 41516
Email: yates@iol.ie
Website: www.woodhillhouse.com

Woodhill House is in a wonderful position up a valley from Ardara. It is an historic country house, standing on a site dating from the seventeenth century, overlooking the Donegal Highlands. It was formerly the home of the Nesbitts, Ireland's last commercial whaling family. The present owners bought the house about 13 years ago, and improvements are ongoing. The two front rooms are large, simply furnished and have wonderful views. There is a friendly informal atmosphere, and the house is surrounded by more than 1.5 hectares of gardens, including a walled garden, which is open to guests. Pets can be kennelled. The high-quality restaurant is open from Easter to the end of October, and there is a licensed, smoking bar. Excellent French-style cuisine is served, using fresh Irish produce and fish from Killybegs, Ireland's principal fishing port. There are several places to eat in Ardara and Irish music is often heard at most of Ardara's 13 bars. The area is well known for its Donegal tweeds and woollen goods. Salmon and trout fishing, shooting, pony trekking, golf, excellent bathing beaches are to be found in this area. The Wildlife Reserve should be of special interest. Mastercard, Eurocard, American Express, Diners accepted.

OWNER John & Nancy Yates OPEN March – November 31 ROOMS 4 double, 3 family, 2 single; all en suite. TERMS €57; reduction for children; single supplement €12.50 MEALS lunch and dinner

Bruckless House

Bruckless, Co. Donegal
Tel: 073 37071 Fax: 073 37071
E-mail: bruck@iol.ie
Website: www.iol.ie/~bruc/bruckless.html

This classic eighteenth-century house stands in a secluded spot in an award-winning garden and cobbled yard, and is a well-known Connemara Pony Stud Farm. It offers gracious living and guests are encouraged to sit around and chat with the owners, who are happy to share their knowledge of the area. The bedrooms are large and elegantly furnished. The spacious drawing room and dining room overlook green lawns and the sea. Both rooms have turf fires, which are lit at the first sign of a chill in the air. There are no TVs in the house, but most guests are happy with this 'TV-free zone'. In this beautiful and unspoiled area of Ireland's Atlantic coast, there are plenty of archaeological sites to explore. Fishing, golf and horseback riding are also available. Visa, American Express, Eurocard, Mastercard accepted. Twelve miles west of Donegal town.

OWNER Joan & Clive Evans OPEN April – September
ROOMS 2 double, 2 single; 2 en suite. TERMS B&B €44.50

Castlereagh House

Bruckless, Co. Donegal
Tel: 073 37202 Fax: 073 37202
Email: castlereaghhouse@eircom.net

This very pleasant early nineteenth-century house stands in well-kept gardens with panoramic views of the Atlantic Ocean and the Blue Stack Mountains. It continues to offer the highest standard of accommodation. The house is quite luxurious, has rich red carpets, is well furnished and very comfortable. The bedrooms are tastefully decorated in soft pastel wallpapers, and one is on the ground floor - all have fine views. There is a comfortable lounge, which displays an antique sideboard. Breakfasts are served on Royal Albert china in the bright dining room. Elizabeth is a most attentive host who is always happy to give advice on what to see and do in the area and to recommend local establishments for evening meals. This is an ideal base for touring Glencolumbkille, Slieve League and Glenveagh National Park. Golf, fishing, horseback riding and an Art Gallery are available within a short drive. This superb value accommodation is an excellent choice for touring this scenic area. Castlereagh House is non-smoking. Visa, Mastercard accepted. Situated on the N56 coast road, 4 km from Killybegs.

OWNER The Henry Family OPEN Easter – October 1 ROOMS 2 double, 1 twin; all en suite. TERMS €31.50; reduction for children; single supplement €8.50

BUNDORAN

Casa Mia
West End, Bundoran, Co. Donegal
Tel: 072 41684

Casa Mia is a large, two-storey house within walking distance of the beach and town. This continental-style house is run by Mary Hamrogue, a friendly, bubbly lady. The bedrooms, all with Sky TV, are bright and cheery with yellow, purple and green duvets. Smoking is only allowed in the bedrooms. The guest lounge is spacious and is comfortably furnished. Breakfast only is served, but there is a good choice of eating establishments in town, which is within walking distance. Close to Belleek, horse-riding, golf and fishing

OWNER Mary & Malachy Hamrogue OPEN All year ROOMS 2 double, 1 twin, 1 family; all en suite. TERMS €£25.50; reduction for children; single supplement €6.50

Conway House
4 Bay View Terrace, Bundoran, Co. Donegal
Tel: 072 41220

This Georgian-style house is conveniently located to all the amenities in this popular seaside town, including Water World. There is a relaxed and informal atmosphere. Mrs McGureen prepares the meals while Mr McGureen maintains the house and keeps it freshly decorated; in his spare time he restores antiques. Two of the bedrooms, and the dining room and lounge have sea views. The dining and lounge rooms both have their original fireplaces, which are lit on chilly days. There is plenty to keep the visitor busy, and this is an ideal base from which to explore this scenic area. Horseback riding and golf are offered within a kilometre.

OWNER Dorothy McGureen OPEN March – September ROOMS 4 double, 1 family; 4 en suite. TERMS €21.50; reduction for children; single supplement €4

CARRICK

Rockville House
Roxborough Coast Road, Carrick, Co. Donegal
Tel: 073 39107 Fax: 073 39107
Email: rockvilledonegal@eircom.net

This friendly four-bedroom bungalow stands in an elevated position, with panoramic views of Donegal Bay and Ben Bulben. The cliffs at Bunglas, the highest marine cliffs in Europe, are 5km away. This is a popular destination for tourists from many parts of the world, and energetic Maureen Hughes arranges walking tours in the Kilcar area. Teelin, an Irish-speaking area, lies close by and attracts people who wish to learn to speak the Irish language. The house is about 1km from the closest beach and from the village of Carrick. The family room has wonderful views, as does the lounge, which has a dining table at one end and sliding doors opening onto the patio, which has a barbecue. Smoking is only allowed in the lounge. The well-appointed bedrooms are small, spotlessly clean, and are all on the ground floor. Laundry facilities are available. Evening meals are no longer available, but Maureen Hughes has an arrangement for meals for her guests at the village restaurant. Tasty substantial meals are served on plates made for Rockville House at a local pottery. A four-bedroom self-catering cottage is also available. From Carrick take the Coast Road, Rockville is one mile from Carrick on the left side.

OWNER Maureen Hughes OPEN All year ROOMS 1 double, 1 twin, 1 family; 2 en suite. TERMS €25.50; reduction for children; single supplement €12.50

CARRIGANS

Mount Royd Country Home
Carrigans, Co. Donegal
Tel: 074 40163
Email: jmartin@mountroyd.com
Website: www.mountroyd.com

An attractive creeper-clad country house, set back off the road, standing in a large landscaped garden, with pet Jacobs Sheep in the field. The large bright rooms are on the first floor, beautifully decorated with coronets, co-ordinated colours of blue/pink/white and cream, rich fabrics and duvets, and antique furniture. All bedrooms have tea makers and TV, as well as views of the rolling hills, and the River Foyle. For guests who prefer a bath to a shower, a combination bathroom is available.

The cosy, predominantly red, sitting room, with a real fire, offers a pleasant spot to unwind after a busy day. Breakfasts are a banquet: there is a help-yourself starter buffet, followed by a wide menu choice, i.e. smoked salmon, omelettes, French toast, plus a well presented traditional Irish breakfast. As one guest comments "does it get any better than this?" Little wonder that Josephine was voted "Landlady of the Year".

This is extremely good value, and if you are planning on spending time in this area, Mount Royd would be an excellent choice. Book in for several days and enjoy the hospitality, good food and first class accommodation. Evening meals are not served, but there is a pub and restaurant within a mile. This is a family friendly house, and a cot and highchair are available. Guests have use of the garden and tennis court. Be sure to visit The Grian of Aileach prehistoric stone fort, which dates from 2000 B.C., Moonreach Presbyterian Church, one of the oldest in Ireland, and Lifford Visitors Centre. The Giants Causeway is just an hour's drive away. Historic Derry City, with its famous walls, is just a 15 minute drive. Smoking designated area only

From Derry, take A40 to Carrigan house on left on the R236. Also signed off the A139 and A14.

OWNER Josephine Martin OPEN February 1 – November 30 ROOMS 4 double/twin/family; all en suite. TERMS from €20 €24–25.50; reduction for children; single supplement €6.50

CASTLEFINN

Gortfad
Castlefinn, Co. Donegal
Tel: 074 46135

This 300-year-old Georgian house stands in its own tranquil grounds and combines old-world charm with modern comforts. The house has been in the same family for seven generations and is furnished with old-fashioned possessions and has stained-glass windows. Dolly Taylor is a kindly, hospitable lady who has been offering her special brand of hospitality for almost 30 years; little wonder that she has guests returning year after year. Guests are usually greeted with a complimentary hot drink and home-baked scones and fruitcake upon arrival. Breakfast only is served, but there are several excellent establishments close by, and Dolly is happy to make recommendations if required. Guests can visit the tweed-weaving area of the Glenties and the 10,000 hectares of the National Park at Glenveagh Castle as well as Derek Hill's art collection at Church Hill. There are two golf courses within 10 km and salmon, trout and coarse fishing in the River Finn.

OWNER Dolly Taylor OPEN Easter – September ROOMS 3 double, 1 twin, 1 family; 4 en suite. TERMS €22; reduction for children

DONEGAL

Arranmore House
Killybegs Road, Donegal, Co. Donegal
Tel: 073 21242

Arranmore House stands in its own grounds in an elevated peaceful location with lovely views, yet it is only a three-minute walk to the town centre. Mrs Kenney, who hails from England, is a friendly lady who takes excellent care of her guests, and runs a comfortable house with a pleasant atmosphere. The guest lounge has an open fire, and substantial breakfasts only are served in a separate dining room. The good-sized bedrooms are well furnished, spotlessly clean, and are all on the ground floor. Guests are greeted with a hot drink upon arrival and Doreen Kenney is happy to offer assistance with local sightseeing.

OWNER Mrs Doreen Kenney OPEN Easter to mid-November ROOMS 2 double, 1 twin, 1 family, 2 single; all en suite. TERMS €19; reduction for children

Belle View
Ballyshannon Road, Donegal town, Co. Donegal
Tel: 073 22167

Belle View is an attractive bungalow standing in half a hectare of grounds, in a peaceful location overlooking Donegal Bay and the Bluestack Mountains. The house has been upgraded since last edition. Mary Lawne is an attentive host who welcomes guests with a hospitality tray featuring tea and home baking. The bedrooms have comfortable beds and good-sized bathrooms. Breakfast only is served, and the dining room has tea-making facilities. There is a wide choice of eating establishments in Donegal town.

The guest lounge, which overlooks the mountains and the bay, has an open fire and tea-makers. There are some lovely walks close by and boating and water sports are available at nearby Lough Eske, and there is a pitch and putt course adjacent to the house. The nearby Donegal Craft Centre is of special interest. On the N56 Ballyshannon - Sligo Road, situated near the Craft Village.

OWNER Mrs Mary Lawne OPEN April – November ROOMS 2 double, 2 family; 2 en suite. TERMS €25.50 26.50; reduction for children; single supplement €6.50 MEALS light meals can be provided

Shanveen House
Killybegs Road, Donegal, Co. Donegal
Tel: 074 21127

Shanveen House stands in an elevated position overlooking the Blue Stack Mountains and is a three-minute walk from the town centre. It is across from the eighteenth-century Presbyterian church. The bedrooms are spotlessly clean and all have chairs and individual wardrobes. Although there are only two en suite bedrooms, another does have its own shower. There is a comfortable lounge with Victorian furnishings, and a piano. The atmosphere at Shanveen House is warm and pleasant and Anna McGarrigle does everything possible to ensure her guests feel welcome and comfortable. A waterbus tour of Donegal Bay can be taken, as well as guided tours of Donegal's Castle. For the energetic, horseback riding and cycling are also available.

OWNER Anna McGarrigle OPEN April – October 31 ROOMS 2 double, 1 twin, 1 family; 2 en suite. TERMS €20.50; reduction for children; single supplement €4

St Ernan's House Hotel
St Ernan's Island, Donegal, Co. Donegal
Tel: 073 21065 Fax: 073 22098
Email: info@sainternans.com
Website: www.sainternans.com

St Ernan's, a classic Georgian house, was built in 1826 by John Hamilton, a nephew of the Duke of Wellington. It is situated on what was an island; the island is now linked to the mainland by a short causeway and covers some 3.25 hectares. It is an elegant, lovely country house in a beautiful location, offering peace and tranquillity in wonderful surroundings. It was converted into a hotel in 1983 and has been in the O'Dowds' hands since 1987; it is licensed. The individually styled bedrooms are beautifully pro-portioned and very spacious; most bedrooms have views of sea and countryside. Dinner featuring fresh produce is beautifully presented in the large dining room, and the elegant drawing room, with a log fire, is an informal spot in which to relax after a busy day. Smoking is not permitted in the dining room, and cigar- and pipe-smoking are not allowed on the premises. For guests who are seeking quality accommodations combined with peace and tranquillity, St Ernan's is an excellent choice. Not suitable for children under six years. Access, Visa, Mastercard, Eurocheque accepted.

OWNER Brian O'Dowd OPEN Easter – October 31 ROOMS 6 double, 6 twin; all en suite. TERMS from €101.50; single supplement negotiable MEALS Dinner

DOWNINGS

Baymount Bed & Breakfast
Downings, Co. Donegal
Tel: 074 55395

Mary McBride is a local lady who was in fact born in the small house at the bottom of the road. Mary and her husband purchased this house 25 years ago. The house stands above the narrow country road and has spectacular views over the bay to the mountains. When it was built the McBrides had 12 children, many of whom have now left home, allowing the option of running a bed & breakfast establishment. The lounge, a large bright room, enjoys the same magnificent views as the dining room, which has separate tables as well as a TV and a sitting area and sliding doors onto the terrace; a great place to sit on fine days. An iron is available on request.

OWNER Mrs Mary McBride OPEN Easter – August 31 ROOMS 4 double, 1 twin, 1 single; 1 en suite. TERMS €20.50–21.50; reduction for children

DUNFANAGHY

Rosman House
Dunfanaghy, Co. Donegal
Tel: 074 36273 Fax: 074 36273
Email: rosman@eircom.net

Rosman House, an attractive modern dormer bungalow, stands in a superb spot with spectacular views of Horn Head, Muckish Mountain and Sheephaven Bay. It has a large well-landscaped garden, and is within walking distance of the village. Roisin McHugh, formerly a teacher, takes great pride in her establishment, and her husband runs the 40-hectare dairy and sheep farm. Improvements are ongoing and the house has been freshly decorated. The spacious lounge, where smoking is permitted, opens onto a patio and gardens.

   The bedrooms are individually decorated with co-ordinated floral colour schemes. There are five ground floor rooms. Breakfast and pre-arranged dinners are served in the elegant dining room on separate tables, which overlook Horn Head. Pet accommodation is available. There are some enjoyable scenic walks close by and an 18-hole golf course. Visa accepted. Through Dunfanaghy village on the Falcarragh Road, turn right, immediately after Art Gallery.

OWNER Mrs Roisin McHugh OPEN All year ROOMS 2 double, 2 twin, 2 family; 2 en suite. TERMS €26.50–28; reduction for children; single supplement €6.50–12.50 MEALS Packed lunches

DUNGLOE

Barr a' Ghaoith
Quay Road, Dungloe, Co. Donegal
Tel: 075 21389 Fax: 075 21389

Barr a' Ghaoith means "top of the wind," an apt description for this house, which sits in an elevated position with panoramic views. This extremely good value accommodation is very much a family-run establishment where all the family joins in to share the work. There is a separate dining room and a comfortable lounge with a VCR and games provided. The house is well maintained and the bedrooms are fresh and clean. Tasty freshly prepared breakfasts include home-baked bread and home-made preserves. Close by activities include angling, golf and hill walking. Tennis courts and a leisure centre are also available. Pitch and putt and deep-sea fishing can be arranged. This must be one of the best value bed & breakfast accommodations in Donegal, and is a popular venue; early reservations are suggested.

OWNER Susan & John Gallagher OPEN All year ROOMS 1 double, 1 twin, 1 family. TERMS €15; reduction for children

FALCARRAGH

Sea View House
Upper Ray, Falcarragh, Co. Donegal
Tel: 074 35552

This attractive bungalow is set in 1.25 hectares of land in an elevated position, surrounded by open countryside and sweeping views of the mountains and sea. On clear days Tory Island can be seen. Jean McFadden is extremely helpful and accommodating, and guests are greeted with a complimentary hot drink upon arrival. The house is immaculate and has been upgraded: the dining room, which overlooks the view, and the lounge, which has a real fire, have new carpet and furniture. The bedrooms are of a good size and have colour-co-ordinated floral fabrics. All are now en suite and two have power showers. Breakfast only is served, and includes home-baked bread, but advice on local eating establishments for dinner is provided. Guests are well taken care of here. This is a wonderful spot in which to relax and to explore the local area. There are some lovely walks close by. Cots are provided.

OWNER Jean McFadden OPEN Easter – September ROOMS 3 double, 1 single; 3 en suite. TERMS €21.50; reduction for children; single supplement €1.50

GLENCOLUMBKILLE

Corner House
Cashel, Glencolumbkille, Co. Donegal
Tel: 073 30021

Corner House is situated in the centre of the village and, as the name implies, located on the corner. Mrs Byrne is a pleasant and considerate host who also runs the adjoining shop, and her son runs the pub. The house looks quite modest from the outside but is surprisingly spacious inside. It has an enormous dining room and a small upstairs lounge. The house is well maintained; the bedrooms are average in size, are immaculate, fresh and bright. Smoking is allowed in the lounge and the bedrooms. The surroundings are beautiful and this is a great spot for hill walking. A lovely old grandfather clock stands in the hallway and there is an interesting doll collection displayed in a cabinet on the landing.

OWNER Mrs J. P. Byrne OPEN April – September ROOMS 2 double, 2 twin, family; 3 en suite. TERMS €25.50–32.50; reduction for children; single supplement €8.50

GWEEDORE

Min-a-Locha
Bloody Foreland, Gweedore, Co. Donegal
Tel: 075 32279
Email: minalocha@eircom.net

This purpose-built modern bungalow, although it does have a second storey, overlooks what is said to be the best views in Ireland, the Bloody Foreland and the Atlantic Ocean. The house was purpose-built for B&B and offers every comfort in a peaceful and tranquil setting. The bedrooms have a medieval décor and are of a good size, as are the bathrooms. The beds have attractive colourful duvets. All of the curtains and bed covers were made by Kathleen Duggan, who extends a warm welcome and prides herself on personal attention to her guests' needs. The spacious lounge has a Victorian-style fireplace where turf fires burn on cool evenings; guests may smoke in lounge only. Breakfasts are served in the bright and airy dining room, overlooking the view, and include home-baked bread and scones. Three-course and light dinners, often featuring fresh local seafood, and good home-cooking are also served, if pre-arranged. There are sandy beaches, hill and coastal walks, cycling and day trips to the Islands. This is a perfect place from which to explore this dramatic and rugged area. A baby-sitting service can be arranged. Traditional Irish music can be found at several local venues.

OWNER John & Kathleen Duggan OPEN April 1 – October 31 ROOMS 2 double, 2 twin, 1 family with private bath/shower; all en suite. TERMS €23; reduction for children; single supplement €5 MEALS Dinner

INISHOWEN

Fernbank
Redcastle, Inishowen, Co. Donegal
Tel: 077 83032 Fax: 077 83164

Fernbank, built in 1970, with later additions, is extremely good value and is situated in an elevated position with spectacular views of Lough Foyle. Elizabeth, who is from Buncrana, has been offering her special brand of hospitality for 30 years; there is a home-away-from-home atmosphere and the house is immaculate. A hot drink is available at just about any time, and Elizabeth is happy to give advice on what to see and do in the area. The bedrooms are all on the ground floor and some have lough views. The sitting room and dining room have pine ceilings and the rooms are bright and cheery. Smoking permitted in lounge only. Greencastle, with its maritime museum and award-winning fish restaurant, is 11 km away. Situated on the main Derry–Moville Road, 9 miles from Muff.

OWNER Elizabeth McLaughlin OPEN All year ROOMS 2 double, 2 family; all en suite. TERMS €28; reduction for children

McGrory's

Culdaff, Inishowen, Co. Donegal
Tel: 077 79104
Email: mcgr@eircom.net
Website: www.mcgrorys.ie

McGrory's is a family run establishment that was totally refurbished in 1999, and provides first class accommodation. The bedrooms are all of a good size, most have cherry wood furniture, comfortable beds, attractive fabrics and duvets. All have TV, direct dial telephones, hair dryer, tea makers and luggage rack: rooms in the oldest part of the house have exposed stone walls. McGrory's is also a pub and a restaurant. The McGrory family are all musical, and Mac's Backroom Bar has earned an excellent reputation as one of Ireland's finest live music venues. Opening acts from around the world have appeared at Mac's, as well as Ireland's top performers, Altan and Paul Brady, The Saw Doctors, and Kieran Goss to name but a few. Concessions are given to residents who are attending a gig at the Backroom Bar. Live music is performed every Wednesday and Saturday - quite a success story for a village of just 200 people.

   The Front Bar hosts traditional sessions on Tuesday and Friday. Fresh local sea food features heavily on the menu in the restaurant, as well as steaks and lamb. Vegetarian and special diets are catered for. Angling and Golf are close by; special golfing rates have been negotiated with Ballyliffen Golf Club. Visa, Mastercard accepted. Easily located in Culdaff village.

OWNER McGrory Family OPEN All year ROOMS 10 double/twin; all en suite. TERMS from €38; reduction for children; single supplement €12.50

St John's Country House

Fahan, Inishowen, Co. Donegal
Tel: 077 60289 Fax: 077 60612

St John's was built in 1785, and lovingly restored by the owners in 1980. The idyllic setting is two acres of lovely grounds and landscaped gardens on the shores of Lough Swilly. The spacious bedrooms have large en-suite bathrooms, most with bath and shower, and large fluffy towels. The five double bedrooms are beautifully and luxuriously furnished, with the perfect blend of modern comforts, including telephone, TV and hairdryer, and the charm of a bygone era. They have king-size beds, with crisp white cotton sheets, warm duvets, rich drapes and carpets, and an additional bonus of Lough Swilly and mountain scenery. The elegant restaurant overlooking the view has won international fame for its imaginative, freshly prepared food. As the restaurant is open to the public, guests planning on dinner should reserve in advance. There is also a non-smoking dining-room. Log fires burn in the bar lounge, an excellent spot for a pre- or after-dinner drink. St. John's is not suitable for children. The ambience is informal and inviting, the owners, who have been here for 23 years, are charming and helpful.

St Johns would be an excellent choice for exploring this unspoilt corner of Ireland. Owner, Reg Ryan, comments he found "his little corner of heaven" and after staying here, am sure you will agree with him. A boat is available for folks interested in fishing: golfers are well catered for, with six courses close by. The prehistoric ring fort of Grianan of Aileach dates from around 1700 B.C., and is well worth a visit.

As the locals say: "up here it's different". Visa, Mastercard accepted. Situated in the village of Fahan on the main Derry to Buncrana Road, R238.

OWNER Reg Ryan & Phil McAfee OPEN All year except for Feb 15 – March 10, & 3 days at Christmas ROOMS 5 double; all en suite TERMS from €51–95; single supplement €19

INISHOWEN PENINSULA

Barraicin

Malin Head, Inishowen Peninsula, Co. Donegal
Tel: 077 70184 Fax: 077 70184

Barraicin takes its name from the field on which it was built by the Doyles in 1971, and means "the square toe-cap". It stands in a superb position, near Ireland's most northerly point, about 1km from the sea, and has lovely sea views. The cosy dining room, where guests share two tables, overlooks the pretty garden, which has an old pump. The Doyles are a delightful couple who have a great sense of humour, and guests feel immediately at home in this warm and friendly house. The bedrooms, all on the ground floor, are clean and bright. The large, sunny lounge has an open fire and sea views, and a TV is available on request: smoking is only allowed in the lounge.

Malin Head is a thriving fishing area and two important government services are located here, the Meteorological Station and the Radio Station, which plays a major role in the safety of local fishermen.

It is within easy reach of Inishowen's five golf links, including the internationally known Ballyliffen Glashedy Golf Links. Barraicin is 6 miles from Malin village, opposite public telephone in Malin Head.

OWNER Maurice & Marie Doyle OPEN Easter – November 30 ROOMS I double, I twin, I family; I en suite. TERMS €16–22; reduction for children; single supplement €5

INVER

Cloverhill House
Cranny, Inver, Co. Donegal
Tel: 073 36165 Fax: 073 36165

Cloverhill House is approached by a private drive bordered with high yew hedges and is an attractive long, low, modern white-washed house in an elevated position which has lovely river views.

The extensive gardens are beautiful and there are fruit trees and strawberry fields. There is an enormous and very pleasant sitting/dining room with a turf fire. The bedrooms are spacious and well furnished; three are on the ground floor. An annex bedroom with en suite bathroom is available, ideal for guests who prefer more privacy. Evening meals are available if ordered in advance, and can be enjoyed with a glass of wine. Home cooked evening meals use fresh fruit and vegetables from the House garden. A ten minute walk brings you to a sandy beach and fishing river. Fishing, golfing and mountain climbing activities are available locally.

OWNER W.T. Coyle OPEN All year ROOMS 3 double, 3 twin; 2 en suite. TERMS €25.50–28; reduction for children; single supplement €12.50

KILLYBEGS

Bannagh House
Fintra Road, Killybegs, Co. Donegal
Tel: 073 31108
Email: bannaghhouse@eircom.net

This modern house stands in an elevated position in a small front garden and has wonderful views of the harbour, town and near and distant hills. Killybegs is a large fishing port, and the harbour always seems to be full of enormous fishing boats, making this an ideal place for fresh fish.

Melly's café does an excellent fish and chip meal in vast portions. The lounge and dining room also have bay views. Smoking is permitted in the TV lounge. The bedrooms, all on the ground floor, are well-appointed and tastefully furnished. Phyllis Melly works hard at creating a comfortable home for guests, and is happy to give advice on local activities and to recommend local restaurants.

OWNER Phyllis Melly OPEN April – October ROOMS 2 double, 1 twin, 1 family; all en suite. TERMS €25.50; reduction for children; single supplement €6.50

Hollycrest Lodge
Donegal Road, Killybegs, Co. Donegal
Tel: 073 31470
Email: hollycrest@hotmail.com

Guests continue to enjoy the relaxing atmosphere and warm welcome found here at this attractive Georgian-style house, which sits off the road in a large, well maintained garden. Guests are welcome to make use of the garden, which is a pleasant spot in which to relax on fine days. Anne Keeney is a very personable lady who enjoys meeting people, and nothing is too much trouble to ensure her guests are comfortable. The house is well maintained and decorated and furnished to a high standard. The colour-co-ordinated bedrooms are on the ground floor and one has a brass bed.

There is a guest lounge with TV and a separate dining room where filling breakfasts are served. Smoking is allowed only on the sun porch. Evening meals are not served, but there are plenty of eating establishments close by. Visa, Mastercard accepted. N56 from Donegal to Killybegs, situated on right hand side, on road 2L from Killybegs.

OWNER Anne Keeney OPEN February 1 – November 30 ROOMS 3 double, 1 twin, 1 single; 3 en suite. TERMS €34.50; reduction for children; single supplement €9

Hillcrest
Ballyshannon Road, Laghey, Co. Donegal
Tel: 073 21837 Fax: 073 21674
Email: sheilagatins@unison.ie

Hillcrest is a pleasant place to stay – the welcome is warm and friendly, a hot drink usually greets guests upon arrival and the house is spotlessly clean. It is a modern bungalow and stands on the side of a hill in an attractive garden. All the bedrooms, which are on the small side, have pretty front-facing views and are located on the ground floor. The small TV room has comfortable chairs and a piano, which guests are welcome to play. Smoking in lounge only. From Ballyshannon on the N15, Laghey sign-posted on left, turn right at Esso station, left at the junction. Hillcrest is the third house on right.

OWNER Mrs Sheila Gatins OPEN Easter – September 30. ROOMS 1 double, 1 twin, 1 double/ single; 2 en suite. TERMS €23–25.50; reduction for children

LETTERKENNY

Hillcrest House
Lurgybrack, Sligo Road, Letterkenny, Co. Donegal
Tel: 074 22300 / 25137 Fax: 074 25137

Hillcrest is a friendly house, where a warm welcome is extended and guests are greeted with a complimentary hot drink and cakes upon arrival. The house is situated on the main Sligo Road, a kilometre from Letterkenny. The house is potentially noisy, but there are great water, mountain and town views. The Maguires are a friendly and helpful couple who have five children. They take excellent care of their guests, and are helpful in every way. The four rooms, although a little small, are spotlessly clean and comfortable; four of them are on the ground floor. Hillcrest offers good value and a high standard of accommodation. Breakfast only is served at separate tables in the bright dining room, and there is a wide choice for evening meals close by. The Maguires are happy to recommend places to eat and to assist guests with daily activities. Visa, Mastercard, American Express accepted.

OWNER Larry & Margaret Maguire OPEN All year ROOMS 2 double, 2 twin, 2 family; 5 en suite. TERMS €21.50–23; reduction for children; single supplement €6.50–12.50

Rinneen
Woodland, Letterkenny, Co. Donegal
Tel: 074 24591

Rinneen, which means "little plot of land at the top of the hill," is a cheery and bright bungalow, with panoramic views of Lough Swilly, the mountains and green fields, where contented sheep graze. The house has a home-away-from-home ambience and the good-sized bedrooms have modern furniture, and floral and autumn colours. There is a real fire in the cosy lounge, which overlooks the view. An additional bonus is Mary McBride, a congenial and helpful host, almost always on hand to assist with itineraries, and who is particularly interested in literature. Excellent breakfasts are served in the dining room; dinners are not available, but Mary is happy to make suggestions for local pubs and restaurants for evening meals.

OWNER Mary McBride OPEN April – October ROOMS 1 double (en suite), 1 family, 1 single. TERMS €21.50–24; reduction for children; single supplement €6.50

White Gables
Derry Road, Letterkenny, Co. Donegal
Tel: 074 22583

White Gables is a spacious house in an elevated position overlooking the river and the town. There is a pleasant view from the dining room/lounge, which has a small sitting area and a table for breakfast which faces the window. Smoking is allowed in designated area. The small bedrooms are clean and simply furnished; two are on the ground floor. There is a pleasant garden that guests may sit in on fine days, and a conservatory with comfortable wicker furniture has been added.

OWNER Mrs Cabrini OPEN All year ROOMS 2 double, 2 twin, 2 family; 4 en suite. TERMS €20.50–25.50; reduction for children; single supplement €5

LIFFORD

The Hall Green Farmhouse
Port Hall, Lifford, Co. Donegal
Tel: 074 41318 Fax: 074 41318
Email: hallgreenfarmhouse@eircom.net

This traditional farmhouse has undergone several improvements. The exterior has been painted terra-cotta and there are new period-style windows. The bedrooms are decorated with pretty wallpapers and matching fabrics. There is an ideal family suite consisting of two self-contained en suite bedrooms. All the beds are orthopaedic and have electric blankets. The dining room, which is to the rear of the house, was the original farmhouse kitchen, dating back over 100 years. The house has old-fashioned furnishings, and there are uninterrupted views over and beyond the River Foyle. The cosy lounge, where smoking is permitted, has TV and a fireplace. Salmon and trout fishing are available in the River Finn, which runs through the farm.

Golf, walking, bird-watching and a fully equipped leisure centre are close by. A visit to the Lifford Old Courthouse, Visitor and Clan Centre is worthwhile. This is a friendly, non-smoking house with a home-away-from-home atmosphere. Light meals are available if requested. Visa, Mastercard accepted. From Lifford take N14 for 3 km, then R265 for 2 miles.

OWNER Mervyn & Jean McKean OPEN January 6 – December 15 ROOMS 1 double, 2 family, 1 double/single; 2 en suite TERMS €23–25.50; reduction for children; single supplement €6.50–10 MEALS Dinner

The Haw Lodge
The Haw, Lifford, Co. Donegal
Tel: 074 41397 Fax: 074 41985

This traditional farmhouse with its newly restored exterior is easily located on the main road about 2.5 km from Lifford. The original farmhouse kitchen dates back 100 years and is now used as the dining room. The interior has also been completely restored, and the garden extended, so guests can relax and enjoy the wonderful views.

The bedrooms are prettily decorated with co-ordinating colours; one is on the ground floor and has a close by toilet and washbasin. There is also an ideal family suite, consisting of two bedrooms with en suite facilities; all the beds are orthopaedic, and a cot is available. The cosy TV lounge has a fireplace. Evening meals are no longer served, but there are some excellent local venues for meals, and Eileen is happy to make recommendations. Salmon and trout fishing are available in the river Finn, which flows through the farm. A fully equipped leisure centre can be found nearby, as well as golf, walking and bird-watching activities. Of special interest is the Lifford Old Courthouse, Visitor and Clans Centre. Visitors can also browse around the pine and gift showroom.

This friendly house with its home-away-from-home atmosphere would be an excellent choice from which to explore this interesting and scenic area. Access, Visa, Mastercard, Eurocard accepted. On Lifford to Sligo N15 Road, at roundabout in Lifford take N15 road for one and half miles, watch for house sign; the house is yellow and on the right hand side of the road.

OWNER Eileen Patterson OPEN March 1 – December 31 ROOMS 1 double, 1 twin, 1 family, 1 single; 2 en suite. TERMS €21.50–24; reduction for children; single supplement €4–6.50

Admiralty House

Carrownaffe, Moville, Co. Donegal
Tel: 077 82529

Admiralty House, a beautifully restored Georgian house, was in a derelict condition when it was purchased by the McFeelys. The restoration took over two years, and the result is a beautiful country house set in a pleasant wooded garden, with views of Lough Foyle. The entryway is very attractive, and has marble floors as does the lounge. There are rich colours throughout and stained-glass windows depicting various sea scenes.

A bonus at Admiralty House is the warmth of the friendly owners. The house is furnished in keeping with its character; most of the pieces were found by the owners at various venues around the country. The bedrooms are individually decorated and are warm and comfortable. The conservatory, with its wicker furniture, is the only new addition to the house. The owners, who have three children, are extremely helpful and provide a portfolio of places to visit in the area. Breakfasts only are served, but there are plenty of places to eat in Moville, an eight-minute walk away. Of local interest is the Greencastle Maritime Museum, a Norman Castle and Napoleonic fort. Mastercard, Visa accepted. Take the Derry Road from Moville, 1½ miles out of Derry. Look to the right – the house is yellow and white, and overlooks Lough Foyle.

OWNER Suzanne McFeely OPEN May 1 – September 30
ROOMS 2 double, 1 twin, 1 family. TERMS €23; reduction for children; single supplement €2.50–6.50

Ardeen

Ramelton, Co. Donegal
Tel: 074 51243 Fax: 074 1243
Email: ardeenbandb@eircom.net
Website: www.ardeenhouse.com

This splendid country house built in 1845 is situated in its own grounds overlooking Lough Swilly. It stands in a well-tended pleasant lawned front garden in a peaceful and tranquil spot. Improvements are ongoing, and since last edition a new bathroom and an upgraded shower are complete. The spacious bedrooms are individually and elegantly decorated in lemon, blue and buttermilk; all have patchwork quilts made by the owner, Anne Campbell. The drawing and dining room are furnished with antiques and have open fires.

The house at one time belonged to a private nurse of King George V and, more recently, to two doctors. Anne Campbell is an excellent host who knows just how to make her guests feel at home. She formerly ran a village shop, but now concentrates on running her very successful bed & breakfast. Self-catering is available. There is a tennis court for guests' use.

There are several places for an evening meal in Ramelton, which has been designated a National Heritage town, and is a pleasant, short stroll away. The county Genealogical Centre is located in the old Meeting House, which is one of the oldest Presbyterian churches in Ireland. Visa, Mastercard accepted.

OWNER Mrs Anne Campbell OPEN Easter – October ROOMS 2 double, 1 twin, 1 family, 1 single; 3 en suite. TERMS €31.50; reduction for children; single supplement €6.50

Crammond House

Market Square, Ramelton, Co. Donegal
Tel: 074 51055

Crammond House is easily located in this unspoiled historical village. Its origins date from 1760, and has been a grocery and hardware shop, as well as a wholesale tea importers. It was home to the same family for four generations, and of special interest are the old photographs of the old shopfront, which the warm and welcoming present owner, Ena Corry, is happy to show guests.

The house has undergone a tasteful restoration; the rooms are well furnished and it has all-modern comforts and is spotlessly clean. Smoking is not permitted in the dining room. The bedrooms are bright, decorated mostly with floral wallpapers, and the non–en suite rooms all have sinks. There is a pleasant and friendly atmosphere, and recommendations on places to eat in the village, as well as information on what to see and do in the area, is provided. A hot drink is offered upon arrival, and at other times on request. Easily located in the town square.

OWNER Mrs Ena Corry OPEN April 1 – October 30 ROOMS 1 double, 1 twin, 1 en suite family. TERMS €21.50–24; reduction for children; single supplement €6.50

Gleann Oir

Ards, Ramelton, Co. Donegal
Tel: 074 51187

This modern house is situated in a hilly area and has spectacular views of farmland and hills. It is a quiet and peaceful, simply furnished family home. Mrs Crawford has seven children, and children are very welcome here; they can wander around the farm if accompanied by an adult. There are 14 hectares and the farm is quite an attraction, with sheep, two milking cows and arable land.

There is a comfortable sitting room with TV and open fire, as well as a small dining room where excellent breakfasts and pre-arranged dinners are served, and an additional family room. There is no licence, but guests may bring their own wine. Two of the bedrooms are on the ground floor.

OWNER Rosemary Crawford OPEN Easter – October 31 ROOMS 2 double, twin, 2 family; all en suite. TERMS €21.50; reduction for children; single supplement €4

COUNTY GALWAY

Galway contains the widely renowned area of Connemara, which stretches northward from Galway city up to Killary Harbour and is bordered on the east by beautiful Lough Corrib, which boasts an island for every day of the year.

Galway, the "city of the tribes," and the nearby popular resort of Salthill, which overlooks the famous Galway Bay, have lovely beaches, a promenade for walking and lots of restaurants: an ideal holiday spot.

Wild Connemara has inspired song and poetry. Today, Galway, Connemara and the west of Ireland are a haven for ancient customs and culture. You will hear lilting and evocative Irish music in the pubs and often the Irish language being spoken. Travel offshore and you become immersed even deeper into Ireland's traditional way of life, with trips to Inishbofin, County Clare, Achill and the Aran Islands.

There's plenty to see and do in the west of Ireland: pony trekking, dramatically located golf courses, angling (which is well catered for, with abundant salmon and trout in clean waters). If you are interested in sixteenth-century castles, visit the ruins of Ardamullivan Castle, 7.5 km south of Gort, an O'Shaughnessy stronghold. Fiddaun Castle, 7.5 km south southwest of Gort, is another of their strongholds.

Clarinbridge is a popular place in September, when it hosts the Oyster Festival. Portumna, a market town, is at the head of Lough Derg.

For the more adventurous, a climb up the Slieve Auchty Mountains is well worth the view.

Two castles worth seeing are Derryhivenny Castle, 4.5 km northeast of Portumna. Built in 1653, it is well preserved, as is Pallas Castle, 9 km from Portumna on the Loughrea Road.

Ballinasloe is well-known for the October Horse Fair, which lasts for eight days and includes carnival events and show-jumping exhibitions.

Corrib View Farm
Annaghdown, Co. Galway
Tel: 091 791114 Fax: 093 55356

This 100-year-old, friendly farmhouse, situated in a peaceful area near Lough Corrib, offers good old-fashioned hospitality. It has received the Agri-Tourism Regional Award. The bedrooms are clean and comfortable and have big fluffy towels. The lounge is warm and there is a separate dining room where breakfasts are served at separate tables. For guests who prefer a continental breakfast, there is a reduction in price. Evening meals are no longer available, but Regina's Pub, 3km away, serves light meals and full dinners. This is a family-run bed & breakfast and guests are made to feel immediately at home.

OWNER Mary Scott Furey and Family OPEN April 1 – October 31 ROOMS 2 double, 2 twin, 1 family, 1 single; 3 en suite TERMS €25.50; reduction for children; single supplement €10

Cashel House
Cashel, Co. Galway
Tel: 095 31001 Fax: 095 31077
Email: cashelhh@iol.ie
Website: www.cashel-house-hotel.com

Situated at the head of Cashel Bay, this gracious, nineteenth-century country house is set in 20 hectares of award-winning gardens and woodland walks. It has gained an international reputation for good food and luxurious comfort in a quiet, relaxing atmosphere. Carefully cooked fresh garden and sea produce,

such as fresh lobsters, clams, mackerel, salmon and scallops, are its specialities, and there is a carefully chosen wine list. Meals are tastefully presented in the elegant dining room with open turf fires.

This would be an excellent choice for a special occasion or honeymoon. Luxury and tranquillity combined with the romantic setting would be a magical experience. General and Madame de Gaulle spent two weeks of their Irish holiday here in 1969. The house is furnished with antiques and other fine treasures, and the bedrooms are beautifully appointed. There are several areas in which to sit, including a conservatory and a patio area. Smoking is permitted in designated areas only. Guests may walk along the seashore, through woods and streams, and drive through the beautiful scenic Connemara. All major credit cards accepted. Situated one and a half miles west of Recess, turn south of N59, and Cashel House is sign-posted from there.

OWNER Dermot & Kay McEvilly OPEN February - December
ROOMS 32 rooms (mixed); all en suite. TERMS B&B from €71;
reduction for children; single supplement (seasonal)
MEALS full dinner and lighter meals

CLARINBRIDGE

Springlawn B & B
Stradbally, Clarinbridge, Co. Galway
Tel: 091 796045 Fax: 091 796045
Email:springlawn@hotmail.com

This attractive house with dormer windows stands in a hectare in the heart of oyster country. Clarinbridge holds an annual Oyster Festival on the weekend of the 2nd Sunday in September. There is a wooded area behind the house, and the sea is within walking distance. The good-sized bedrooms maintain a high standard and have modern comfortable furnishings. Maura McNamara, who has been running her successful bed & breakfast for 11 years, takes a personal interest in her guests and is happy to provide information on golf, fishing and pony trekking, all of which are within a 15-minute drive. This non-smoking house has a TV lounge and a separate dining room where breakfasts, pre-arranged dinners and light meals are served at modest prices. As an alternate, there are three restaurants close by. There is no public phone, but guests may use the owners' on request. All major credit cards accepted. Springlawn is 1 mile off the N18 on the Limerick side of Clarinbridge village.

OWNER Maura McNamara OPEN March 1 – November 30
ROOMS 1 double, 1 twin, 1 family, 1 single, triple; 3 en suite
TERMS €25; reduction for children; single supplement €8
MEALS light teas and dinners

Ardmore House
Sky Road, Clifden, Co. Galway
Tel: 095 21221 Fax: 095 21100
Email: info@ardmore-house.com
Website: www.ardmore-house.com/

This luxurious farmhouse is set in beautiful scenic countryside
overlooking the sea. It is warm and inviting and Kathy Mullen is a
delightful and pleasant host – guests here are assured of true
Irish hospitality. The immaculate bedrooms are well decorated
and have comfortable beds. There are two lounges, one with TV
and an open fire, and one quiet lounge for chatting or reading.
This is a non-smoking house.

  Sea-food is a speciality for evening meals, and light meals are
also available. Dinners must be ordered in advance, and special
diets can be catered for. Lake and deep-sea angling, pony
trekking, beautiful walks and golf are all available in the area.
Scenic farm walks to the cliff and picnic areas can also be taken.

OWNER Kathy Mullen OPEN April 1 – October 1 ROOMS 2
double, 1 twin, 3 family; all en suite. TERMS €25.50–28; reduction
for children; single supplement €12.50 MEALS Dinner

Mallmore House
Clifden, Co. Galway
Tel: 095 21460 Email: mallmore@indigo.ie

This lovingly restored Georgian house (formerly the home of
the Darcy family, the founders of Clifden, and his excellency, the
Archbishop of Tuam), is set in 14 hectares and is within walking
distance of the sea. The house overlooks the bay, and most of
the bedrooms have lovely views. All the bedrooms are on the
ground floor and are spacious and comfortable. The large lounge
has a turf fire and is a peaceful place in which to relax after a
busy day, or have a smoke. Award-winning breakfasts are served
in a separate dining room, and for other meals there are several
establishments in Clifden.

  Kathleen Hardman is a considerate and helpful host and guests
are assured of personal attention. The world-famous Connemara
ponies are bred at Mallmore and can be seen in the grounds, and
the woodland is a haven for a great variety of wildlife. 1 mile
from Clifden on the Ballyconneely Road.

OWNER Kathleen Hardman OPEN April 1 – October 31
ROOMS 3 double, 2 twin, 1 family; all en suite TERMS €25.50;
reduction for children; single supplement €6.50

Ocean Villa
Kingstown, Sky Road, Clifden, Co. Galway
Tel: 095 21357
Email: oceanvilla@eircom.net

Ocean Villa is situated in a wonderful position overlooking the
sea and hills. The house is immaculately maintained and the
welcome here is warm and friendly. Carmel Murray is a most
hospitable host who greets guests with a hot drink upon arrival,
and is happy to spend time assisting guests in every way. The
bedrooms are of a good size, have comfortable beds, tea making
facilities, and are warm and comfortable.

This is a peaceful and tranquil location and there is plenty to
see and do from here, golf, mountain climbing pony trekking, fishing, and beach walks, all of which, can be arranged by your hosts.
Home cooked meals are on offer, fresh fish is often on the
menu, and special diets can be catered for with advance notice.
Smoking is permitted in designated areas only. Take a left turn at
centre of Clifden for Sky Road, pass Abbeyglen Castle Hotel,
drive for five more miles on upper Sky Road, then following
finger signs for Ocean Villa.

OWNER Mrs Carmel Murray OPEN March 1 – October 31
ROOMS 6 double/twin/family; 4 en suite. TERMS €23–25.50;
reduction for children; single supplement €6.50–8 MEALS dinner

Sunnybank House
Sunnybank, Clifden, Co. Galway
Tel: 095 21437 Fax: 095 21976
Email: info@sunnybankhouse.com
Website: www.sunnybankhouse.com

This charming period house of character, whose history is part
of Clifden town, commands an elevated position in well tended,
landscaped grounds over-looking Clifden town.

The immaculate, well-appointed bedrooms are tastefully decorated and furnished to a high standard. Smoking is not permitted
in bedrooms. There are two ground floor rooms with their own
sitting rooms. There is also a spacious lounge which has some
antique pieces, including a grandfather clock and soft, comfortable furnishings, and there is an additional lounge with TV. The
house is bright and decorated mostly with pastel shades.
There is a heated swimming pool, a sauna, tennis courts and
mature gardens for guests' use. Evening meals are not served,

but the charming owners, Jackie and Marion O'Grady, have an award-winning seafood restaurant with a bistro bar that is open for lunch and dinner daily. Sunnybank would be an ideal base from which to explore this beautiful area of Ireland. The house is not suitable for children. Visa, Mastercard accepted. N59 from Galway, turn right at Esso station, pass church, take first left, house is 200 m on the right.

OWNER Jackie & Marion O'Grady OPEN March 1 – November 1 ROOMS 6 double, 4 twin, 1 single; all en suite. TERMS €38; single supplement €12.50

The Quay House
Beach Road, Clifden, Co. Galway
Tel: 095 21369 Fax: 095 21608
Email: thequayhouse@iol.ie
Website: www.thequayhouse.com

Quay House is the oldest building in Clifden and was built over 200 years ago for the Harbour Master. Since that time it has been a Franciscan Monastery, and a convent. It is now run by a charming couple, Paddy and Julia Foley, and the ambience is informal and comfortable. The house is non-smoking. The spacious bedrooms are individually themed, have antique furniture, original paintings, and large bathrooms, with both a shower and bath. Several bedrooms have working fireplaces, most of them overlooking the harbour. The studios have balconies, and small fitted kitchens. All bedrooms have TV, phone and tea makers.

Quay House is full of items of interest, including family portraits, and period furniture, and other treasures. The house was in a dilapidated condition until 9 years ago, When Paddy and Julia undertook the job of tastefully refurbishing the house, skilfully combining modern amenities with old world charm. A tiger's head greets guests in the entry hall, and Buster, the pug, also resides here. This is a wonderful place to stay, as guests have every comfort. Breakfast is served in the conservatory overlooking the garden, a great spot from which to start the day. Special diets can be catered for at breakfast. There are several establishments in the area for evening meals. There is a good selection of wines. Two ground floor bedrooms have wheelchair access. Visa, Mastercard accepted.

OWNER Paddy & Julia Foyle OPEN mid-March – end October (other months by arrangement) ROOMS 14 rooms double/twin/family; all en suite. TERMS €57–63.50; reduction for children; single supplement €19

Ballykine House
Clonbur, Co. Galway
Tel: 092 46150 Fax: 092 46150
Email: ballykine@eircom.net

Ballykine House is situated on the road between the picturesque villages of Cong and Clonbur, and is known as the gateway to Connemara. The house continues to maintain its high standard and offers good value accommodation. It overlooks the famous fishing lake of Lough Mask. It has its own private grounds of gardens and lawns, surrounded by beautiful woodlands. The oldest part of the house belonged to the Guinness family; the house and the land were purchased by the family in 1940, with an addition in 1992: there is a wine license. Mr and Mrs Lambe are a very congenial couple who have created a warm and inviting atmosphere. There is a cosy sitting room and open fire, and a conservatory to relax in with tea and coffee makers provided. Smoking is only permitted in the conservatory.

There are wonderful forest walks (guides can be provided) as well as walks to the summit of magnificent Benlevi. The immediate area is a fisherman's paradise. Restaurants are within walking distance of the house. Golf is available at famous Ashford Castle and Ballinrobe. Take N84 from Galway to Cong; from Cong take R345 to Ballykine House.

OWNER Ann Lambe OPEN April 1 – November 1 ROOMS 2 double, 2 twin, 1 family; all en suite. TERMS €25.50; reduction for children; single supplement €7.50

Cregg House
Galway Road, Connemara, Co. Galway
Tel: 095 21326 Fax: 095 21326
Email: cregghouse@eircom.net

This immaculate dormer bungalow stands in an elevated position on half a hectare of grounds. The house has a spectacular view of Roundstone Bog and the mountains beyond. Mary O'Donnell continues to maintain her high standards and the bedrooms are prettily and individually decorated with soft pastel colours. The O'Donnells have been offering their special brand of hospitality for over 13 years; guests feel very much at home here, and enjoy chatting round the turf fire, which is lit at the first sign of a chill in the air. Excellent breakfasts include fresh fruit, home-made yoghurt and soda bread. An ideal base from which to tour Connemara, there is a fishing river less than five minutes away and golf and horseback riding are also available. Visa accepted. On N59, main Galway Road.

OWNER Mary O'Donnell OPEN Easter – November 1 ROOMS 3 double, 2 twin, 1 family; 5 en suite. TERMS €24; reduction for children; single supplement €7.50

Killary House
Leenane, Connemara, County Galway
Tel: 095 42254 Fax: 095 43591

Killary House has lots of character, and is situated on 800 acres, part of a working sheep farm, overlooking Killary Harbour. This is an idyllic location for families, and folks interested in outdoor activities. Leenane is a small village, and was the location for the film, The Field, starring Richard Harris. Evening meals are not served, but there are plenty of establishments close by that serve good food. Special diets are catered for at breakfast. The bedrooms are all spacious, and furnished with antiques. Tea-making facilities are available in the bedrooms. Smoking is permitted only in designated areas in the house. There is also a very large sitting room with TV. The welcome here is warm, guests return here often, enjoying the informal ambience and Mary's hospitality. There are lovely views all round the property, and pleasant of walks can be taken from the farm. Sign-posted at Leenane.

OWNER Mary King OPEN March – October ROOMS 7 double/family/twin; 4 en suite. TERMS €26.50; reduction for children; single supplement €6.50

Lakeside Country House
Oughterard, Connemara, Co. Galway
Tel: 091 552846 Fax: 091 552846

This warm and friendly, immaculately kept house is in a superb position on the shores of Lough Corrib with panoramic views of the lake and its many islands. This is a working farm of sheep and cattle, and there is also a donkey and a Connemara pony. An additional bonus are the delightful and charming owners, Josie and Mary O'Halloran – little wonder guests return here often to enjoy their special brand of Irish hospitality. The bedrooms, all on the ground floor, are of a good size and have patchwork quilts or Country Diary duvets. Smoking is permitted in the sitting room only. There is a bog on the property which provides the turf for the fireplace in the sitting room. Breakfasts only are served in the dining room with pine furniture, and there are several options for evening meals close by. Josie can easily be persuaded to take guests up the river, and there is an angling centre almost adjacent to the property.

There is a picnic area by the lake and in the garden by the fountain/waterfall. You may arrive here as a guest, but you will leave as a friend. It is a wonderful spot from which to explore this beautiful area. Travel down Golf Course – Aughnanure Castle Road and follow signs for Lakeside Country House. Visa, Mastercard accepted.

OWNER Mary O'Halloran OPEN March 1 – November 30 ROOMS 2 double, 1 twin, 1 family; all en suite TERMS €25.50–28; reduction for children; single supplement €8.50

Waterfall Lodge
Oughterard, Connemara, Co. Galway
Tel: 091 552168
Email: kdolly@eircom.net

This superb period residence stands in a secluded setting, with beautiful grounds ablaze with colour in spring and summer, and a cascading waterfall. The river Owen Riff runs through the property, and private game fishing for salmon and trout is available to guests. A visit to the Glengowla Silver and Lead Mines, Ireland's only show mine, is well worth a visit.

The house is furnished with antiques, including a grandfather clock, and the tastefully furnished bedrooms are reached by a pitch pine stairway. Breakfasts only are served in the elegant dining room at separate tables, and the spacious TV lounge has a cast-iron and marble fireplace. Tea and coffee making facilities are in the lounge and guests may help themselves at just about any time. Kathleen Dolly is a delightful lady and is very knowledge-able about the area. The atmosphere is friendly and informal – this is a non-smoking house. This is a popular bed & breakfast establishment and early reservations are recommended.
Take N59 from Galway city to Oughterard; Waterfall Lodge is the first house on the left after the bridge.

OWNER Kathleen Dolly OPEN All year ROOMS 3 double, 2 twin, 1 family; all en suite. TERMS €31.50; reduction for children; single supplement €6.50

Cregg Castle
Corrandulla, Co. Galway
Tel: 091 791434
Email: creggcas@indigo.ie

Cregg Castle, the last fortified castle to be built west of the Shannon, sits in a peaceful and tranquil spot on 67 hectares of

wildlife preserve, also home to several other animals, such as pet sheep, dogs, a donkey and chickens. This is a very lived-in, casual, informal property, and there are no strict rules here. Guests may walk in the woods and spot the wildlife, or go farther afoot and take a walk by the river. Breakfasts, which include free-range eggs and home-baked bread, are served until noon, and dinners are served in the Great Hall with its huge log fire. Smoking is permitted in the Great Hall only. The emphasis here is on relaxation, and guests are encouraged to get to know each other, enjoying conversation and the occasional musical evening. This is an ideal place for those who want to be involved in Irish music. Owners Pat and Ann Marie are experienced musicians and are delighted to play with or for guests. Most of the bedrooms are of a good size and have comfortable beds.

This is a unique property with many original features, such as the huge locks and security bars, the foot scraper with the rampant black cat of the Blake's crest and the shutters on the big windows. The Blake crest is also on the fireplace with its black marble. Outside in the courtyard is a Queen Anne bell tower; in the inner yard is the original forge and the remains of an oven for firing pottery. A spring well provides the castle with water. Cregg Castle's welcome, as described in their brochure, is exactly right – "Hail Guest, we ask not what thou art; if friend we greet thee hand and heart; if stranger, such no longer be, our friendly faith shall conquer thee." Cregg Castle is a place to capture Ireland's history and culture. Visa, Access, Mastercard accepted. Directions from Dublin/ Limerick: take Tuam/ Sligo turn off at Oranmore roundabout (five miles from Galway). Turn right for Tuam at Claregalway and then first left for Corrandulla.

OWNER Anne & Marie Broderick OPEN March – November 30 ROOMS 2 double, I twin, I family, I single; 4 en suite TERMS €51; reduction for children; single supplement €19 MEALS dinner

Carraig Beag

1 Burren Hill Heights, Knocknacarra Road, Salthill, Galway
Tel: 091 521696

This luxurious, red brick house is just off the promenade and has excellent views of the bay. The bedrooms are a good size and are furnished with every comfort in mind. There are attractive, rich wood doors and a handsome staircase. Breakfasts are served at separate tables in the elegant dining room, which has a beautiful crystal chandelier and marble fireplace. The owners, Paddy and Catherine Lydon, are an added bonus. They are a very helpful and accommodating couple.

Catherine and Paddy often take walks along the promenade in the evening; guests may join them, but beware, you might find it hard to keep up with them! This good value bed & breakfast offers a high standard of accommodation at modest prices, and it is well situated for all of the local amenities. Mastercard accepted. Follow the promenade from Galway to Salthill. First building after the seafront is the Spinnaker House Hotel, on your left. Turn right after the Spinnaker into Knocknacarra Road; Carraig Beag is the second house on the right, and is sign-posted.

OWNER Catherine & Paddy Lydon OPEN All year except for Christmas ROOMS 2 double, 2 twin, 1 family; all en suite. TERMS €29–33; reduction for children; single supplement €10–20

Dun Roamin

Gratton Road, Galway, Co. Galway
Tel: 091 582570

The Bogan family named their modern, attractive, red brick house after their decision to stay put and enjoy Galway and the beautiful scenic countryside. The house has a warm and welcoming atmosphere and the rooms are clean with comfortable beds and warm duvets. The guest lounge is cosy and breakfasts only are served in a separate dining room, consisting of cereals, fruit and a traditional Irish platter. Smoking is only allowed in the lounge. Dun Roamin is located less than two minutes from the beach, restaurants and other amenities. Jo Bogan is a down-to-earth, friendly lady, and a helpful and considerate host. Guests are welcomed with a hot drink upon arrival.

OWNER Mrs Jo Bogan OPEN All year ROOMS 2 double, 2 twin; all en suite. TERMS €25.50; reduction for children; single supplement €12.50

Eureka

Bushy Park, Galway, Co. Galway
Tel: 091 523555 Fax: 091 523229

Eureka is set back off the main road in a quiet position, yet is just five minutes from Galway town on the road to Connemara. This attractive modern house is very well maintained and an added bonus are the accommodating owners, John and Mary Connell. Mary is very knowledgeable about the area and enjoys sharing information with guests. The bedrooms are well maintained and decorated to a high standard. The front rooms have views of the lake, river and golf course. The small sun lounge has a TV and a conservatory has been added for guests' use. A complimentary hot drink and biscuits are offered upon arrival. Breakfast only is served, and guests not wanting the traditional Irish breakfast have a choice of yoghurts and fresh fruit. There is a restaurant close by for evening meals, and bar food is also served. The house is directly opposite the Glenlo Abbey golf course. Visa, Access, Mastercard accepted.

OWNER John & Mary Connell OPEN May 1 – September 30 ROOMS 2 double, 1 double/single; all en suite. TERMS €23–25.50; reduction for children; single supplement €7.50–10

Killeen House

Bushypark, nr. Galway, Co. Galway
Tel: 091 524179 Fax: 091 528065
Email: killeenhouse@ireland.com
Website: www.killeenhousegalway.com

This charming house, built in 1840, is approached by a tree-lined driveway. It nestles in 10 hectares of beautifully landscaped gardens that extend down to Lake Corrib. Catherine Doyle is a wonderful host with a flair for décor and a passion for antiques. The house has been tastefully refurbished, combining all-modern comforts without detracting from the original ambience. The rooms are enormous and luxuriously appointed. One room reflects the Victorian era, another the Edwardian. There are direct dial telephones in all bedrooms. The elegant drawing room has the original marble fireplace and an interesting teapot collection: smoking is only permitted in the drawing room.

A varied breakfast is tastefully presented in the dining room. For those who enjoy gracious living in a tranquil atmosphere, Killeen Lodge is an excellent choice. A path from the house leads down to the shores of Lough Corrib. All major credit cards accepted. Situated on the N59 four miles from Galway city centre.

OWNER Catherine Doyle OPEN All year ROOMS 4 double, 1 twin, 1 family; 5 en suite. TERMS from €57; single supplement from €25.50

Mandalay by the Sea

10 Gentian Hill, Galway, Co. Galway
Tel: 091 524177 Fax: 091 529952

This beautiful, new Georgian-style house is in a superb location
overlooking the bay and the Aran Islands. Owner Georgianna
Darby is from Rhode Island in the USA. Mandalay is furnished
and decorated to extremely high standards; there are rich wood
furnishings and antiques. The rooms are spacious, two have
balconies and all have views. The entry hall and the kitchen have
Liscannor stone floors from the Burren. There are two lounges,
one with a piano and TV. There are lots of plants and dried
flower arrangements throughout the house. Excellent breakfasts
are served in the bright dining room. For nature lovers there are
some very pleasant walks close by, and a bird sanctuary can be
seen in front of the house. Visa, Mastercard accepted. Mandalay
by the Sea can be found off 336 Coast Road, 2 miles from
Galway city.

OWNER Georgina Darby OPEN All year ROOMS 2 double, 2
twin, 2 double/single; 5 en suite. TERMS €20.50–25.50; reduction
for children; single supplement €6.50

Seaview

Beach Court, Gratton Road, Galway, Co. Galway
Tel: 091 582109 Fax: 091 582109

This detached, attractive white house faces the seafront. The
front bedrooms overlook the sea; they are all colour-co-ordinated and are spotlessly clean, and two have orthopaedic beds.
There is a balcony for guests' use and a small TV lounge. The
house is a five-minute walk from the town centre and directly
across from the beach. Mrs Bready Tracey is an accommodating
host and there is plenty of information provided on what there
is to do and see in the area. This is good value accommodation
in a central position. All major credit cards accepted.

OWNER Mrs Bready Tracey OPEN All year ROOMS 2 double, 1
twin, 1 family; all en suite. TERMS €21.50; reduction for children;
single supplement €7.50–10

LEENANE

Delphi Lodge

Leenane, Co. Galway
Tel: 095 42222 Fax: 095 42296
E-mail: delfish@iol.ie

This magnificent 1830s house was beautifully restored in 1988,
and is now one of the finest sporting lodges in Ireland. Set in
400 hectares with three loughs in a stunning lakeside location,
and surrounded by ancient woodlands and towering mountains,
it is the ultimate Connemara retreat.

The house has antique pine furniture and the bedrooms have lovely views. Originally the sporting estate of the Marquis of Sligo, Delphi is now the home of Jane and Peter Mantle. Jane is a Cordon Bleu cook who specialises in local seafood. The Lodge has a strong emphasis on salmon and trout fishing, and Delphi is one of the finest game fisheries in Ireland. Fly-fishing for salmon is available, but must be pre-booked. The fishing season runs from spring to September. Outside the fishing season the lodge is popular with shooting parties, ramblers and golfers. Horseback riding and hunting can also be arranged. Superb, safe and uncrowded beaches are within a 20-minute drive, and the Lodge is conveniently placed for visiting Westport and all the sites of Connemara. A huge snooker room and a magnificent library are open to guests. Evening meals are served at an old oak table and the wine cellar is extensive. Not suitable for children. French spoken. There are four charming country cottages available for self-catering. Visa, Mastercard accepted.

OWNER Peter Mantle OPEN January 10 – December 15 ROOMS 6 double, 6 twin; all en suite. TERMS B&B from €60; single supplement; MEALS dinner

Glen Valley Farm and Stables
Glencroff, Leenane, Co. Galway
Tel: 095 42269 Fax: 095 42365
Email: gvhouse@yahoo.com

This friendly, award-winning, modest farmhouse is found down a rather bumpy road in a remote location amidst lovely country-side, nestled in the foothills of Lettershanbally Mountain. The house is non-smoking. The rooms are spacious, clean and simply furnished. The small, cosy lounge has turf fires. This is an ideal base for those who enjoy hill walking. Pony trekking is available on the farm, which is run by Mrs O'Neill. Substantial breakfasts are provided, and Mrs. O'Neill is happy to make recommendations and dinner reservations for the restaurants which can be found a short drive away. N59 Clifden Road, four and half miles from Leenane Village.

OWNER Josephine O'Neill OPEN May 1 – October 31 ROOMS 2 double, 2 twin, 1 family; 3 en suite, 1 private bath. TERMS B&B €25.50–28; reduction for children; single supplement €12.50

MOYCULLEN

Moycullen House and Restaurant
Moycullen, Co. Galway
Tel: 091 555566 Fax: 091 555566
Email: info@moycullen.com
Website: www.moycullen.com

Moycullen House lies on a narrow, quiet road, on one of the highest points in the area overlooking Lough Corrib. It is on the edge of Connemara, making it an ideal location for touring, trips to the Aran Island and Lough Corrib. It was built in the 1930s by Lord Campbell, and has great oak doors with the original iron locks. The servants' bells still exist in the sitting room. During the time of remodelling for the new dining room and restaurant, two stone fireplaces were exposed.

The restaurant on the premises, which is open to the public has full bar facilities, and an outstanding wine list. The award winning restaurant is run by Marie's son Richard, who is the chef, and his wife, Louise. Dinners are not served on Wednesday, table d'hote 25.95 and an a la carte menu is available. The house stands in 12 hectares of rhododendrons and azaleas, and a pure spring provides the house with water. The bedrooms are large, tastefully decorated and well furnished, most with period fireplaces. There is an elegant and comfortable sitting room which has an old stone fireplace, and also a conservatory. Philip and Marie are charming hosts who can organise coarse, trout and salmon fishing as well as boats on Lough Corrib. There are four 18-hole golf courses within a half hour's drive. American Express, Visa, Laser and Mastercard accepted.

OWNER Marie & Philip Casburn OPEN March – early January ROOMS 2 double, 2 twin, 1 family; 2 en suite. TERMS €51; reduction for children negotiable; single supplement €12.50 MEALS full à la carte menu

OUGHTERARD

Corrib Wave Guest House
Portacarron, Oughterard, Co. Galway
Tel: 091 552147 Fax: 091 552736

Corrib Wave House has been upgraded to a three-star guest house with wine license, situated in picturesque surroundings overlooking the lake and Connemara mountains. This is a peaceful and tranquil spot, part of a working sheep farm of 10 hectares. The bedrooms, all of which overlook the view, have been upgraded with sturdy seating, made by owner Michael Healy, and have good-sized bath-rooms. The lounge, where smoking is permitted, has an open fire and there is a separate dining room where breakfasts and excellent evening meals, if pre-arranged, are served. This is an ideal spot for people who enjoy the outdoors; there are lovely walks close by, and salmon, trout and coarse fishing. There are boats for hire, and ghillies can be arranged. Swimming can be enjoyed on the lake, and there is an 18-hole golf course within a kilometre. The house is conveniently located near Galway and Connemara. Visa, Mastercard, Eurocard accepted. Corrib Wave Guest House is off the N59, 1 1/2 km east of Oughterard.

OWNER Michael & Maria Healy OPEN February – October 31 ROOMS 3 double, 4 twin, 3 family; all en suite, TERMS €31.50; reduction for children; single supplement €10 MEALS dinner

ROUNDSTONE

The Angler's Return
Toombeola, Roundstone, Connemara, Co. Galway
Tel: 095 31091 Fax: 095 31091
Email: lynnhill@eircom.net

Nestled at the foot of Derrada Hill, between the mountains and the sea, and overlooking a fresh water tidal pool, The Anglers Rest dates back to the 1900s. It has thick stone walls, log fireplaces and an interesting history. It was first built as a single storey cottage known as "The Fishery". John Robertson, a Scottish gentleman, leased the building and started a salmon cannery on the small island in the Owenmore River. It was rebuilt as a hotel in 1839, and has been run as a guesthouse by the same family since 1964. It stands in five hectares, with woodlands and colourful gardens. The lounge, with terracotta tiles, has a log fireplace, and is a good spot in which to relax. There are no TVs, but there are plenty of books to read. The ambience is free and easy, there are no petty rules, and guests are well taken care of. The spacious bedrooms have lake and garden views: they are not en-suite, but do have sinks, and there are two bathrooms exclusively for guests. One new bedroom does have its own shower and toilet. Breakfasts feature home-made yoghurt, honey, home-baked bread, home-made marmalade and preserves. Free range eggs are also on the menu. Smoking is permitted in the lounge. It is an artist's and hill walker's paradise. Sea fishing can be arranged locally and brown trout lakes can be fished at no charge to guests. Connemara is one of the most unspoilt and beautiful landscapes in Europe. Golfing, beaches, restaurants and pubs are a short drive away. From Galway take N59 Galway/Clifden Road, turn left on R341 at Roundstone/Ballynahinch Road Castle sign, 4 miles from there.

OWNER Lynn Hill OPEN March 1 – November 30 ROOMS 2 double, 2 twin; 1 en suite with own bathroom. TERMS €31.50–35.50; single supplement €12.50 MEALS dinner, snacks

The Connaught

Barna Road, Salthill, Galway, Co. Galway
Tel: 091 525865 Fax: 091 525865
Email: tconnaught@eircom.net

This pleasant, friendly residence is set back off the road in a quiet position. It is a well maintained house, redecorated throughout to a high standard. The well-appointed bedrooms are nicely furnished, and all new comfortable orthopaedic beds with electric blankets. The lounge has rich red carpeting and there is a bright dining room where an extensive menu of substantial, freshly prepared breakfasts can be enjoyed. An extremely cordial and helpful couple, the Keaveneys do everything to ensure their guests are comfortable and well taken care of. There is a warm and friendly atmosphere and guests feel relaxed and very much at home here. The Connaught offers good value bed & breakfast, and this would be an ideal place from which to explore this diversified and beautiful area. Drive along the promenade in Salthill, with Galway Bay on the left. Continue on until you reach T-junction, turn left at Barna Road. House is approximately 500 yards on right hand side.

OWNER Colette & Tom Keaveney OPEN March 17 – October 31 ROOMS 3 double, 1 twin, 2 family; 5 en suite. TERMS €25.50–28.50; reduction for children; single supplement €8 (high season)

Ard Mhuirbhi

Aille, Inverin, Spiddal, Co. Galway
Tel: 091 593215 Fax: 091 593326

Ard Mhuirbhi, which means "seashore height," offers quality accommodation. The house is located on the sea side of the coast road on a small, peaceful road, and is set in mature, landscaped gardens. The entrance to the house is through a small porch full of colourful potted plants and flowers. The bedrooms, all of which are on the ground floor, are large and well furnished. They have large wardrobes, soft pastel colours and co-ordinated fabrics, and two have excellent views of the Burren and the bay. All bedrooms have TV and electric blankets. The lounge is well furnished and breakfast is served on the patio on fine days. The house is immaculately maintained and is delightful in every way. Owner Ria Feeney has thought of just about everything for her guests' comfort and is an attentive, courteous host. There are no TVs in the room, but one is available on request. This is a tranquil place to return to after a busy day and guests can enjoy walks on the beach three minutes from the house, or the moors and bog, which are just a five-minute drive away. Convenient for touring Connemara and for trips to the Aran Islands. Access, Visa, Mastercard accepted. Situated 5 km west of Spiddal village on the R336 coast road.

OWNER Rita Feeney OPEN February – mid December ROOMS 2 double, 1 twin, 2 family; 4 en suite. TERMS €27; reduction for children; single supplement €7

Cala 'n Uisce
Greenhill, Spiddal, Co. Galway
Tel: 091 553324 Fax: 091 553324
Email: moyafeeney@iol.ie

Cala 'n Uisce means "little harbour," which is apt, as the house is in a picturesque setting facing the bay. The house was designed by owner Pádraig Feeney and has leaded windows and a red brick exterior. High standards are found here, and the house continues to be exceptionally well maintained. This is a non-smoking establishment. There are three ground floor bedrooms, attractively decorated with co-ordinated fabrics; all bedrooms have tea-making facilities and TV. Many interesting paintings of local scenes, by Mrs Feeney and other family members, are on display throughout the house. The lounge, which has a turf fire, leads out onto a patio. The dining room, where a tasty breakfast is served on linen table-cloths and pretty china, overlooks the bay.
  Pádraig Feeney's father was a cousin of John Ford, who directed *The Quiet Man*. This is an Irish-speaking area, and the Feeney family speaks Irish. Cala 'n Uisce is a most comfortable and peaceful place; the house stands in half a hectare of land-scaped gardens, and there are beautiful bog areas and sea walks close by. No smoking in the bedrooms. No pets. Visa, Mastercard accepted. Situated 2.5 km west of Spiddal village.

OWNER Moya Feeney OPEN April – October ROOMS 3 double, 1 twin, 2 family; all en suite. TERMS €25.50; reduction for children; single supplement €7.50

Cloch na Scith – Thatched Cottage
Kellough, Spiddal, Co. Galway
Tel: 091 553364 Fax: 091 553890

This cosy, 130-year-old, traditional thatched cottage, part of a working farm, has played host to actress Julie Christie and the Swedish ambassador. There are thick stone walls, uneven floors, plenty of history and an old-world charm. Owner Nancy Hopkins-Naughton offers one of the warmest welcomes in Ireland. She is a delightful, down-to-earth host and guests are greeted with a hot drink on arrival, often with home-made cake. The family are Irish speaking and into Irish music. The lounge/dining room has turf fires, and a Galway wedding shawl which belonged to Nancy's grandmother hangs on the wall. Breakfast, and four-course home-cooked dinners if ordered in advance, are served on old pine tables and blue willow china. Guests may bring their own wine to dinner. Nancy is an absolutely delightful lady; there are no petty rules here and guests are treated as friends, so it is little wonder that many of her guests are repeat visitors. Smoking is not permitted. The bedrooms are comfortable with firm beds; two are on a lower floor and one room is quite large with its own bathroom. The beach is two minutes away and there are maps provided for folks interested in walking. Cloch na Scith has been featured on TV's Holiday programme. A one-bedroom, self-catering cottage is available.

OWNER Nancy Hopkins-Naughton OPEN March 1 – September 30 ROOMS 1 double, 1 twin, 1 family; 2 en suite. TERMS €28; reduction for children; single supplement €20.50

Col Mar House
Salahoona, Spiddal, Co. Galway
Tel: 091 553247 Fax: 091 553247

This comfortable secluded country home stands in mature gardens and private woods, close to the sea and the beach. Children are welcome here, there is a playground, cot, and a highchair available. Special diets can be catered for at breakfast. Dinners are not served, but there are plenty of venues for evening meals close by.

Irish is spoken in this non-smoking house. The bedrooms are of a good size, have comfortable beds, and are furnished in keeping with the house; tea-making facilities are provided in rooms. Guests are welcome to enjoy the garden.

There is a sandy beach, golf and fishing nearby, and this location is handy for touring Connemara. Maureen Keady is a warm and hospitable host, a hot drink is offered on arrival, and there is a good supply of information on what to see and do in the area. Situated 1.5km west of Spiddal.

OWNER Maureen Keedy OPEN May – September ROOMS 5 double/twin/family; all en suite. TERMS €24.11; reduction for children; single supplement €7.50

Suan Na Mara
Stripe, Furbo, Spiddal, Co. Galway
Tel: 091 591512 Fax: 091 591632
Email: suannamara@tinet.ie Website:
www.irishholidays.com/suannamara.com

A most attractive custom built dormer bungalow, designed with high standards, stands in its grounds, with a lawned garden, complete with fish pond, old water pump, and seating for guests. The house is luxuriously furnished, and there is a ground floor bedroom, which has a colourful patchwork quilt. All rooms have extras, such as fruit bowls, bottled water, and a choice of drinks, along with TV, hairdryer and tea- and coffee-making facilities. The showers are all power showers. There is a sitting room, which has a fireplace, plenty of comfortable seating, and a bright dining-room where imaginative breakfasts, and dinners, are served. Fresh flowers adorn the tables when possible, and meals are served on fine china on linen tablecloths. Just about everything has been thought of to provide the finest in accommodation. Brian Clancy is a qualified chef, who has worked in many fine hotels; his superb meals can now be enjoyed at Suan na Mara. Dinners have to be booked in advance and any special dietary requirements made known. This award winning property is situated 8 miles from Galway, and just a few minutes walk to the beach. This non-smoking house is an ideal base for touring the west of Ireland, and there is pony trekking, golf and fishing nearby. Trips to the Aran Islands can be arranged. Laundry and ironing facilities are available. A high chair and baby cot can be provided.

OWNER Brian and Carmel Clancy OPEN All year ROOMS 4 double/twin; 3 en suite. TERMS €30–33; reduction for children; single supplement €7.50–10 MEALS dinner

TUAM

Gardenfield House
Tuam, Co. Galway
Tel: 093 24865

This rambling, comfortable period house dates from 1860 and is part of a 26-hectare working farm of sheep and cattle. The atmosphere is casual, friendly and welcoming. The house is in a tranquil setting and is approached up a gravel drive through fields dotted with sheep. The rooms are all good-sized, and are individually decorated in burgundy and gold, and a mixture of soft pastel shades. There are tall ceilings, and the dining and sitting rooms have the original casement shutters. Free-range chickens provide the eggs for breakfast and Esther, who is a good cook, prepares excellent evening meals, with plenty of organic vegetables; lamb from the farm is often on the menu. Vegetarians can be catered for with advance notice. Both the small, snug sitting room and the lounge have coal fires. There are two self-catering units available.

OWNER Mrs Esther Mannion OPEN All year ROOMS 1 double, 1 twin, 1 family; 2 en suite. TERMS €21.50; reduction for children; single supplement €6.50 MEALS dinner

COUNTY LIMERICK

Bordered on the north by the expanses of the Shannon, Limerick is a peaceful farming county with its fair share of relics from the past.

The origins of the city of Limerick go back to the days of the Vikings. Always a principal fording point for the Shannon River, it has played an important part in Irish history, particularly during the 1690s. Old English Town and the old Irish part of the city across the river are the most interesting parts of the city to explore, particularly around St John's Square with its Georgian architecture. The most noteworthy sight to visit is the Granary, a restored eighteenth-century warehouse, which houses the tourist office as well as restaurants, shops and an exhibition gallery. King John's Castle with its massive rounded tower, St Mary's Cathedral, dating from 1172, and the Hunt Collection at the National Institute for Higher Education can also be visited. Adare has some splendid ruins to see, the finest one being the Franciscan Friary. Others include the Trinitarian Abbey, the Augustian Abbey and St Nicholas Church. It is a most attractive town, with pretty thatched cottages and lovely views of Desmond Castle and Adare Manor on the river.

It is thought the "limerick" may well have come from Croom, which was the meeting place of eighteenth-century Gaelic poets, who wrote extremely witty verse.

ADARE

Adare Lodge
Kildimo Road, Adare, Co. Limerick
Tel: 061 396629

Agnes Fitzpatrick is a charming lady who has created an informal and welcoming atmosphere at this luxurious mock-Tudor house on a quiet side street, surrounded by an award-winning garden. The picturesque centre of Adare village, with its thatched cottages, is just a two-minute walk away. The house is tastefully appointed and the bedrooms are exquisitely decorated, and provide Ballygowan water and sweets. Guests are well looked after here and can enjoy high standards with a taste of luxury at affordable prices. Excellent breakfasts are served in the bright, attractive dining room, and there is a conservatory lounge and an additional lounge with plenty of literature on the area and a good supply of books for browsing. Evening meals are not available here, but Agnes Fitzpatrick has menus of local restaurants available and is happy to suggest venues for evening meals. All the bedrooms are on the ground floor, and are suitable for the slightly less mobile. On pleasant days guests can enjoy a cup of tea on the patio.

OWNER Agnes Fitzpatrick ROOMS 2 double, 2 twin, 2 family; all en suite. TERMS €28.50; reduction for children; single supplement €16

Clonunion House
Limerick Road, Adare, Co. Limerick
Tel: 061 396657

This traditional eighteenth-century farmhouse is 100 m off the main road in tranquil surroundings, and is part of a working sheep, deer, beef and tillage farm. At one time it was the stud farm belonging to Lord Dunraven, and interested guests can see the Horse Cemetery, with its horse-shoe- shaped headstones, where several famous stallions were buried. The house is furnished in keeping with its character; three bedrooms have the original fireplaces, and one a high bed. They are clean and com-fortable. Deer now inhabit the paddocks and there is a viewing stone where interested guests can watch the fallow deer. Breakfast only is served, but there are plenty of venues for evening meals and Irish music in Adare, Ireland's prettiest village, which is just 2 km away. Visa, Access, American Express accepted.

OWNER Mary & Michael Fitzgerald OPEN April 1 – November 1 ROOMS 1 double, 1 twin, 1 family; all en suite. TERMS €23; reduction for children; no single supplement in single room

LIMERICK

Clonmacken House
Off Ennis Road, Limerick, Co. Limerick
Tel: 061 372007 Fax: 061 327785
E-mail: clonmack@indigo.ie

This large, purpose-built, attractive yellow-and-green-trim guest house stands in its own grounds in a quiet setting, yet is just five minutes' drive from Limerick City. Brid McDonald thoroughly enjoys her bed & breakfast business; guests receive a warm wel-come in this friendly and hospitable house. Excellent standards of décor prevail and the house is comfortably furnished. The bedrooms are standardised and have attractive rose-patterned duvets, and multichannel TV. The comfortable lounge has soft furnishings and dainty wallpapers. Bunratty Castle is a 10-minute drive and Shannon Airport is a 15-minute drive. Breakfast only is served, but a pub serving evening meals is just 200 m away. Visa, Mastercard accepted.

OWNER Brid & Gerald McDonald OPEN All year ROOMS 3 double, 3 twin, 2 family, 2 double/single; all en suite. TERMS €23–28.50; reduction for children; single supplement from €7.50

Trebor
Ennis Road, Limerick, Co. Limerick
Tel: 061 454632 Fax: 061 454632

Trebor, which is the name of the owner's son spelt backward, is a well maintained, comfortable turn-of-the-century townhouse. The bedrooms are spotless and tastefully decorated with colour-coordinated wallpapers and fabrics. Breakfast includes fresh-squeezed orange juice, muesli or porridge and homemade breads, followed by a cooked breakfast. Mrs Joan McSweeney takes excellent care of her guests and is happy to give advice on what to see and do in the area. Trebor is popular with cyclists. Drying facilities are available. Evening meals are available (vegetarian and special diets catered for) if arranged in advance. Access, Visa, Mastercard accepted.

OWNER Mrs Joan McSweeney OPEN April 1 – November 1 ROOMS 2 twin, 2 family; all en suite. TERMS €23; reduction for children; single supplement €6.50 MEALS dinner

NEWCASTLE WEST

Ballingowan House
Newcastle West, Co. Limerick
Tel: 069 62341

This light and airy Georgian house, known to locals as the "pink house", stands back a good distance from the road behind a well-landscaped front garden. The bedrooms are quite spacious, are colourfully coordinated, and have multichannel TV. Two have a bath and shower and the rear rooms overlook peaceful countryside. One bedroom is on the ground floor. The lounge is bright with a blue and terra-cotta décor, interesting coving, and a marble fireplace. The conservatory area, which is full of colourful potted plants in summer, is a good spot in which to relax with a book and a cup of tea. Breakfast only is served at a large table, and tea is offered upon arrival and by request at other times. The owners are most accommodating and guests receive lots of personal attention; there is plenty of information on what to see and do in the area. Self-catering units are also available.

OWNER Carmel O'Brien OPEN All year ROOMS 2 double, 1 twin, 1 triple, 1 double/single; all en suite TERMS €24; reduction for children; single supplement €4

COUNTY MAYO

County Mayo is a maritime county, with the Atlantic Ocean making deep inroads into its coastline on the west and on the north. The sea influences the shape of its beauty, from the long, narrow fjord of Killary Harbour to the island-studded Clew Bay. Castlebar is the country town of Mayo and a good centre for touring. The most interesting building in the town is that occupied by the art centre and the education centre. It was formerly a chapel, the cornerstone of which was laid by John Wesley in 1785.

Westport is a gem of a town. The architect is not known, although some locals believe him to be a French architect left behind from Humbert's expedition in 1798. The main feature is the Octagon, a fine piece of planning. In the centre stands a Doric pillar, mounted on an octagonal granite base, on which the statue of George Glendenning once stood. Innisturk Island can be visited from Roonah Point. It is an exceptionally attractive island with a lovely harbour; there is a glorious beach on the south side.

Killary Harbour is a striking example of a fjord. Its 8 km sweep cuts deep into the surrounding mountains.

At Knock there is the Knock Fold Museum, which pays tribute to the area's forefathers. The collections and exhibitions on show help us to understand what life was like for our ancestors.

ACHILL ISLAND

Aquila
Sraheens, Achill Island, Co. Mayo
Tel: 098 45163
Email: aquila@ireland.com

This cosy, clean, modern bungalow is situated in an elevated position, with magnificent views of Achill Sound and the Corraun Mountains. The bedrooms are well-appointed, prettily decorated and have comfortable beds. One very popular room is the converted attic room, but it is not for everyone, as the approach is via a very narrow staircase. There are four rooms on the ground floor. Smoking is permitted in the bedrooms.

There is a comfortable sitting room and lounge with TV/VCR and an open turf fire. Cots are available. The house is located near five "Blue Flag" beaches, and two Outdoor Pursuit Centres. Self-catering is available. Drive onto Achill Island, take the second left turn; house is sign-posted.

OWNER Mrs Kay Sweeney OPEN March 1 – September 30
ROOMS 2 double, 1 twin, 1 family, 1 single; 4 en suite
TERMS €24; single supplement €6.50 MEALS tea and scones

BALLINA

Ashley House
Ardoughan, Ballina, Co. Mayo
Tel: 096 22799 Fax: 096 22799
Email: ashleyhousebb@hotmail.com

Ashley House is an attractive, Georgian-style dormer bungalow
situated off the main road, set in a beautifully landscaped garden.
Guests are welcome to sit out on fine days, and the dining room
overlooks the award winning garden.. It was established as a bed
& breakfast over 13 years ago and has built a good reputation
for offering a high standard of accommodation. The bedrooms
are well-appointed and are all on the ground floor. Carmel
Murray is a friendly lady with a good sense of humour. The
dormer was converted several years ago into private quarters
for the family. The owner's son is an enthusiastic fisherman and
can advise guests on the best spots. Carmel is into dancing and
could easily be persuaded to give guests a lesson and/or a
demonstration. A self-catering unit is available. Visa, Mastercard
accepted. Ashley House is 1 km from Ballina town on the N59
Belmullet Road.

OWNER Carmel Murray OPEN All year ROOMS 2 double, 1
twin, 1 family; all en suite. TERMS €25.50; reduction for children;
single supplement €6.50

Belvedere House
Foxford Road, Ballina, Co. Mayo
Tel: 096 22004

This spacious, modern two-storey house stands in its own
grounds, a 10-minute walk from the town centre. The bedrooms
are of a good size, are attractively decorated and clean and have
orthopaedic beds. There is a very large dining room and lounge
with a TV and fireplaces. The owners are attentive and work
hard to maintain the high standards. Breakfast only is served, but
there are many fine eating places in the area. Ballina is situated
on the lower reaches of the River Moy, directly between Lough
Conn/Cullen and Killala Bay. Bicycles are available for hire locally.
For guests who would like a day trip to Dublin, there is a good
local bus service. Ballina is a bustling town and there are several
venues where traditional Irish music can be heard. On main
Dublin Road - N6 heading to Ballina.

OWNER Mary Reilly OPEN All year ROOMS 2 double, 2 twin, 2 family; 5 en suite. TERMS €24; reduction for children; single supplement €7.50

The Hawthorns
Belderrig, Co. Mayo
Tel: 096 43148 Fax: 096 43148
Email: camurphy@indigo.ie

Located in the picturesque village of Belderrig (between Ballina and Belmullet), beside the sea and small fishing port, this clean and cosy bungalow stands in an open area with wonderful views of Ben Head and the Twang Mountains. There are cliff walks close by and the sea is a five-minute walk. Owner Carmel Hawthorn is a local lady who enjoys sharing her knowledge of the area with interested guests. The house is within driving distance of the Ceide Fields.

The bedrooms, all on the ground floor, are spotlessly clean. Smoking is permitted in the bedrooms. The lounge has a turf fire, which is lit on cool days, and breakfasts, dinners and light meals are served in the bright dining room. Vegetarians can be catered for; all meals must be ordered in advance. This is a pleasant family home – the Hawthorns have three children. Self-catering is available. Baby-sitting can be arranged.

OWNER Carmel Hawthorn OPEN All year ROOMS 2 double, 1 twin; 2 en suite. TERMS €23; reduction for children; single supplement €9 MEALS dinner, light meals

Kingfisher Lodge
Mount Falcon, Foxford Road, Ballina, Co. Mayo
Tel: 096 22718
Email: kingfisherlodge@eircom.net

This family-owned charming country house stands in extensive grounds 6.5 km from Ballina. It is nestled between two mountain ranges and surrounded by unspoiled beaches. It opened in 1990 and has been successful since the beginning; many guests are repeat visitors. Kingfisher Lodge has fast become known as one of the premier guest houses in the area. An extension, combining 2 family rooms, has been added. There is a sitting room and reading room with a real fire. The bedrooms are beautifully decorated; one has a four-poster bed with a floral and lace canopy. This is exceptionally good value, the perfect combination of superb hosts, pleasant surroundings and comfortable accommodation. Kingfisher Lodge is an ideal base for anglers; Kevin Gallagher, a full-time fishing guide with 25 years experience fishing the River Moy, will assist with all the arrangements for a fishing holiday and secure the correct permits. Ghillie service is available upon request. Freshly prepared, home-cooked modestly priced evening meals are available if arranged in advance. There are five golf courses in the area and Ballina is a lively town where traditional Irish music can be found most nights. Early reservations are recommended at this popular establishment. Take the Foxford to Ballina Road, turn left after Mountfalcon Castle, signed at the end of the road.

OWNER Kevin & Bernadette Gallagher OPEN March 1 – September 30 ROOMS 2 double, 2 twin, 4 family; all en suite TERMS €30.50; reduction for children; single supplement €9 MEALS dinner

BALLYCASTLE

Ballyglass B&B
Ballycastle, Co. Mayo
Tel: 096 43343

This old stone house was totally gutted for the purpose of building a holiday home for the down-to-earth owners, Jim Hennelly and Carmel Kelleher, but with more tourists visiting this beautiful and interesting region, they opened the house as a bed & breakfast instead. This is good-value, clean, no fancy frills accommodation; the bedrooms are simply furnished. Jim cooks breakfast and takes care of guests, Carmel works outside the home, but helps out when she can. The dining room is adjacent to the cosy lounge with its turf fires. Jim also makes clocks from pine, yew and oak, which are on display, and are available for purchase. There are archaeological digs going on and Jim will take interested people along to see them, and to the second tallest stone in Ireland, which is close by. An ideal spot from which to visit the Ceide Fields, Belderrig prehistoric farm, fifteenth-century Moyne abbey, or take a walk on the Western Way.

OWNER Jim Hennelly & Carmel Kelleher OPEN May 4 – October 1 ROOMS 2 double, 1 twin, 1 family; 2 en suite TERMS €19; reduction for children; single supplement €12.50

Keadyville
Carrowcubbic, Ballycastle, Co. Mayo
Tel: 096 43288

Keadyville is in a beautiful location overlooking Downpatrick Head and the sea. Mrs Kelly went into business as more tourists came to the area to visit the interpretative centre of the fasci-nating Ceide Fields, which are older than the pyramids. The top floor, all in pine, was added to the property in 1992 and a conservatory was added in 1997. The rooms are average in size and are clean and comfortable, and all offer scenic views. One bedroom is on the ground floor. The friendly owners are local people and greet guests with a cup of tea, and are happy to provide information on the area. There is a cosy lounge/dining room where a fire is lit on chilly days; smoking is only allowed in the lounge. Evening meals are available if pre-booked. There are self-catering units available. Take the Ballycastle/Belderrig Road; house is sign-posted.

OWNER Michael & Barbara Kelly OPEN All year ROOMS 2 double, 2 twin; all en suite. TERMS €23; reduction for children; single supplement €10 MEALS dinner

BANGOR

Hillcrest House
Main Street, Bangor, Erris, Co. Mayo
Tel: 097 83494

This is a modern, cosy bungalow, located in the centre of the village, very close to the Owenmore River. Mr and Mrs Cosgrove are a very congenial couple, and Mr Cosgrove was born in the village. The restaurant, which is part of the house, is very popular with the locals. Special diets are catered for if pre-booked. Mrs Cosgrove, who does all the cooking, has built up an excellent reputation for providing good food. The bedrooms are comfortable and hot water bottles are provided. The property is non-smoking. This is a popular spot with fishermen, with river and lake fishing close by. Visa accepted. On the N59 from Mulrany to Belmullet.

OWNER Evelyn Cosgrove OPEN All year ROOMS 2 double, 2 twin TERMS €24; reduction for children; single supplement €6.50 MEALS dinner, high tea

CASTLEBAR

Primrose Cottage
Pontoon Road, Castlebar, Co. Mayo
Tel: 094 21247

If you are looking for that "special place" to stay, Primrose Cottage, situated in a peaceful spot, would be a good choice. Sisters Monica and Teresa Nealon are a delightful team, taking excellent care of their guests in a "home from home" ambience. They are both retired, and having travelled extensively, wanted to ensure that all the comforts they found lacking, during their travels, were provided. There are lots of items of interest throughout the house, including paintings of local scenes, candles, dolls and books. Although the house is non-smoking, it is not suitable for children. The bedrooms are of a good size, with pine furnishings, electric blankets and comfortable beds. Tea makers, hair dryers and a portfolio on what to see and do in the area complete the facilities. The ground floor room has a King-size bed.

There is an imaginative breakfast menu, which is prepared to order, and home made scones and preserves are offered on arrival. The guest lounge has a real fire, and there is lots of Irish literature to read.

Monica and Teresa are knowledgeable about the area, and are happy to assist guests with itinerary planning. Evening meals are not served, but there several venues for evening meals in Castlebar. Situated on the edge of town on the R310.

OWNER Monica & Teresa Nealon OPEN January 1 – December 18 ROOMS 3 double/twin; all en suite. TERMS €26.50–33; single supplement €6.50

CHARLESTOWN

Ashfort
Galway/Knock Road, Charlestown, Co. Mayo
Tel: 094 54706
Email: ashfort@esatclear.ie

Ashfort is an impressive two-storey Tudor-style house set off the road in spacious grounds. The bedrooms are well-appointed, and have rich wood furnishings. The house is decorated to a high standard throughout; there are plush carpets and a luxurious lounge for guests to relax in. This is an ideal base from which to explore the unspoiled area of the west of Ireland, and there are lots of things to see and do in the area. Owners Carol and Philip O'Gorman are a delightful couple who are always happy to assist guests with itinerary planning, and to make recommendations for evening meals. Guests are greeted with a hot drink upon arrival. The bedrooms are roomy and comfortable.

Ashfort is modestly priced for the comfort and high standards found here; guests would be well advised to book in for several nights and use this as a base. Knock Shrine is a 20-minute drive. Situated on the N17/N5, 5 miles from Knock Airport.

OWNER Carol & Philip O'Gorman OPEN March 1 – December 31 ROOMS 2 family, 3 double/single; all en suite. TERMS €25.50; reduction for children; single supplement €6.50

Hillview

Belmullet Road, Crossmolina, Co. Mayo
Tel: 096 31609

A spacious country house is an elevated position, flowers boxes a blaze of colour in spring and summer, with stunning views of Nephin Mountain and the surrounding countryside, . This is a working and dairy sheep and the surrounding fields are dotted with sheep. The house is well maintained and non-smoking. The large bedrooms have modern furniture, and great views. The sitting room has Sky TV, VCR and videos. Breakfast times are flexible (you can sleep in here), evening meals, including vegetarian choices, are served, if pre-arranged, and there are other venues for meals close by.

Maureen is an attentive host, happy to assist guests in every way. Darkey, the dog, is friendly. The tranquil surroundings also offer Golf and fishing in Lough Conn, and is within easy driving distance of the Ceide Fields. Hillview is 1 mile from Crossmolina.

OWNER Joe & Maureen Loftus OPEN March – October ROOMS 4 double/twin/family; all en suite. TERMS from €24; reduction for children; single supplement €6.50 MEALS dinner (if booked)

Kilmurray House

Castlehill, Crossmolina, Co. Mayo
Tel: 096 31227

Kilmurray House is a large, attractive, welcoming farmhouse on 22 hectares of dry stock farm-land, beautifully situated under Nephin Mountain. It is hard to believe that the house was a ruin before Joe and Madge lovingly restored the interior, cleverly combining modern conveniences and a traditional setting. The original oak staircase and wooden doors have been retained, as has the fireplace in the lounge, made by a local craftsman. The house is the recipient of two awards: the "Farmhouse of the Year" and the "BHS and Bord Fáilte Award." Smoking is permitted in bedrooms only. The bedrooms are large, tastefully decorated with matching fabrics and comfortably furnished. A turf fire burns brightly in the lounge on chilly days. It's an ideal base from which to explore this scenic area, and a fisherman's delight – the farm has its own boats for guests' use on Lough Conn. Breakfast only is served, but there are several restaurants and pubs in the area for evening meals. Very enjoyable Irish musical evenings are less than 0.5 km away. The Heritage Museum for tracing ancestry is 2.5 km away. Baby-sitting is available. Sign-posted from Crossmolina town.

OWNER Madge & Joe Moffat OPEN April 1 – October 1
ROOMS 2 double, 2 twin, 2 family, 2 single; 4 en suite. TERMS
€26.50; reduction for children; single supplement €8.50

Beach View House
Ross, Killala, Co. Mayo
Tel: 096 32023

Beach View House as the name indicates has views of the bay,
and is within a two minute walk of Blue Flag Beaches. It is quiet
and peaceful, an ideal spot for bird watching and outdoor activities. Mary is a congenial host; her guests are well taken care of,
and made very much at home in the cosy ambience. The bedrooms, all on the ground floor, have soft pastel colours of green,
blue and pink, with co-ordinated duvets and curtains all made by
Mary. Hairdryers are available. All the rooms have garden views.
There is a turf fire in the cosy lounge, which has a TV and VCR,
and tea is available on request. Smoking is only allowed in the
lounge. Dinners have to be pre-booked, with special diets
catered for, and there are plenty of choices for food within a
very close drive. Mary has been offering her special brand of
hospitality since 1981, with many visitors returning for yet
another peaceful break. A garage is available for pets.
Northbound from Killala, take the first right off R341.

OWNER Peter and Mary O'Hara OPEN All year ROOMS 4
double/twin/family; all en suite. TERMS €23–25.50; reduction for
children; single supplement €6.50 MEALS dinner (if booked)

Gardenhill Farmhouse
Killala, Co. Mayo
Tel: 096 32331 Fax: 096 32331

This is a large, modern farmhouse, set in 20 hectares of mixed
farming, standing back off the road in a peaceful location. The
spacious bedrooms are colour-co-ordinated and have tasteful
furniture; one bedroom is on the ground floor. Owner Mary
Munnelly is a registered nurse, and an alternative medicine
practitioner skilled in reflexology. The cosy lounge has an open
fire and hearty breakfasts are served in the dining room, which
overlooks the distant hills. Smoking is allowed on the patio only.
Evening meals can be served, if pre-arranged, and feature tasty
home cooking, with local salmon often on the menu. Tea making
facilities are provided in the hallway. The Interpretative Centre
for the Ceide Fields is within an easy drive and there is golf,
deep-sea and shore fishing and miles of sandy dunes and beaches
at Killala Harbour.

Turn left in the centre of Killala town, continue for half a mile. House sign-posted.

OWNER Kevin & Mary Munnelly OPEN June 1 – August 31 ROOMS 2 double, twin, 2 family, 1 single; all en suite. TERMS €25.50; reduction for children; single supplement €6.50

KNOCK

Ashford Manor
Claremorris Road, Knock, Co. Mayo
Tel: 094 88514

Ashford Manor is a large, attractive house with hanging baskets, potted plants, and leaded windows. The congenial owners, James and Mary Flatley, are a friendly couple who formerly ran an adjacent hotel prior to its conversion to a convent, and have been successfully running this establishment for seven years. The house is beautifully maintained and immaculately kept. The entryway has rich carpets, and the relaxing sitting room has tasteful furniture and rich red carpet. The bedrooms are of a good size and are well furnished. Breakfasts are excellent and are cooked on the Aga. On fine days guests can enjoy a cup of tea outside where seating is provided.

OWNER James & Mary Flatley OPEN March 1 – October ROOMS 2 double, 2 twin, 2 family; all en suite. TERMS from €19; reduction for children; single supplement €6.50

Drumeagles
Ballyhaunis, Knock, Co. Mayo
Tel: 094 88393

This large, spacious modern house is set back off the road in its own grounds. The house was built in 1990, but has some traditional features, such as interesting coving and ceiling roses. Kathleen Henry, who had a bed & breakfast in another residence, had this house specifically designed to ensure her guests had the finest accommodation in a comfortable and pleasant ambience. A mahogany staircase leads to the bright, colour-co-ordinated bedrooms, where there are rich fabrics, curtains and light pastel colours of peach, green and pink. Kathleen, a local lady, is happy to assist guests with itineraries and to make suggestions for evening meals. Guests are greeted with a hot drink upon arrival. The sitting room is pleasantly furnished and the house offers excellent value accommodation. It is just a pleasant seven minutes' walk to Knock Shrine and a 20-minute drive to the airport.

OWNER Kathleen Henry OPEN Easter – October 1 ROOMS 2 double, 3 twin, 1 family; all en suite. TERMS €22; reduction for children; single supplement €5.50

Moher House
Liscarney, Co. Mayo
Tel: 098 21360
Email: moherbandb@eircom.net

Marion O'Malley is a delightful lady who knows just how to make her guests feel at home, offering a cup of tea and some of her delicious home-baked scones upon arrival. The redecorated house has bedrooms all en suite, with pretty duvets, electric blankets and hot water bottles. Excellent breakfasts and dinners are served, using the best cuts of meat provided by Mr O'Malley, who is a local butcher. Vegetarian meals are served by request, dinners must be ordered in advance. There is a pleasant sitting room with an open fire where guests receive a complimentary Irish coffee after dinner. This is an ideal area for walking and there are four designated walks. Moher House is located off the Western Way Walking Trail, and a pickup and drop service is available to the trail. The more adventurous can climb Croagh Patrick Mountain, with its magnificent view of 365 islands. Fishing is available in Moher Lake across the road from the house. Transport to the pub in the evening is also offered. Visa accepted. Take the N59 heading south out of Westport on the Westport/Clifden Road.

OWNER Marion O'Malley OPEN March 17 – October 31
ROOMS 1 double, 2 twin, 1 family; all en suite TERMS €25.50; reduction for children; single supplement €6.50 MEALS dinner and packed Lunch

Rivervilla
Shraugh, Louisburgh, Co. Mayo
Tel: 098 66246 Fax: 098 66246

Rivervilla is a bungalow situated in a peaceful and secluded spot along the banks of the Runrowen River, on a 10-hectare sheep farm. The house is non-smoking. Salmon and trout fishing are available as well as lovely river-side walks. A real home-away-from-home atmosphere pervades here, and home-baked breads are a feature. Evening meals are no longer served, but there are several excellent restaurants nearby.

The bedrooms are tastefully decorated, some have glorious views of Shreffy Mountain and Croagh Patrick. Of special interest is the Great Famine and Granville interpretive centre. There are some excellent places for evening meals in Louisburgh.
Visa, Eurocard accepted.

Sign-posted on Louisburgh/Westport Road 335 or via Chapel Street, Louisburgh, pass Spa shop continue past O'Malleys Builders, signed from there.

OWNER Mary O'Malley OPEN May 1 – September 31 ROOMS 1 double, twin, 1 family, 1 single; 2 en suite. TERMS €25.50–28; reduction for children; single supplement €6.50

NEWPORT

Loch Morchan
Kilbride, Newport, Co. Mayo
Tel: 098 41221

This old-style farmhouse is part of a working sheep and cattle farm situated in a quiet location with good views all round, just 10 minutes from Clew Bay. The house is fresh and bright, the bedrooms average in size with comfortable beds. One of the nicest things about Loch Morchan Farm is Mrs Chambers herself, a delightful lady who is a most caring and attentive host; the bed & breakfast was established over 19 years ago, with many guests returning for the special hospitality found here. There are several good eating establishments close by. The area is excellent for sea, river and lake fishing, with special rates for fishing groups. An 18-hole golf course is close by.

OWNER Celena Chambers OPEN May 1 – October 31 ROOMS 1 double, 1 twin, 2 family; 1 en suite. TERMS €19; reduction for children; single supplement €2.50

WESTPORT

Altamont House
Ballinrobe Road, Westport, Co. Mayo
Tel: 098 25226

Altamont House is a pre-Famine wisteria-covered farmhouse situated within a five-minute walk of the town centre. The standards continue to improve at this pleasant, welcoming house; established as the first guest house in the area, it has built up an excellent reputation for offering good service at reasonable prices. The spotless bedrooms are prettily decorated, and the rooms to the rear of the house overlook the lovely garden, as does the lounge, which has an open fire. The prize-winning gardens are a popular spot with guests. A sun-lounge and patio has been added. Breakfasts are served in the attractive dining room, where a silver service is employed, and when possible there are fresh flowers on the table. Evening meals can be had at several good pubs and restaurants close by.

OWNER Mrs Rita Sheridan OPEN March 16 – November 16
ROOMS 2 double, 3 twin, 1 family, 2 double/single; 5 en suite
TERMS €21.50; reduction for children; single supplement €6.50

Brooklodge B&B
Deerpark East, Newport Road, Westport, Co. Mayo
Tel: 098 26654
Email: Brooklodgeb&b@eircom.net

This spacious house is situated in a quiet residential area 2.5 km
from the town centre. This is a relaxed and friendly house, and
guests are encouraged to make themselves at home. Owners
Michael and Noreen Reddington are extremely pleasant, and
early breakfast can be provided if required, or if you prefer, a
cooked breakfast is available until 10 a.m. The lounge has a turf
and coal fire in the restored Victorian fireplace, a pleasant spot in
which to unwind after a busy day. Smoking is only allowed in the
lounge. The bedrooms are good-sized, have a soft pastel décor
and are tastefully furnished. There is a good choice of pubs and
restaurants in town, a five-minute walk away. Visa, Mastercard
accepted. Third turn to right after petrol station on N59 to
Newport.

OWNER Michael & Noreen Reddington OPEN March 1 –
November 30 ROOMS 4 twin; all en suite. TERMS €24; reduction
for children; single supplement €8.50

Cloneen House
Castlebar Street, Westport, Co. Mayo
Tel: 098 25361

Easily located in the heart of Westport, with its terracotta, deep
south exterior, and large colourful display of flowers, to the front
of the house, and the balcony. The bedrooms, are decorated with
warm autumn colours, co-ordinated fabrics and bedspreads,
made by Mrs. Reidy. All have TV, telephone, hairdryer, and ironing
facilities. Well presented breakfasts are served at separate tables
in the bright dining room, and there is also a very large lounge
with comfortable furnishings. Smoking is allowed only in the
lounge. The Irish Museum, which is close by, should be on your
list of things to see.

OWNER Mrs C. Reidy OPEN All year ROOMS 16
double/twins/family; all en suite. TERMS €30.50–34.50; reduction
for children; single supplement €£2.50–6.50

Moher House

Liscarney, Westport, Co. Mayo
Tel: 098 21360
Email: moherbanb@eircom.net

Marion O'Malley is a delightful lady who knows just how to make her guests feel at home, offering a cup of tea and some of her delicious home-baked scones upon arrival. The bedrooms are clean with pretty duvets; there are electric blankets, hot water bottles, and the house has been freshly redecorated. Excellent breakfasts and dinners are served, using the best cuts of meat provided by Mr O'Malley, who is a local butcher. Vegetarian meals and special diets are catered for by request; dinners must be ordered in advance. There is a pleasant sitting room with an open fire where guests receive a complimentary Irish coffee after dinner. Smoking is not permitted.

Moher House is located off the Western Way Walking Trail, A pickup and drop off service is available. The more adventurous can climb Croagh Patrick Mountain, with its magnificent view of 365 islands. Transport to the pub in the evening also offered. Fishing is available in Moher Lake across the road from the house. Visa accepted. Take the N59 heading south out of Westport Westport/Clifden Road.

OWNER Marion O'Malley OPEN March 17 – October 31 ROOMS 1 double, 2 twin, 1 family; all en suite. TERMS €25.50; reduction for children; single supplement €6.50 MEALS dinner and packed lunch

Riverbank House

Rosbeg, Westport, Co. Mayo
Tel: 098 25719

An inviting, spacious house with attractive black shutters, flower baskets and window boxes, situated in a peaceful spot adjacent to a river. The rooms are a good size and are clean and comfortable with modern furnishings. New windows and wooden floors have been installed since the last edition. There is a relaxing guest lounge with an open fire. Kay O'Malley is pleased to help guests plan activities or day trips. Freshly prepared tasty breakfasts with home baked bread are served in the sunny dining room; evening meals are not available, but there are several choices for evening meals close by. Local amenities include shooting at the Tirawley Game Reserve, bathing, boating, trout and salmon fishing and golf. Visa, Mastercard accepted. On T39/R335, turn left at the harbour.

OWNER Kay O'Malley OPEN April 1 – October 30 ROOMS 4 double, 2 twin, 2 family; 6 en suite. TERMS €25.50; reduction for children; single supplement €6.50–9

Rosbeg Country House

Rosbeg, Westport, Co. Mayo
Tel: 098 25879 Fax: 098 25879

This eighteenth-century house with its friendly old-fashioned
ambience is situated in a wonderful location on Clew Bay.
Several original features remain, such as ceiling roses and casement shutters. Furnished with antiques, the spacious bedrooms
are individually decorated with rich, warm, co-ordinated fabrics
and wallpapers. The parlour-like lounge has sea views, as do
some of the bedrooms. Kay O'Briain is a gracious host who has
been welcoming guests into her inviting home for over 20 years.
Breakfasts are served to the soft sounds of classical music. This
is a wonderful place to relax and unwind; it is quiet and tranquil,
and the only sound to be heard in the morning are the birds
singing. Activities in the area include walks along the award-
winning beaches, swimming, hill climbing and fishing. Venues for
evening meals are within walking distance.

OWNER Kay O'Briain OPEN Easter – September ROOMS 3
double, 2 twin; all en suite. TERMS €25.50–31.50; single
supplement €12.50

Seapoint House

Kilmeena, Westport, Co. Mayo
Tel: 098 41254 Fax: 098 41903

Seapoint House is situated in a beautiful, unspoiled setting overlooking an inlet of Clew Bay. Most of the rooms have views of
the sea and mountains. The garden has been upgraded and
improved since the last edition. There is a very large lounge and
a fireplace, a reading room, and a tastefully decorated dining
room, which leads out onto a sun porch. The upgraded bedrooms are functional and spotlessly clean and self-catering is
available. Fishing, sailing, walking and an 18-hole golf course are
available nearby and there is a pony for children to ride.
Baby-sitting can usually be arranged. This is a non-smoking
house. Visa, Mastercard accepted.

OWNER The O'Malley Family OPEN May 1 – October 1
ROOMS 2 double, 2 twin, family; all en suite. TERMS €31.50;
reduction for children; single supplement €9.50

COUNTY SLIGO

County Sligo is located in one of the most beautiful and least explored regions of Ireland, surrounded by rugged mountains and rolling hills. The landscape is a patchwork of picturesque lakes, lush forests and sparkling rivers, its coastline dotted with peaceful coves.

Sligo's seaside resorts stretch along the coast from Innishcrone to Mullaghmore, with sandy beaches, fishing, golfing, beautiful walks and horseback riding – there is so much to do in this uncrowded corner of Ireland.

Explore the Glenriff Horseshoe, the Ladies Brae, visit Lissadell House, and for the more adventurous, climb to the summit of Queen Maeve's Cairn.

Tour the loughs – Arrow, Gill, Easky, Gara, Glencar, Templehouse and Talt – and feast your eyes on Sligo's beauty. W. B. Yeats, the poet, is buried at Drumcliffe. He called Sligo "The Land of Heart's Desire," and after you have visited, you will too.

BALLYMOTE

Temple House
Ballymote, Co. Sligo
Tel: 071 83329 Fax: 071 83808

Temple House is approached through an impressive gateway bordered by white iron railings. The drive meanders through parkland to this large Georgian mansion. It is set in 400 hectares of farmland and woodland, and there is a large garden where organic vegetables are grown for the evening meal. The estate has been in the Perceval family since 1665, the present house having been redesigned and refurnished in 1864. The entrance through a portico leads to a large entry hall with tiled floor and shooting gear. This in turn leads to a second, larger hall, off which is an enormous dining room and three sitting rooms, all with open fires. The larger room has lovely views over the garden to the lake and ruins of a castle built by the Knights Templar in 1200. The enormous bedrooms are furnished with antiques and

family portraits. Some have original bathroom fittings, curtains and carpets, etc., which consequently are faded and worn, but this all lends charm and atmosphere to the house. The Percevals are very friendly people. Mrs Perceval does all the cooking and Mr Perceval runs the farm, which is stocked with sheep, Kerry cattle and poultry, providing the kitchen with fresh meat, bacon, eggs, vegetables and fruit. Almost everything is home-grown and home-made, including yoghurt, jams and cream cheese. Evening meals, if pre-arranged, are served at 7:30 p.m. Please note Mr Perceval is chemically sensitive, so guests are asked to avoid all perfumed products. All credit cards except Diners.

OWNER Mrs D. Perceval OPEN April 1 – November 30 ROOMS 3 double, 1 twin, 1 single; 4 en suite. TERMS €65; reduction for children negotiable if sharing; single supplement €15 MEALS dinner

CLIFFONEY

Villa Rosa
Bunduff, Cliffoney, Co. Sligo
Tel: 071 66173 Fax: 071 66173

This friendly family home has wonderful views of the Donegal Mountains and Bundoff Beach, and overlooks a bird sanctuary and megalithic tombs. The property is well maintained and is decorated to a high standard. It offers clean and comfortable accommodation. There is a TV lounge and an en suite bedroom on the ground floor. John McLoughlin is a qualified chef and has built up an excellent reputation for providing good food. Cookery and lace-making demonstrations are available for groups of six or more, and there are several sea and hill walks locally, as well as a nearby golf course and diving facilities. John and Beatrice pride themselves on the personal touch, doing everything possible to ensure guests enjoy their stay. Guests feel very much at home here. The house is nestled in its own grounds and the ever-changing scenery and views are superb. This is an excellent choice for folks looking for a peaceful and tranquil holiday. American Express, Visa, Eurocheque accepted.

OWNER Beatrice McLoughlin OPEN March 1 – October 31 ROOMS 2 double, 2 twin, 2 family; 4 en suite. TERMS €23; single supplement €9 MEALS Dinner

COOLLOONEY

Union Farm
Coollooney, Co. Sligo
Tel: 071 67136

This 300-year-old house, painted pale blue, stands in a very neat front garden in quiet, peaceful countryside and has lovely views.

The house is part of a 20-hectare cattle farm and is well kept, with an old-fashioned parlour-like lounge, which has a piano and TV. There is a separate dining room where freshly prepared, tasty breakfasts are served. Low doorways and thick walls abound, and the small, spotlessly clean bedrooms are modestly furnished. Evening meals or high tea are served at 7 p.m. if arranged in advance. Union Farm offers good value accommodation and fishing is available on the property, which is inhabited by sheep and swans.

OWNER Des & Tess Lang OPEN March 1 – October 15 ROOMS 1 double, 2 twin, 1 single, 1 triple; 2 en suite. TERMS €20.50; reduction for children 20%; single supplement €2.50 MEALS dinner

DRUMCLIFFE

Benbulben Farm
Barbaribbon, Drumcliffe, Co. Sligo
Tel: 071 63211 Fax: 071 73009

This large, modern house nestles in the foothills of Benbulben Mountain in a well tended landscaped garden, surrounded by a 36-hectare sheep farm. There are unparalleled views and 250 square kilometres of beautiful Yeats country – his last resting place is Drumcliffe churchyard, which is within view of the farm. This is very much a family home, and the Hennigans are very congenial people, offering a hospitality tray upon arrival. The rooms are spotlessly clean and simply furnished with fitted wardrobes and firm beds, and most have views. This is perfect walking country (there is a nature walk on the farm), and there are 30 mapped hill walks in the vicinity.

   Transport can be arranged to take visitors to starting points and back to base in the evening. If you're looking for a tranquil holiday, you may wander round the farm, visit the small museum on the property and enjoy some local lane walks. There is a TV lounge and a bright dining room where breakfasts, light meals and pre-arranged dinners are served. There is no licence but guests are welcome to bring their own wine. Sligo also has some fine examples of early megalithic tombs. Benbulben Farm would be a good choice from which to explore this scenic area. Visa, Mastercard accepted. Take the N15 from Sligo, turn right at Drumcliffe Creamery, sign posted from there.

OWNER Anne Hennigan OPEN April 1 – September 30 ROOMS 2 double, 2 twin, 2 family; 5 en suite. TERMS €25; single supplement €7.50 MEALS dinner, light meals

Urlar House
Drumcliffe, Co. Sligo
Tel: 071 63110

This Georgian house is approached up a private drive in a peaceful location. The house is spacious and well maintained. The TV lounge, where smoking is permitted, has an original marble fireplace and two archways with the original Wedgwood figure design. The bedrooms vary in size; there is a family suite, consisting of double and twin rooms with en suite facilities, that is ideal for friends or family travelling together. Mrs Healy is the proud recipient of the northwest Agri-Tourism Award and a Galtee Breakfast Award. Excellent breakfasts are served family style on a large antique table, and consist of yoghurts, stuffed pancakes, omelettes, or a traditional Irish breakfast. There is an enclosed sun porch for the children to play in, which leads onto the garden.

OWNER Mrs Gemma Healy OPEN April – October ROOMS 2 double, 2 twin, 1 family, 1 single; 2 en suite. TERMS €28–31.50; reduction for children; single supplement €7.50

RIVERSTOWN

Coopershill
Riverstown, Co. Sligo
Tel: 071 65108 Fax: 071 65108
E-mail: ohara@coopershill.com

Approached through parks and woodland, a long drive winds its way to this Georgian mansion, which has been home to the O'Hara family for seven generations since it was built in 1774. Peacocks strut on the front lawn and there are splendid views over woods, hills and the River Arrow, which runs through the property. The house has been restored by the present owners to an extremely high standard, without in any way detracting from its ambience. Much of the furniture is original, family portraits adorn the walls and the rooms are extremely large and luxurious.

Candlelit dinners are served in the elegant dining room, which has enormous sideboards with gleaming family silver. There is a lounge and a spacious drawing room with a log fire. Five of the bedrooms have four-poster or canopy beds. Walks can be taken on the 200-hectare estate, where there is an abundance of wildlife. Coarse fishing is available on the River Arrow, and a boat is available for trout fishing on nearby Lough Arrow. There is a championship golf course nearby, beautiful uncrowded beaches and megalithic monuments. If you are looking for somewhere to stay for a special occasion, Coopershill would be an excellent choice.

OWNER Brian & Lindy O'Hara OPEN April 1 – October 31
ROOMS 7 double, 5 twin; 7 en suite. TERMS €58.50–67.50;
reduction for children negotiable; single supplement €12.50
MEALS dinner, afternoon teas

Ross House
Riverstown, Co. Sligo
Tel: 071 65140 Fax: 071 65140

This 100-year-old country house in peaceful surroundings is
approached down a quiet country lane. Mrs Hill-Wilkinson is a
friendly woman who enjoys baking and welcomes guests into her
kitchen. Home cooked meals are available on request from 7.30
pm and a cup of tea is available later in the evening: special diets
can be catered for if pre-arranged. It is a comfortable family
home. Guests have use of a TV lounge with a turf fire. Smoking is
allowed in the lounge only. One of the bedrooms is small; the
other three are average in size, clean and comfortable.

There are two large en-suite bedrooms on the ground floor,
suitable for guests with disabilities. There is a tennis court for
guests' use. This is a wonderful place for children; there is a
donkey, hay-making and cattle on this mixed 48-hectare farm.
Many visitors come to Lough Arrow for the fishing. Fishermen
can hire boats, tackle and engines at the farm. There are beautiful
beaches close by and many ancient monuments to visit throughout County Sligo, at Creevykeel and Deerpark for instance. The
archaeological sites at Carrowmore and Carrowkeel are of
special interest.

OWNER Nicholas & Oriel Hill-Wilkinson OPEN March 16 –
November 1 ROOMS 1 double, 2 twin, 2 family, 1 single; 2 en
suite. TERMS €25.50–29; reduction for children; single supplement
€7.50 MEALS dinner

SLIGO

Aisling
Cairns Hill, Sligo, Co. Sligo
Tel: 071 60704

This immaculate bungalow, whose name means "Irish Dream,"
stands in its own grounds in an elevated location on the south
side of Sligo. The bedrooms are average in size and are comfortably furnished. They are all on the ground floor and now have TV
and dressing gowns. Des and Nan are a very congenial and
accommodating couple who work together as a team. Nan
cooks breakfast while Des enjoys chatting with guests and help-
ing them plan daily activities. Breakfast only is served, but there

are plenty of eating establishments in Sligo. There is a comfortable lounge with a coal fire.

OWNER Des & Nan Faul OPEN All year ROOMS 2 double, 2 twin, 1 family; 3 en suite. TERMS €20.50–22; single supplement €6.50

Lissadell
Mail Coach Road, Sligo, Co. Sligo
Tel: 071 61937

This red brick new house is within walking distance of the town centre and offers a high standard of accommodation. The rooms are of a good size, well furnished and tastefully decorated. Mary formerly ran a bed & breakfast establishment by the same name in the area for several years and brings her expertise to this new property. Mary is friendly and accommodating and is willing to help her guests in every way to ensure they have a comfortable stay. Freshly prepared breakfasts only are served, but there are several establishments within walking distance for evening meals. Lissadell is a good base from which to explore Yeats' country.

OWNER Mary Cadden OPEN All year ROOMS 2 double, 1 twin; all en suite. TERMS €28–30.50; single supplement

Tree Tops
Cleveragh Road, Sligo, Co. Sligo
Tel: 071 60160 Fax: 071 62301
Email: treetops@iol.ie
Website: www.sligobandb.com

This well maintained, spacious, modern, attractive house stands in a secluded location with a pretty garden and fishpond just eight minutes' walk from the town centre. The immaculate bedrooms are large, tastefully decorated, well furnished and have orthopaedic beds. There is a collection of prints and paintings on display. Wholesome breakfasts are served in the dining room/lounge, which has period furniture. There are some lovely walks and views close by. Tree Tops would be a good choice as a base from which to explore this interesting area.

OWNER Ronan & Doreen MacEvilly OPEN January 15 – December 15 ROOMS 2 double, 3 family; all en suite. TERMS €28-29.50; reduction for children 20%; single supplement €10.50

TOBERCURRY

Cruckawn House
Ballymote Road, Tobercurry, Co. Sligo
Tel: 071 85188 Fax: 071 85188

This friendly, welcoming home is set back off the road and stands in its own grounds overlooking a golf course; there are clubs and caddies for hire, and the green fees are moderate. Maeve Walsh is a friendly, outgoing lady who knows how to make her guests feel at home, and greets them with a complimentary hospitality tray. Maeve is also director of the North West Tourism Organisation and an expert on local attractions. The rooms are a little small, but are spotlessly clean and comfortable.

There is a pleasant TV lounge and a separate dining room where freshly prepared, substantial breakfasts are served. Evening meals are no longer served, but there are several establishments close by for evening meals. Separating the dining room from a small sun lounge are sliding glass doors with the family crests of the owners' families engraved in the middle of each door. Laundry facilities are provided. Local amenities include salmon and trout fishing, game shooting, mountain climbing, horseback riding and pony trekking. Tubbercurry is quite a lively place, where traditional Irish music and dance can be enjoyed Tuesday and Thursday and on weekends from May to September. Visa, Access, Mastercard accepted.

OWNER Joe & Maeve Walsh OPEN March – October ROOMS 2 double, 2 twin, 1 family; all en suite. TERMS €22; reduction for children 33%; single supplement €9.50

Pine Grove
Ballina Road, Tobercurry, Co. Sligo
Tel: 071 85235

This attractive, large house has been repainted white and green and has had Georgian-style windows installed. It stands in a pretty front garden on the edge of town on the Ballina Road. Mrs Kelly is a good cook and caters for non- residents for lunch as well as evening meals, served in a large dining room overlooking a patio. Breakfasts are substantial and will set you up for the day. The house is simply furnished with old-fashioned furniture. There is a TV lounge with an open fire. There is no licence, but guests are welcome to bring their own wine. This is a popular venue and early reservations are recommended. On pleasant days guests are welcome to make use of the garden. Visa, Mastercard, Eurocard accepted. Situated on the Ballina Road, 300 m off the N17. Knock Airport is 11 miles away.

OWNER Teresa Kelly OPEN All year ROOMS 1 double, 2 twin, 2 family; all en suite. TERMS €28; reduction for children; single supplement €9 MEALS dinner

COUNTY CARLOW

One of the smallest counties in Ireland, Carlow lies just below Wicklow and is in an area of rich farmland.

The county town, Carlow, has had an eventful history, which includes being captured by Cromwell in 1650. Now the town manufactures beet sugar and has quite a few noteworthy sights, including the ruin of a Norman castle, a Gothic Revival Catholic church, the Carlow Museum and the fine courthouse with a Doric portico fashioned after the Parthenon.

There is a ruined twelfth-century church at Killeshin, with a fine Romanesque doorway, and fourteenth-century Ballymoon Castle, which has apparently never been occupied.

BAGENALSTOWN

Kilgraney House
Bagenalstown, Co. Carlow
Tel: 0503 75283 Fax: 0503 75595
Email: kilgrany@indigo.ie

Bryan Leech and Martin Marley have created a most delightful fantasy world in their charming Georgian house, overlooking the lovely Barrow valley. Kilgraney Country House is full of wonderfully chosen pieces of fabric, furniture and art from all around the world, with a strong Philippine influence, and each of the six comfortable bedrooms is furnished and decorated with unique imagination. This is a delightful place to spend a weekend, and in fact Bryan and Martin specialise in creating memorable weekend getaways. Guests can experience wonderful home-cooked six course dinners using both exotic products and home grown fruits, herbs and vegetables. Breakfast, served in the sunlit morning room, offers both traditional and healthy options. No smoking or pets. Unsuitable for small children. Access, Visa and Mastercard accepted. The house has a wine licence. Just off the R704, Kilgraney is halfway between Bagenalstown (Muine Bheag) and Borris.

OWNER Bryan Leech and Martin Marley OPEN March – November ROOMS 6 double/twin/singles; all en suite . TERMS €44 MEALS dinner

Lorum Old Rectory
Bagenalstown, Co. Carlow
Tel: 0503 75282 Fax: 0503 75455

Dating from the eighteenth century, Lorum Old Rectory is set in 7.5 hectares nestling beneath the Blackstairs Mountains. It is surrounded by open countryside, with views as far as Tipperary. The bedrooms are spacious, furnished with antiques, and all have

their original fireplaces, hairdryers, telephones and tea and coffee making facilities. Five-course imaginative dinners are available, by prior arrangement, with home-grown organic vegetables, and the house does have a wine licence. The tiny snug room with a fireplace is the only room where smoking is allowed. There is a comfortable, informal atmosphere, and Don and Bobbie Smith are a friendly couple. Don likes to organise cycling holidays, which include cycle hire, airport pickup and daily baggage transportation. Work continues on the garden, and guests have use of a croquet lawn. No pets. Access and Visa cards accepted. The Old Rectory is 6.5 kilometres from Bagenalstown on the R705 Borris road.

OWNER Bobbie & Don Smith OPEN January 1 – December 15 ROOMS 3 doubles, 2 double/twin; all en suite . TERMS €51; single supplement €14 MEALS dinner €35

BALLON

Sherwood Park House
Kilbride, Ballon, Co. Carlow
Tel: 0503 59117 Fax: 0503 59355
Email: info@sherwoodparkhouse.ie

This lovely Georgian house is set in peaceful countryside, and has a large garden and pleasant views. Patrick and Maureen Owens are a most welcoming, gentle couple and have friendly dogs. Sherwood Park has an especially beautiful winding staircase, and an unusual raised hallway features an old, flat-topped piano. The drawing room also has a piano, and excellent, home cooked five-course dinners are elegantly served by candlelight in the very large dining room. Guests may bring their own wine, and dinner must be ordered in advance. The bedrooms are spacious and comfortable and have some lovely furniture, including several four-poster beds. Families are well catered for, and the rooms have en suite bathrooms with both baths and showers. They each have hairdryer, trouser press and tea and coffee making facilities. No smoking, and pets can be accommodated in a small kennel. Visa, Mastercard, American Express and Eurocheques are accepted. Altamount Gardens are nearby, and golf, fishing and riding can be enjoyed locally. The house is just off the N80.

OWNER Patrick & Maureen Owens OPEN All year ROOMS 1 twin, 3 triple, all en suite . TERMS €40.50; single supplement €8; reductions for children; MEALS dinner €25.50

BORRIS

Step House
Main Street, Borris, Co. Carlow
Tel: 0503 73209 Fax: 0503 73395

This early Georgian town house stands right in the centre of Borris. It was originally the dower house to the castle, the entrance gates to which are on the opposite side of the street. It is heavily decorated and furnished with a lot of pieces, some of which are antiques. Both the drawing room and the dining room, which leads from it, have ornate fireplaces. Most of the bedrooms, all with TV. lie at the back of the house, some with nice views, and one has a four-poster bed. Borris is close to the Leinster Way and there are great walks along the River Barrow. The house is not suitable for children. Pets by arrangement, smoking in lounge only. Visa and Mastercard accepted.

OWNER James & Cait Coady OPEN 17 March – 20 December ROOMS 3 doubles, 2 twins; all en suite. TERMS €31.50–44.50; single supplement €6.50–12.50

CARLOW

Barrowville Town House
Kilkenny Road, Carlow , Co. Carlow
Tel: 0503 43324 Fax: 0503 41953

A friendly welcome, professional service and comfort in a lovely in-town setting are what visitors can expect at this attractive, eighteenth century town house. The Dempseys, experienced in hotel ownership, did the whole house up (which was a major undertaking), and created a place of elegance and comfort. The en suite bedrooms have hairdryers, telephones, TV, shoe shine and tea and coffee making facilities. Exquisitely presented, sumptuous breakfasts are served in the attractive conservatory overlooking the lovely, private back garden. There is also a small sitting room, which has a TV and tea and coffee making facilities and a door out to the garden, which is a nice place to take a stroll. Barrowville is on the main Kilkenny road, just a three minute walk from the centre of town. No pets. Smoking permitted only in the sitting room. Visa, Access and American Express accepted.

OWNER Randal & Marie Dempsey OPEN All year ROOMS 2 double, 2 twin, 21 single, 2 family; all en suite – 5 have bath and shower . TERMS €31.50–35; single supplement €10

COUNTY CAVAN

Cavan is an undiscovered county, an angler's delight with its unlimited opportunities for coarse and game fishing. Large areas of Cavan seem to have more water than land. The undulating landscape and picturesque settings are dotted with wooded islands providing much of the county's delightful scenery. There is plenty to see and do, including a museum in Virginia, which has 3,000 items dating back to 1700. Saint Killian's Heritage Centre and Fore Abbey are other sites of interest. Cavan Crystal can be bought in the factory shop on the outskirts of Cavan town. Derragara Museum is situated on the Annalee River, and exhibits a full-size mud and wattle homestead.

BELTURBET

Rockwood House
Cloverhill, Belturbet, Co. Cavan
Tel: 047 55351 Fax: 047 55373
Email: jbmac@eircom.net

A charming country house standing in three of secluded woodland gardens. The house was built in the style of an older house that previously stood on the property, using the original stone, and wood in the building of the new house. The house is furnished with a mixture of modern and antique pieces, and the good sized bedrooms have comfortable beds and pastel duvets. Bedrooms do not have TV, but there is one in the guest lounge where fires burn on cool evenings. Traditional freshly prepared breakfasts are served in the dining room, which overlooks the garden.

Tea and coffee are available on request, guests are well taken care of here by Susan Macauley who enjoys having people in her home. Plenty of information is provided on what to see and do in the area. Visa, Mastercard accepted. Situated on the N24 two miles from Butlersbridge and six miles from Cavan.

OWNER James and Susan Macauley OPEN All year ROOMS 2 double, 2 twin; all en suite. TERMS from €28; reduction for children 25%; single supplement from €7.50

Ross Castle

Mountnugent, Co. Cavan

Tel: 049 8540237 Fax: 049 854023

Email: Rosshouse@eircom.net

Website: www.ross-house.com

This fascinating castle is situated amidst majestic trees and has magnificent views of Lough Sheelin, a lake famous for its brown trout. The castle was built in the sixteenth century, and later fell into a derelict condition. It was restored in 1864 by Anna Maria O'Reilly, a lineal descendant of Myles O'Reilly (known as "The Slasher"), who used the tower in the castle the night before being killed by Oliver Cromwell's troops.

It has a fascinating history and offers unique and interesting accommodation. It is entered through a gateway to an inner courtyard and surrounded by a stone wall. On the ground floor is a large entrance hall connecting the tower and the sitting room. There is an open fireplace, and French windows offer a beautiful view across the lake. One double bedroom has access to its own terrace. The tower is ideal for friends or family travelling together; there are two double en suite bedrooms, plus an additional toilet, and a sitting room – access is by 65 winding stone steps. The rooms are furnished with antiques and the ambience is peaceful. Teamakers are available in the sitting room and evening meals can be taken at nearby Ross House. In addition, guests are able to make use of the rest of the facilities such as boat hire, tennis court, sauna and jacuzzi for a modest charge. A self-catering cottage is also available. Under new management, smoking is permitted.

This is exceptionally good value accommodation and early reservations are highly recommended. Visa, Mastercard, Eurocheque accepted.

OWNER Benita Walker OPEN All year ROOMS 1 double, 2 twin, 1 family; 4 en suite. TERMS €40; children under 3 free, under 12, €30; single supplement €13

Ross House

Mountnugent, Co. Cavan

Tel: 049 8540218 Fax: 049 8540218

Email: rosshouse@eircom.net

Website: www.ross-house.com

This charming, Virginia creeper–covered old manor house dates from the 1600s and stands in beautiful grounds on the shores of Lough Sheelin. It was built as a dormer House and belonged to the Nugent family, who were the Lords of Delvin.

The spacious bedrooms, centred around the courtyard, are in the tastefully restored carriage houses. They have antique furniture, and three rooms have a conservatory and four have their own fireplace. Smoking is permitted in specific bedrooms and the dining room. After a busy day sightseeing, guests may, for a modest charge, enjoy the sauna and/or jacuzzi. This is a wonderful place and must be one of the best value bed & breakfast properties in Ireland. A Christmas package is available, but very early reservations are essential.

Guests have access to a sandy beach which provides safe bathing. The private pier with boats for hire gives fishermen the opportunity to fish waters of this well stocked lake. Ross House is fast being recognized for its fine Equestrian Centre, part of the 145-hectare farm which offers pony trekking, a horse-back riding arena and a tennis court.

Ulla Harkort is a very congenial and accommodating host. Delicious four-course dinners are prepared, if ordered in advance, using fresh produce and local meats; vegetarian and light dinners are also available. If you are looking for high standards, good food and a tranquil setting with lots of old-world charm, then Ross House should be your first choice. Visa, Mastercard accepted.

OWNER Ursula Liebe-Harkort OPEN All year, ROOMS 1 double, 2 single, 5 double/single; all en suite. TERMS €35; reduction for children – free up to 2 years, 30% thereafter; single supplement €13 MEALS dinner, lighter meal

VIRGINIA

The White House
Old Castle Road, Virginia, Co. Cavan
Tel: 049 8547515 Fax: 087 4181322
Email: mchugo@esatclear.ie

This warm, traditional-style house is in a lovely situation adjacent to the beautiful Deerpark Lakeland Forest, a well-known spot for hiking, horseback riding, golfing, fishing and water sports. It stands in a large garden where there is a display of old farming implements from Mr McHugo's father's farm in Galway. The bedrooms are clean and tidy with bright wallpapers and comfortable beds. Satellite TV and tea-making facilities in all bedrooms. There is a conservatory and lounge for guests' use. Smoking is only allowed on the patio. Breakfasts are excellent and feature smoked salmon and scrambled eggs, fresh fruits and yoghurts or a full Irish breakfast. Emily pampers her guests, with nothing being too much trouble to ensure their stay is comfortable. Tea and scones are served on your arrival. This is a popular venue for fishermen and tourists. Cavan has 365 lakes, one for every day of the year, so if fishing is your interest you have come to the right place! A visit to Cavan Crystal is worthwhile and the local museum has 3,000 items dating back to 1700.

OWNER Emily McHugo OPEN January 1 – October 1 ROOMS 2 double, 1 twin, 1 family; all en suite. TERMS €20; reduction for children 25–50%; single supplement

COUNTY KILDARE

County Kildare is famous for horse breeding and training, which takes place on the Curragh, a great plain leading into a boggy area, the Bog of Allen. Many horse-race meetings are held here, including the Irish Sweep Derby, the Irish 2000 Guineas, the Irish Oaks and the Irish St Leger. The town of Kildare is the centre for horse breeding and has a well-preserved Church of Ireland cathedral and round tower.

At Robertstown, the eighteenth-century buildings along the Grand Canal have been restored to look as they did when this was a great water thoroughfare. Here is it possible to visit Europe's largest falconry. Two of Ireland's greatest Georgian houses, Carton and Castletown, are located at Cellbridge. A music festival takes place in June at Castletown, as does one of the hunt balls held during the Dublin Horse Show week.
The very pretty village of Leixlip has many associations with the Guinness family; the twelfth-century Norman castle belongs to Desmond Guinness.

Remains of a Franciscan Abbey can be seen at Castledermot, and Athy has many historic sights worth explor-ing, including the sixteenth-century Woodstock Castle, just out of town. Moone High Cross, one of Ireland's most beautiful high crosses, is at Moone Abbey, 12 km from Athy.

ATHY

Coursetown Country House
Stradbally Road, Athy, Co. Kildare
Tel: 0507 31101 Fax: 0507 32740

Pride of ownership and attention to detail are prevalent at Coursetown House, originally a 200 year old farmhouse. What remains of the old brickworks that stood beside the house is a church like bell in a mini tower, which is still in use. The farm consists of 200 acres of arable land and an immaculately main-tained and interesting garden surrounds the house. Of the 4 rooms one has been designed specifically with the wheelchair user in mind. The remaining 3 en suite rooms are upstairs and have every possible amenity including a full range of toiletries.

The plainly furnished breakfast room has doors out to a patio and the pretty garden, where breakfast is served on fine days. The lounge has a full range of books to appeal to the tourist. No children under 8. No smoking. Major credit cards accepted. Coursetown House can be found off the R428, 3 kilometres from Athy.

OWNER Iris & Jim Fox OPEN All year ROOMS 4 doubles, twins TERMS €38; single supplement €6.50

Tonlegee House
Athy, Co. Kildare
Tel: 0507 31473 Fax: 0507 31473
Email: marjorie@tonlegeehouse.com
Website: www.tonlegeehouse.com

Set in a quiet country position, Tonlegee House was built around 1790 and stands in 2 hectares of grounds. Mark and Marjorie did a great job restoring the house, which had been flatlets, into a place of character and comfort. The drawing room is especially large and pleasant, and the bar has nice old furniture and prints. The bedrooms are comfortable and attractively decorated and have TV, telephones and mineral water. Tea or coffee is served upon arrival. However, it is the food that draws people here. Mark does the cooking, almost single-handedly, which is quite a task as he makes everything possible himself, including pastas, breads and pastries. Organic vegetables and salads come from the walled garden, and fresh fish and game are specialities. Pets by arrangement. Visa, Mastercard and American Express accepted. Tonlegee is sign-posted off the Castlecomer to Kilkenny road.

OWNER Marjorie Molloy OPEN January – mid-November ROOMS 2 single, 2 twin, 8 double; all en suite TERMS €53.50; single supplement €23; reductions for children MEALS dinner

CASTLEDERMOT

Kilkea Lodge Farm
Castledermot, Co. Kildare
Tel: 0503 45112 Fax: 0503 45112
Website: www.kildarehouse.com

Kilkea Lodge, which has belonged to the Greene family since 1740, is approached down a long driveway and is set in rolling parkland with a pleasant, rural aspect. Godfrey runs the 105 hectare farm, and additionally there is a livery yard. It is very much a family home, a typical old country house with guests sharing some of the facilities with family members, and it has a relaxed, informal atmosphere. The comfortable drawing room has a piano and fireplace, and traditional food is served in the dining room. The family room is an enormous studio, converted from an old barn, with its own entrance, four beds, a small loft and a sitting area in the middle - ideal for families or small groups. Kilkea Lodge is not suitable for young children. Kilkea Lodge is suited to those who enjoy country life and animals. Dinner by arrangement for groups of minimum of six people. Pets outside only, and no smoking in the bedrooms. American Express accepted.

OWNER Marion & Godfrey Greene OPEN All year except for Christmas and January ROOMS 4 double, twin, family some with private bathrooms. TERMS €44.50; single supplement €12.50 MEALS dinner from €25

CELBRIDGE

Springfield
Celbridge, Co. Kildare
Tel: 01 6273248 or 01 6288254 Fax: 01 6273123

This substantial Georgian house with Victorian flavours is set in 5 hectares of fields and gardens with horses, dogs and cats. It was the childhood home of Aidan Higgins and is referred to in his book 'Langrish, Go Down', and was at one time gutted by fire and rebuilt following the original plans. The house is luxuriously decorated with six large en suite bedrooms. There is one family room up a narrow spiral staircase, and another has four bunk beds. The master bedroom has a stereo system, jacuzzi for two, a shower with two jets, and an extra large four-poster bed. All rooms have TV, video, telephone, hairdryers and tea and coffee making facilities. Libby has six children, and welcomes families. Visiting children muck in with the family and are fed all together in the enormous kitchen, which was originally the old milking rooms and is also available to guests for take-out food, etc. Breakfast is served in the traditional dining room at one large table, or after 12 p.m. in the kitchen. There is a selection of 150 videos, a one kilometre track in front of the house for runners, and exercise machines. No pets. For directions from Celbridge, cross the Liffey bridge, keep left and follow the main road south for about 2 km. The house is on the right behind electronically controlled gates. Access, Visa and American Express accepted.

OWNER Libby Sheehy OPEN All year ROOMS 4 double, 2 family; all en suite. TERMS €76; reductions for children

Fremont

Tully Road, Kildare, Co. Kildare
Tel: 045 521604

Fremont is a modern bungalow in a private setting, three minutes' walk to the town centre and the twelfth century cathedral. The house is in good decorative order, and the ground floor bedrooms are spotlessly clean, with modern furnishings, shower units and hairdryers.. The comfortable TV lounge has a Leitrim stone fireplace and there is a display of Waterford, Galway and Cavan crystal in the bright dining room. Mrs. O'Connell is a considerate host who enjoys meeting people, and she extends a warm welcome to everyone. The Irish Stud and Japanese Gardens can be reached in 15 minutes on foot. Pets outside only and smoking is allowed in the TV lounge. Fremont is sign-posted from the centre of town.

OWNER Frieda O'Connell OPEN March 17 – October 30 ROOMS 2 double, 1 twin; 1 en suite, 2 public bathrooms. TERMS €24; single supplement €5

Moyglare Manor Hotel

Moyglare, Maynooth, Co. Kildare
Tel: 01 6286351 Fax: 01 6285405
Email: info@moyglaremanor.ie
Website: www.moyglaremanor.ie

A lovely long driveway flanked by majestic trees, with horses and sheep grazing in fenced fields to each side, leads to this impressive eighteenth century stone built mansion. Inside there are a series of small reception rooms and hallways stuffed with antique furniture, ornaments and flowers, giving it a rather dark and sombre air. The bedrooms are spacious, comfortable and well equipped with hairdryers, telephones and mineral water. The cuisine at Moyglare attracts many visitors. Beautifully presented food is served in the two elegant dining rooms by candlelight, and there is an extensive wine list. Small conferences can be catered for. There are several golf courses in the vicinity, and riding and hunting can be arranged. Moyglare is the nearest country house hotel to the airport. All major credit cards accepted. No pets. The property is two kilometres from the church in Maynooth.

OWNER Nora Devlin, Shay Curran – Manager OPEN All year except for Christmas ROOMS 16 double or twin; all en suite. TERMS €140; single supplement MEALS lunch, dinner from €38

Cloncarlin Farm House
Nurney Road, Monasterevin, Co. Kildare
Tel: 045 525722

This 200 year old attractive house was built by Lord Drogheda to entertain his guests, and is reached up a long tree-lined driveway. It is set in pretty countryside in an elevated position, and is part of a 68 hectare mixed farm. When the McGuinnesses bought it ten years ago it was pretty derelict. The comfortable bedrooms have pleasant views, and there is a lounge and dining room. Fishing is available on the Barrow River, and there are riding stables close by. The Japanese Gardens and National Stud are a 15 minute drive away. Pets and smoking outside only. The house is sign-posted off the Dublin/Cork road.

OWNER Marie McGuinness OPEN February 1 – December 1 ROOMS 1 single, 5 double/twin, 2 en suite. TERMS €23–25.50; single supplement; reductions for children

Barberstown Castle
Straffan, Co. Kildare
Tel: 01 6288157 Fax: 01 627027
Email: castleir@iol.ie
Website: www.barberstowncastle.com

Dating from the early thirteenth century, this historic castle was one of the first great Irish country houses to open for guests, becoming a hotel in 1973. The castle keep is a venue for banquets, and larger groups of up to 150 people are entertained in the sixteenth century banqueting hall. The Elizabethan part dates from the second half of the sixteenth century, and the Victorian house was built in the 1830s. It is said that a man is interred between the top of the stairs and the roof of the tower. His family did this to prevent their eviction as tenants, as the lease stated that if he was put underground, it would expire. The bedrooms are spacious and comfortable and each is individually decorated. All rooms have hairdryer, trouser press, telephone, TV and modem line. Barberstown has a good reputation for its food, which is creative and beautifully served. It is an interesting and relaxing place to stay, within easy reach of Dublin and the airport. No pets. Major credit cards accepted. From Dublin exit the N4 for Maynooth and Straffan.

OWNER Kenneth C. Healy OPEN February – December ROOMS 22 doubles/twins; all en suite. TERMS €100–127; single supplement €20; reductions for children MEALS dinner €50 & a la carte

The K Club

Straffan, Co. Kildare
Tel: 01 601 7200 Fax: 01 601 7299
Email: hotel@kclub.ie
Website: www.kclub.ie

The ultimate in luxury, elegance and service, The Kildare Hotel & Golf Club is a superb country mansion. It stands in gracious parklands, manicured gardens, and an 18-hole Arnold Palmer designed championship golf course, which will be the venue for the Ryder Cup in 2005. The 700 acres stretch to the River Liffey, and the island in the river can be reached by a series of paths and bridges. The origins of the house go back to 550 AD, and the present building was restored and opened in 1991 as a luxurious hotel and country club. No expense has been spared with the refurbishment of public rooms and bedrooms alike. The highest quality materials have been used, interesting paintings hang on the walls, Waterford glass is used from chandeliers to tooth mugs and every possible comfort and thought has gone into bedrooms and bathrooms The service is impeccable, the staff efficient, and It has a friendly and relaxing atmosphere. The amenities are endless, and every taste and activity is catered for from, of course golf, to salmon fishing, indoor tennis, health and leisure club with indoor swimming pool, snooker, squash, bicycling and horseriding.

All major credit cards accepted. Wheelchair facilities. The property is sign-posted in the village of Kill and can be found on the way to Straffan.

OPEN All year ROOMS 69 twins, doubles, suites.
TERMS €241–3174 MEALS all available

Windgate Lodge

Barberstown, Straffan, Co. Kildare
Tel: 01 6273415

This attractive, modern, red brick house is set back off the road in half a hectare of landscaped gardens. The house is in good decorative order, and there are two bedrooms on the ground floor. Pat Ryan is a friendly lady and is always eager to offer assistance to guests. Good home cooked breakfasts are served in the dining room, and there is a TV lounge. A self catering unit is also available. With the motorway all the way to the centre of Dublin, this is a good location for either Dublin or the airport. Cars can be left at the railway station three kilometres away at Maynooth, from which there is a good train service into town, and buses also run frequently. Close by there are country walks, golf, riding and a butterfly farm and steam museum. Smoking downstairs only. To reach Windgate Lodge from the N4 west-bound, take the Maynooth exit, turn left and the house is five kilometres on the left.

OWNER Patricia Ryan OPEN All year ROOMS 1 double, 1 twin, 1 family; all en suite. TERMS €31.50; single supplement €6.50; reductions for children

THE CURRAGH

Martinstown House
The Curragh, Co. Kildare
Tel: 045 441269 Fax: 045 441208
Email: meryll@eircom.net
Website: www.martinstownhouse.com

This unusual house was built as a shooting lodge for the second Duke of Leinster, and was constructed in the "Strawberry Hill" Gothic style 200 years ago. It is set in 70 hectares of park-like grounds and farmland and has a wonderful walled garden full of flowers, fruit and vegetables, and a hard tennis court. At the back of the house is an unusual gothic stable yard. Mrs. Long has had some interesting decoration done to the house. The entryway has a faux mural, giving one the feeling of the entrance to a church, and then opens out to countryside views. The house is very comfortable, and furnished with some lovely furniture in a simple, unfussy way. There is a smaller sitting room, and grander, more formal drawing room with a high, decorated ceiling. The bedrooms are spacious and the bathrooms newly tiled, one or two reached up a narrow winding staircase. Dinner, served in the attractive, intimate dining room and cooked by a French chef, is available if arranged in advance. No pets or small children, and no smoking in the bedrooms. American Express, Visa and Mastercard accepted. Martinstown House can be found from the N7 in Kildare by passing the Japanese Gardens, forking right and following the signs.

OWNER Mrs Thomas Long OPEN All year except for Christmas and Easter ROOMS 2 double, 2 twin; 2 en suite, 2 private bath-rooms. TERMS €89; single supplement €12.50 MEALS dinner €38

COUNTY KILKENNY
Kilkenny, the county town, is one of the oldest and most interesting towns in Ireland. It comes alive at the end of August during the Kilkenny Festival, which is one of Ireland's foremost cultural festivals. Kilkenny Castle stands in the centre, dominating the town, and just opposite are the Kilkenny Design Centre workshops, which can be visited.

The cathedral stands on the site of a monastery built by St Canice in the sixth century and from which the city took its name. The Kilkenny Archaeological Society houses its collection in a most interesting Tudor merchant's house – Rothe House – and the City Hall, built in 1761, was formerly the Tolsel or Toll House. The well-known writers Swift, Berkeley and Congreve, were educated at Kilkenny College, a fine Georgian building.

The Kilkenny countryside is pretty and compact, and places of interest to visit are the attractive town of Thomastown, near Dysart Castle, former home of George Berkeley, after whom the city and oldest campus of the University of California is named. Near to Callan on the King's River is Kells, a fortified, turreted and walled collection of early ecclesiastical buildings, and near Urlingford are the ruins of four castles.

CALLAN

Ballaghtobin
Callan, Co. Kilkenny
Tel: 056 25227 Fax: 056 25712
Email: gabbetts@indigo.ie
Website: www.balloghtobin.com

Ballaghtobin, its origins dating back to the 12th century, has been in the Gabbett family for 450 years. Today's house covers different periods, the most recent being the front entrance area, which was rebuilt by Mickey Gabbett's parents. Set in parkland and its 500 acres of farmland, it is surrounded by gardens, which include the ruins of a Norman church, a hard tennis court and croquet lawn. Mickey and Catherine are a delightful and very friendly couple and are delighted to welcome guests to their beautiful home. Flair and imagination has been used in renovating the guests' quarters, which include the drawing room, small sitting room off which is the attractive conservatory, and the delightful bedrooms, two of which have sofa/stools that fold out to become extra beds. They all have hairdryers, trouser presses, TV, tea trays and local reading material. Smoking in drawing room only. Pets in cars. Visa is accepted. Ballaghtobin is off the R699 road between Callan and Knocktopher, but it is as well to get precise directions.

OWNER Catherine & Mickey Gabbett OPEN January – December 1 ROOMS 1 twin, 1 family, 1 double; all en suite. TERMS €44.50–51; single supplement €12.50; reductions for children

Berryhill

Inistioge, Co. Kilkenny
Tel: 056 58434 Fax: 056 58434
Email: info@berryhillhouse.com
Website: www.berryhillhouse.com

This most attractive country house was built by the Dyer family
in 1780 and stands in 80 hectares of farmland with wonderful
views to the Nore Valley and to the hills on the other side. It is a
favourite retreat of actress Mia Farrow who has stayed here
with her six children. Berryhill is not suitable for children under
10 years. Accommodation is in the three exceptional suites – the
frog room, the pig room and the elephant room - one of which
has an outside terrace where one can enjoy the view, and another is on the ground floor with its own entrance. Breakfast is a
speciality and is served in the dining room, which has a fireplace
and bay window. Guests can relax in the long drawing room,
which has a baby grand piano, in front of the log fire with a drink
from the honesty bar. Belinda Dyer is a charming and attentive
hostess, and both she and George, who takes care of the farm,
love meeting people. There is a pleasant garden, a cross-country
croquet course, private fishing, lovely walks and two excellent
restaurants within walking distance. No pets, no smoking in
bedrooms. Minimum two night stay. Mastercard and Visa/Access
accepted. Berryhill is just outside Inistioge.

OWNER George & Belinda Dyer OPEN May 1 – August 1
ROOMS 2 double, 1 family; all en suite. TERMS €57–70; single
supplement €12.50; reductions for children

Cullintra House

The Rower, Inistioge, Co. Kilkenny
Tel: 051 423614
Email: cullhse@indigo.ie
Website: www.indigo.ie/~cullhse/index.htm

This attractive, ivy-covered, 200 year old house is approached by a long driveway through a park of grazing cattle, and has been in Patricia Cantlon's family since the turn of the century. It is an animal and bird sanctuary, and there are a great many friendly cats and a local fox who comes to eat dinner in the garden every evening. The rooms, including a garden conservatory and a converted barn, reflect Patricia's artistic talents. She is also an accomplished cook and serves dinner by candlelight in an unhurried fashion. Guests should bring their own wine. Breakfast can be taken as late as you wish. The studio/conservatory with a small kitchen for making drinks is available for guests and can also be used as a small conference room. There are 93 hectares of farmland, and a private path leads to beautiful Mount Brandon and the ancient Cairn. Pets by arrangement, no smoking in the dining room. Cullintra House is sign-posted off the R700 New Ross to Kilkenny road and is 6 miles from New Ross.

OWNER Patricia Cantlon OPEN All year ROOMS 6 double/twin; 3 en suite, 2 public bathrooms. TERMS €29–38; single supplement €12.50; reductions for children MEALS dinner €23

Garranavabby House
The Rower, Inistioge, Co. Kilkenny
Tel: 051 423613

This attractive country house, parts of which date back to the seventeenth century, is set in a pretty garden and is part of a large mixed farm, mostly sheep and cattle. There are ornamental pheasants, chickens to provide eggs for the house, and lovely views. Garranavabby is a nice, comfortable, well lived in family home, with some faded furnishings, but a welcoming atmosphere pervades. Guests have use of a comfortable sitting room, and breakfast is served in the pleasant dining room with a sideboard full of silver. This is an excellent spot for fishing, hill walking, riding and shooting. Pets by arrangement. No smoking in the bedrooms.

OWNER Johanna Prendergast OPEN All year ROOMS 1 double, 1 twin, 1 family; 2 public bathrooms. TERMS €28.50; single supplement €6.50

Grove Farmhouse
Ballycocksuist, Inistioge, Co. Kilkenny
Tel: 056 58467

In a rural setting this 200 year old farmhouse is surrounded by its beef, sheep and corn growing farmland. With a small, pretty, colourful garden to the front, the house both inside and out is immaculately maintained. The South Leinster Way passes through the farm, which has belonged to the same family for generations. The dining room, where breakfast only is served is particularly large, and there is a pleasant living room. No smoking. Pets by arrangement. All major credit cards accepted. Grove Farmhouse is well signed from the R700 Thomastown to Inistioge road.

OWNER Nellie Cassin OPEN Easter – end October ROOMS 4 double/twin; 3 en suite, 1 private bathroom.
TERMS €21.50–24

JENKINSTOWN

Swift's Heath
Jenkinstown, Co. Kilkenny
Tel: 056 67653 Fax: 056 67654

This splendid house, built in 1650, was lived in by the Swift family until 30 years ago, when it was bought by the present owners, who have done a wonderful job restoring it. It is reached from the main road through an impressive stone archway and down a long driveway, and is surrounded by its own grounds. Brigitte Lennon is originally from Germany, and is a friendly and welcoming hostess. The very large rooms have good, old furniture, and one bathroom is the original bathroom dating from 1845, still with its old fixtures and a splendid loo with a painted porcelain basin and flush handle - which has to be treated with the utmost care as it is very difficult to repair. The single room is Jonathan Swift's old room. There is an incredible billiard room, a comfortable drawing room, and large dining room with one long table where both breakfast and dinner, by request, are served. Tea or coffee are offered to guests upon arrival, and can be ordered at other times. There is a grass tennis court, and nearby fishing is available on the River Nore, as well as golf, riding, and hunting and shooting in season. Pets can be accommodated in the stables. Smoking in certain areas by arrangement. Most major credit cards accepted. Swift's Heath can be reached off the N77, about 6 miles from Kilkenny.

OWNER Brigitte Lennon OPEN February 1 – December 20 ROOMS 1 double, 2 twin; all en suite. TERMS €44.50; reductions for children MEALS dinner €25.50

KILKENNY

Berkeley House
5 Lower Patrick Street, Kilkenny, Co. Kilkenny
Tel: 056 64848 Fax: 056 64829
Email: berkeleyhouse@eircom.net
The previous owners were the ones that rescued Berkeley House from a derelict state and renovated it about eight years

ago. It dates from the 1800s and is right in the very centre of Kilkenny, close to the castle. It offers well equipped, nicely decorated bedrooms, which have phones and TV, and is efficiently, and professionally run. There is an attractive small breakfast room and car parking is available behind the house. No pets. Major credit cards accepted.

OWNER Declan Curtis & Linda Blanchfield OPEN All year ROOMS 2 double, 2 twin, 6 double/twin; all en suite. TERMS €38–47.50; single supplement €9.50–19; reductions for children

Burwood Bed & Breakfast
Waterford Road, Kilkenny, Co. Kilkenny
Tel: 056 62266

This modern bungalow with old fashioned hospitality is set back off the main road with a small front garden. Joan Flanagan is a most accommodating host and is proud of the personal attention she gives guests. A cup of tea or coffee is offered upon arrival and in the evening. The small bedrooms are all on the ground floor and are simply decorated. They have tea and coffee making facilities and hairdryers. There's a comfortable TV lounge for guests and breakfast only is served in the dining room. The large rear parking area has 24-hour surveillance. No pets. No smoking. Burwood can be found on the Waterford road, one kilometre from the centre of medieval Kilkenny.

OWNER Joan Flanagan OPEN May – October ROOMS 3 doubles, 1 twin; 3 en suite, 1 private bathroom. TERMS €25.50; single supplement €7.50; reductions for children

Danville House
New Ross Road, Kilkenny, Co. Kilkenny
Tel: 056 21512 Fax: 056 21512
Email: treecc@iol.ie

This 200 year old Georgian house is set in open countryside, with a pretty garden and a long driveway up from the main road. The house has been split into two, with Kitty Stallard's son and his wife living in one half and taking care of the farm. Kitty is a friendly, cheerful hostess, and the house has a relaxed atmosphere. One bedroom is on the ground floor, and they all have hairdryers. The TV lounge is combined with the dining room, which has a large table where breakfast is served. In summer croquet is set up on the lawn, and there is a walled kitchen garden. Fishing, golf and riding are available nearby. No pets. No smoking only in the dining room. Danville House is one kilometre from Kilkenny on the New Ross road.

OWNER Kitty & Dan Stallard OPEN April 1 – October 31
ROOMS 5 double/twin/single; 4 en suite, 1 private bathroom
TERMS from €23; single supplement €12.50

Dunromin
Dublin Road, Kilkenny, Co. Kilkenny
Tel: 056 61384 Fax: 056 70736
Email: valtom@oceanfree.ie

The standard of maintenance is exceptionally high throughout
the public rooms and bedrooms of this house. There is a wonderful, friendly atmosphere and tea or coffee is offered on
arrival. The bedrooms have recently been completely refurbished
in bright cheerful colours, and are immaculately clean. Guests
enjoy the secluded, landscaped garden, and there are views of
the golf course to the front. Dunromin is well known for its
informality and great musical evenings, set off by Tom Rothwell
playing the accordion. Breakfasts include home-baked breads and
home-made preserves. The house is on the edge of the town,
reached off the N10. No pets. No smoking. Visa and Mastercard
accepted.

OWNER Valerie & Tom Rothwell OPEN March 1 – December 20
ROOMS 4 double/twin; all en suite. TERMS €26.50–28; single
supplement

Hillgrove
Bennettsbridge Road, Kilkenny, Co. Kilkenny
Tel: 056 51453 or 22890 Fax: 056 51453
Email: hillgrove@esatclear.ie

This delightful family home is set back off the New Ross Road,
three kilometres from Kilkenny. Margaret Drennan used to work
for the Irish Tourist Board and knows everything there is to
know about Kilkenny. She is happy to suggest itineraries and help
with planning your stay. The house is furnished in a mixture of
old and reproduction furniture and the en suite bedrooms all

have hairdryers and tea and coffee making facilities. There is a TV lounge and a varied breakfast menu. No pets. No smoking. Visa cards are accepted.

OWNER Margaret & Tony Drennan OPEN February 1 – November 30 ROOMS 2 doubles, 2 twins, 1 family; all en suite. TERMS €26.50; single supplement €7.50; reductions for children

Newlands Country House
Sevenhouses, Danesfort, Kilkenny, Co. Kilkenny
Tel: 056 29111 Fax:
Email: newlands@indigo.ie

The Kennedys originally owned Shillogher House in Kilkenny, then decided to move out into the countryside and designed and built Newlands moving in the mid 1990s. It is set in 28 hectares of farmland, supporting cattle and sheep, and Seamus breeds greyhounds. Although the house has every comfort, and wonderful food, it is the personalities and hospitality of Seamus and Aileen that make a stay here so memorable. The house is very well built and insulated, so one hears no noise from other guests. The bedrooms are very comfortable, with lavish décor; four have whirlpool baths, and they all have telephones, TV, trouser presses, hairdryers, fridges and tea and coffee making facilities. Outstanding breakfasts, orchestrated by Seamus, are served in the conservatory style dining room, which has bright, cheerful colours and an attractive tiled floor. There are special weekend packages available, which include an eight course dinner on Saturday night. These are very popular with people wanting to get away for peace and quiet in comfortable surroundings. Kilkenny is but a short drive away, with all its historical attractions and variety of restaurants. No pets and no smoking. Visa, Mastercard and Access accepted. To find Newlands take the N10 Waterford road from Kilkenny and turn right at the Harvester Pub – the house will be on the right hand side in about half a mile.

OWNER Seamus & Aileen Kennedy OPEN All year except for Christmas ROOMS 3 double, 3 double/twin; all en suite. TERMS €31.50–38; single supplement in summer €19 MEALS dinner on Saturday evenings, & sometimes Wednesday

MADDOXTOWN

Blanchville House
Dunbell, Maddoxtown, Co. Kilkenny
Tel: 056 27197 Fax: 056 27636
Email: info@blanchville.ie
Website: www.blanchville.ie

This elegant Georgian country house stands in its own grounds and is approached by a tree- and shrub-lined private drive. It has a warm and friendly atmosphere and is beautifully furnished with antiques. The large, comfortable bedrooms overlook the lovely green countryside and have hairdryers, tea and coffee making facilities, TV and some rooms have trouser presses. The spacious drawing room with the original wallpaper and service bells has a TV, grand piano and open fireplace. Dinners, if booked in advance, are served in the atmospheric dining room, and are tastefully prepared with home-grown produce. Guests are welcome to bring their own wine. There is a hard tennis court for guests' use and a billiard and games room. Local amenities include golf, racing, fishing and flying at the Kilkenny Air Club.

There are a wide range of archaeological and historical attractions, and Blanchville is at the centre of a Craft Trail incorporating five prominent studio workshops in Co. Kilkenny. A recent addition to the establishment are three most attractive and well appointed self catering units, skilfully converted from the ruins of the Victorian coach house. They are well suited for families with children. No smoking in bedrooms or the dining room. Pets by arrangement. Most major credit cards are accepted. To reach Blanchville take the first right one kilometre after the Pike Pub off the N10 Dublin road. Then left at next crossroads and the entrance is 2 kilometres on the left.

OWNER Tim & Monica Phelan OPEN March 1 – November 1 ROOMS 3 doubles, 2 twins, 1 family; 5 en suite, 1 private bathroom. TERMS €51; single supplement €10; reductions for children MEALS dinner €31.50

Abbey House
Jerpoint Abbey, Thomastown, Co. Kilkenny
Tel: 056 24166 Fax: 056 24192

Abbey House is an attractive building located opposite Jerpoint
Abbey. The house may have been built as early as 1540, and a mill
here dates from the twelfth century. Ruins of the old mill, which
Helen Blanchfield would love to restore, lie behind the house.
The house itself was in very bad condition when the Blanchfields
bought it in 1988, and only one original wall is left after doing
the restoration work. Helen is an amusing, chatty lady with a lot
of energy. The house is spacious, with a drawing room, and
simply furnished bedrooms all equipped with hairdryers, telephones and TV. The pleasant dining room has small tables. Dogs
are allowed in their baskets in bedrooms, smoking only in the
drawing room. Visa, Access, Mastercard and Eurocard accepted.
Abbey House is on the N9.

OWNER Helen Blanchfield OPEN All year except for Christmas
ROOMS 6 double/twin/single; all en suite. TERMS €35–38; single
supplement €6.50–12.50; reductions for children

Ballyduff House
Ballyduff, Thomastown, Co. Kilkenny
Tel: 056 58488

This attractive eighteenth-century manor house is set in lovely
peaceful countryside, reached down a series of country lanes
and entered through a gateway and up a long pot-holed driveway. It stands just above the River Nore and enjoys views of the
river and hills. Mrs. Thomas is a charming young widow with two
children, and is a kind and thoughtful hostess. Ballyduff is a wonderful old family home, with an interesting collection of family
portraits. The bedrooms are huge and comfortably furnished and
have good-sized bathrooms. Breakfast is served in the dining
room, and guests also have use of a wonderful library and drawing room with TV. Arrangements can be made for guests to fish
on the estate's own stretch of the River Nore, and hunting is
also available. No smoking in bedrooms. Visa, Mastercard accepted.

OWNER Mrs. Breda Thomas OPEN All year ROOMS 2 double, 1
twin; all en suite. TERMS €38; reductions for children

Belmore
Jerpoint Church, Thomastown, Co. Kilkenny
Tel: 056 24228

Belmore House is full of character, as are its owners, Joseph and

Rita Teesdale, and their son, Henry. The house has a lovely atmosphere and is full of interesting pictures and books, many about the history of Jerpoint Abbey and other sites dating from the Norman conquest. The house was first built as a shooting lodge by the Earl of Belmore. The family rooms are mostly in the servants' quarters with vaulted ceilings and flagstone floors. The guest rooms mostly have elegant rounded ceilings, are well appointed and have hairdryers, etc. The Teesdales have owned the house since 1953, and farmed their two farms on both banks of the River Nore, Trout and salmon fishing are free for guests. Pets welcome in stables. Smoking allowed in some areas. Major credit cards accepted.

OWNER Rita & Joseph Teesdale OPEN All year ROOMS 2 doubles, I twin; all en suite. TERMS €29

URLINGFORD

Springview House
Urlingford, Co. Kilkenny
Tel: 056 31243

Springview House is most people's ideal of an Irish country farmhouse. Full of peace and comfort it was probably built in the late 1700s or early 1800s, and originally the upper rooms were accessed one room through another. Later a corridor was built and now there are three delightful family rooms, each with a double and single bed and private or en suite bathroom. The Joyce family have lived here since 1916, Mr. Joyce running their two farms with dairy cows and beef cattle, and Eileen Joyce is a charming, friendly hostess. Springview offers good value and can be found 600 metres off the Urlingford to Kilkenny R693 road. No smoking. No credit cards.

OWNER Mrs. Eileen Joyce OPEN April I – November I ROOMS 3 double/twin; 2 en suite. TERMS €25.50; reductions for children

COUNTY LEITRIM
Leitrim is a county of charming beauty, with distinctive hill formations and lovely lakes. This long, narrow county is divided in two by Lough Allen, one of the many lakes of the River Shannon. The county is a very popular place for anglers, and the main topic of conversation everywhere seems to be fishing. Dromahair is a pretty village, located about 12 km from Manorhamilton. The road from here is superbly scenic, with views of Lough Gill and beautiful wooded countryside. Fenagh, which is located in the hills, has the ruins of a Gothic church, all that remains of the monastery St Columba founded as

a school of divinity. You can fish to your heart's content in this area, which is full of lakes, beautiful scenery and wildlife. Carrick-on-Shannon is the centre of river cruising on the Shannon. There is a large marina, several cruising companies, and lots of restaurants and pubs, which during the season have traditional Irish music.

BALLINAMORE

Glenview
Aughoo, Ballinamore, Co. Leitrim
Tel: 078 44157 Fax: 078 44814

Glenview is a most attractive farmhouse on the new Shannon–Erne link, 500m from lock 4, beside the Woodford River. This is a delightful rural setting; there are extensive gardens, a pony, and a donkey and cart for children's enjoyment. A games room and pool table are available for guests' use. The house is efficiently run and guests are always made to feel part of the family. The residence has undergone extensive renovations and there is now a fully licensed restaurant offering the meal of the house and a table d'hôte menu. The lounge has a marble fireplace where log fires burn on cool days, and an antique chaise longue. There are many lakes close by and guests are advised on the best places to fish. A tackle shed, cold room and bait service are provided. Teresa Kennedy has been very successful with her bed & breakfast business for the past 14 years, and is the proud recipient of the BHS Agri-Tourism Award. Three self-catering bungalows are available, two of which have full wheelchair facilities. There is plenty to keep the visitors busy, including barge cruises, walking, golfing, horseback riding, canoeing, a Genealogy Centre and in the local pubs traditional Irish music. Visa, Mastercard, Access accepted.

OWNER Teresa Kennedy OPEN March 1 – October 31 ROOMS 5 twin, 1 family; 5 en suite. TERMS €24–31.50; reduction for children; single supplement €8.50 MEALS dinner

Riversdale Farm Guesthouse
Ballinamore, Co. Leitrim
Tel: 078 44122 Fax: 078 44813

This large, spacious country residence surrounded by an 32-hectare farm overlooks the new Shannon- Erne waterway, which borders the farm for 1km and is adjacent to Aughoo lock. All of the rooms have views and are furnished to a high standard. There are two lounges, one with TV, and both have open fires. Breakfast and excellent dinners are served in the conservatory dining room, which is furnished with chestnut and beech furniture made by a local craftsman. This is a wonderful spot for an all-purpose holiday – in the courtyard of the farm there is a small leisure complex which consists of a heated pool, sauna, and squash court. The cut-stone hay barn has been converted to a large games room, which could also be used for small seminars. The Ballinamore-Ballyconnell canal, which is based at Riversdale Farmhouse, also offers barging holidays; the barges are a modification of the traditional narrowboat, but are wider and offer more living space and comfort. Full details are available from Riversdale Farm, which is run by a member of the Thomas family. Cooking is done by the Ballymaloe-trained family and there is a wine licence.

There is a 9-hole golf course at Ballinamore and five minutes away is Drumcoura City Western Riding Centre. Special breaks are available. Access, Mastercard, Visa accepted.

OWNER Raymond Thomas OPEN All year ROOMS 10 rooms double/ twin/ family; all en suite. TERMS €28; reduction for children 25%; single supplement €9 MEALS dinner

The Old Rectory
Fenagh Glebe, Ballinamore, Co. Leitrim
Tel: 078 44089
Email: theoldrectoryleitrim@eircom.net
Website: www.theoldrectoryireland.com

The Old Rectory dates from the nineteenth century, and stands in 50 acres of private woodland, overlooking Fenagh Lake. The perfect place for folks wanting to get away from the hustle and bustle of city life. It is furnished with antique pieces and the rooms are well maintained and comfortable. There are two en-suite bedrooms, and two standard. TV and tea-makers in all rooms.

Dinners are available, using local produce, meats, and home made desserts. Pre-booking, is essential, and vegetarians are catered for with advance notice. Situated next to Fenagh's historic Abbey. Guests can enjoy walks through the woodland and there is plenty of wildlife to be seen. This is good value, non-smoking accommodation, golf, fishing and horse riding are all close by. Visa, Mastercard accepted.

OWNER Mrs Julie Curran OPEN January 10 – December 1 ROOMS 4 rooms single/twin/family; 2 en suite. TERMS €28–31.50; reduction for children; single supplement from €6.50 MEALS dinner

Ard na Greine

St Mary's Close, Carrick-on-Shannon, Co. Leitrim
Tel: 078 20311

Ard na Greine is an ideal property for people looking for an
angling holiday – this well maintained house is situated in a quiet
cul de sac, yet is within walking distance of the River Shannon
and a choice of 41 fishing lakes. Helen Dee is a most welcoming
lady who runs her B&B in a friendly but efficient manner and
serves a hearty breakfast. Evening meals are not served, but
there are several establishments within walking distance. The
rooms are spotlessly clean in this comfortable modern house,
and there is a video and TV in the guest lounge. Guests are welcome to return at any time during the day and Helen is happy to
help with things to see and do in the area – there is a heated
swimming pool, sports complex tennis courts, and a 9-hole golf
course, and for folks interested in a little night life there are
several local bars and hotels that provide music. Visa accepted.

OWNER Helen Dee OPEN All year ROOMS 4 double, 4 twin, 2
family; 2 en suite. TERMS €25.50–28; reduction for children; single
supplement €4

Caldra Lodge

Carrick-on-Shannon, Co. Leitrim
Tel: 078 21606 Fax: 078 21606

This family-run, beautifully restored Georgian house offers the
highest standards of hospitality and good home-cooked food. It
stands in a secluded spot in 30 hectares of farmland overlooking
the Shannon Waterways and is an ideal location for visiting local
beauty spots. Guests are made to feel immediately welcome; tea
or coffee is offered upon arrival. In addition to the lounges, there
is a conservatory, which is a delightful spot in which to relax on
pleasant days, and both the dining room and lounges have fires
on chilly days. Smoking in designated area.

There are boats and a bait and tackle room for guests' use.
There are 41 coarse fishing lakes within a 8-km radius. Evening
meals must be pre-arranged. Traditional music can be enjoyed in
local pubs. Most major credit cards accepted. Pass the Shannon
Valley Hotel and take the first left; the lodge is sign-posted from
there.

OWNER Maura O'Donnell OPEN March – November ROOMS 3
double, 1 twin, 1 family; 3 (2 with shower) en suite. TERMS
€26.50; reduction for children; single supplement €4 MEALS full
and light dinners

Corbally Lodge

Dublin Road, Carrick-on-Shannon, Co. Leitrim
Tel: 078 20228 Fax: 078 20228

Corbally Lodge is a country-style house furnished with antiques, set in an attractive garden in a peaceful spot. The bedrooms are well maintained and are spotlessly clean and comfortable; two are on the ground floor. The comfy lounge has turf fires and a TV. Mrs Rowley is a friendly, hospitable lady who takes excellent care of her guests. Smoking is allowed in the sitting room. Tasty breakfasts and pre-arranged home-cooked dinners are served in the bright dining room, featuring fresh vegetables, home-baked bread and excellent desserts. The River Shannon is close by and there are numerous lakes in the area. Golf, swimming and local boat hire are also available. Visa, Mastercard accepted. Sign-posted at Carrick-on-Shannon.

OWNER Valerie & P. J. Rowley OPEN March – October ROOMS 2 double, 3 twin; 3 en suite. TERMS €24; reduction for children 25%; single supplement €6.50 MEALS dinner

Lakeview Glebe House

Drumcong, Carrick-on-Shannon, Co. Leitrim
Tel: 078 42034

This old-style country house is adjacent to the Shannon Erne Canal and overlooks Carrickport Lough to the front and Lough Scur to the rear. It has a warm and welcoming atmosphere and the owners, Tom and Nancy McKeown, are hospitable and friendly. The house was originally owned by the parish priest; the house and 2 hectares were purchased by Tom and Nancy in 1972, and they have been welcoming guests into their home since that time. The house has a lived-in feel, the bedrooms are large and modestly furnished and most have lough views. There are seven lakes close by and guests can fish for perch, pike, bream and rudd, while Loughs Carrickport and Scur are within a five-minute walk. Guests have use of a three-bedroom self-catering cottage.

OWNER Nancy & Tom McKeown OPEN April 1 – November 30 ROOMS 2 double, 1 twin, 1 family; 2 en suite TERMS €23; reduction for children 50%; single supplement €2.50 MEALS dinner

COUNTY LONGFORD

The most central county in Ireland, Longford lies in the basin of the Shannon. The landscape is consequently low and flat, interspersed with small streams and lakes dotted with islands. Longford has strong associations with writers, particularly Oliver

Goldsmith, Padraic Colum, Maria Edgeworth and Leo Casey, and is a popular place for coarse fishing.

The town of Longford is spaciously laid out with wide streets, a Renaissance-style court house and a nineteenth-century cathedral, which is built of grey limestone and has impressive towers. Close to Newtonforbes is beautiful Castleforbes, a fine seventeenth-century castellated mansion. St Patrick is said to have founded a church at the old village of Ardagh in a pretty wooded setting, the ruins of which can still be seen.

DRUMLISH

Cumiskey's Farmhouse
Ennybegs, Drumlish, Co. Longford
Tel: 043 23320
Email: kc@iol.ie
Website: www.iol.ie/~kc

Cumiskey's farmhouse is in a rural location, surrounded by stone walls, an excellent choice from which to explore the many places of interest in the area. There is a slab stone entryway, arched doors, leaded windows, and a beamed ceiling. The drawing room has a large stone fireplace with turf fires, and a medieval-themed light. A galleried landing in the lounge is approached via a spiral staircase which leads to the library area. Smoking permitted only in sitting room. A luxury suite is ideal for "romantic getaways"; it has a king size bed, sitting room, corner bath and shower, dressing gowns and slippers, telephone and fridge. All the bathrooms have power showers.

Antique furnishings include a sideboard and chaise longue in the sitting room. Four course evening meals can be taken; vegetarian choices are also on offer, but, must be pre-booked. Breakfast includes buffet starters, followed by a traditional cooked breakfast. This is an interesting, well maintained house. There is a Regional Theatre in Longford and a championship Pitch and Putt Course opened in 2001.

Musical evenings take place on occasion and there is a piano available to guests. Guests may enjoy a glass of wine with their meal as the house has a wine license. Horse riding can be arranged. Access, Visa, Mastercard accepted. Once in the general area, the house is well signed posted.

OWNER Patricia Cumiskey OPEN March – October ROOMS 6 double/twin/family; 5 en suite, 1 own bathroom. TERMS €25.50–51, reduction for children; single supplement €7.50–12

Sancian House
Dublin Road, Longford, Co. Longford
Tel: 043 46187

Sancian House has been welcoming guests for many years; they return often to enjoy the warm and informal atmosphere and high standards found here. A pot of tea and scones is offered upon arrival. The rooms are spotlessly clean and simply furnished. The house sits back off the main road, the front garden is full of roses and there are colourful window boxes. Martha O'Kane is a friendly, outgoing lady who is very knowledgeable regarding family heritage, and is willing to assist guests who are interested in tracing their family history. An 18-hole golf course is located across the street, and it is a five-minute drive to the lovely village of Ardagh.

OWNER Martha O'Kane OPEN All year ROOMS 2 double, 1 twin, 2 single; 3 en suite. TERMS €23; reduction for children; single supplement €6.50 (in double room)

Eden House
Newtownforbes, Co. Longford
Tel: 043 41160

This large Tudor Style red brick house is easily located when reaching Newtownforbes, Although in the village, it is set back off the road double glazing keeping traffic noise to a minimum. The owners built the house for their retirement, but soon decided to open for business and offer rooms for travellers. En-suite facilities were added, and the ground floor room has an adjacent bathroom. The rooms are well appointed and have co-ordinated fabrics. Soft colours predominate, and there is a blue, green, and yellow room, known as the sunshine room. The lounge has a real fire, lit at the first sign of a chill, and the very welcoming hosts offer scones and tea on arrival. Smoking in sitting room only.

Breakfasts are excellent, pancakes, French toast, as well as traditional cooked fare, are on offer, This is a very comfortable home, guests feel immediately at ease. Bike storage is available. There are plenty of venues for evening meals in the village.

OWNER Eileen Prunty OPEN All year except for Christmas ROOMS 5 double/twin/family; all en suite. TERMS €26.50; reduction for children; single supplement €7.50

COUNTY MONAGHAN

Monaghan is a sportsman's paradise, with many lakes and small roads winding round the hills and through Monaghan's pastoral landscape. It is an unspoilt area, rich in farming land, and ideal country for outdoor activities and exploring. Among the prettiest lakes are Lake Muckno, Glaslough Lake, Lough Emy and the Dartry Lakes. Monaghan is a market town, and is home to an award-winning museum which houses the Clogher Cross, a fine example of early Christian metalwork. In July, Monaghan hosts the Fiddler of Oriel Festival of Irish dance and music.

CARRICKMACROSS

Shanmullagh House
Killanny Road, off Dundalk Road, Carrickmacross, Co. Monaghan
Tel: 042 966 3038 Fax: 042 966 1915

Shanmullagh House is an attractive, modern, red brick house in a rural setting with countryside views. With nothing in sight but green fields and mature trees, it is a peaceful and tranquil "away from it all" spot. The property is adjacent to the well-known Nurenmore Hotel and Country Club with its excellent golf course. The house is tastefully decorated throughout and has pine floors, immaculately kept bedrooms and power showers. Mr Flanagan runs a gift shop in town and Margaret Flanagan takes care of the bed & breakfast – and her three delightful young daughters. Excellent breakfasts are served in the dining room which overlooks the view, allowing a peaceful start to the day. Smoking in lounge only.

The owners are a congenial and friendly couple who obviously enjoy what they do, and guests are well taken care of here. Visa accepted.

OWNER Margaret Flanagan OPEN All year ROOMS 2 double, 2 twin, 2 family; 5 en suite TERMS €23; reduction for children; single supplement €5

CASTLEBLANEY

Rockville
Dundalk Road, Castleblaney, Co. Monaghan
Tel: 042 9746161
Website: www.dirl.com/monaghan/rockville-house.htm

Rockville is situated on the outskirts of town on the N2 Dublin–Derry Road. It is set back off the main road, stands in its own grounds, and double glazing keeps traffic noise to minimum. Joan Loughman is a welcoming lady, the ambience is friendly and informal. Tea is offered on arrival, a and nothing is too much trouble to ensure guests have everything they need. There is a separate dining room, with an attractive wood ceiling, and a spacious lounge, which has a real fire when chilly. Smoking is permitted in the lounge only. The rooms are furnished, with a mixture of modern and traditional, and colour co-ordinated with dainty wallpapers; all rooms have TV.

Lough Muckno Park, with fishing, golfing, horse riding, tennis and water-skiing is within walking distance. There are also several venues for evening meals in town. There is seating in the pretty garden for guests' use.

OWNER Joan Loughman OPEN All year except for Christmas ROOMS 2 double, 2 twin; 3 en suite. TERMS €25.50; reduction for children; single supplement €4

NEWBLISS

Glynch House
Newbliss, Co. Monaghan
Tel: 047 54045 Fax: 047 54321
Email: mirth@eircom.net

Glynch House is an impressive Georgian residence set in beautiful countryside, part of an 80-hectare farm where they raise calves and a beef suckling herd. The house has spacious rooms, furnished in keeping with its character, and there is an original marble fireplace in the lounge, where peat fires burn on chilly days. Smoking is only allowed in the study. The original casement shutters are still in working order.

Most of the bedrooms overlook peaceful countryside and a fairy fort. John O'Grady can easily be persuaded to tell guests stories about the fairies. An additional bonus of staying at Glynch Farm are the owners themselves – a down-to-earth, friendly and hospitable couple who have created a wonderful, informal atmosphere, and have a great sense of humour. John obviously enjoys chatting with guests and sharing his knowledge of the area. The house was originally built for a member of the Hugonuck family. New Bliss is an artist's colony; Richard Morris, a well-known architect, left his home for artists and musicians. More details on this interesting aspect can be obtained from John O'Grady. Excellent, freshly prepared breakfasts are served family-style, with special diets catered for by arrangement. There are several eating establishments close by for evening meals. Visa, Mastercard accepted. Take the R183 Clones Road - Glynch House is on the left-hand-side when the overhead bridge comes into view. The bridge is four miles from Clones.

OWNER John & Margaret O'Grady OPEN February 1 –
September 30 (other dates by arrangement) ROOMS 1 double, 2
twin, 1 family, 1 single; 3 en suite. TERMS €31.50; reduction for
children; no single supplement in single room (€6.50 if double
room)

COUNTIES OFFALY AND LAOIS

Both counties lie in the central part of Ireland, with the River
Shannon forming their western border.

Clonmacnois is an important name in Irish history.
St Ciarán founded a monastery here in A.D. 548, which became
one of Ireland's best-known religious centres. A pilgrimage is
held here each September on the feast of St Ciarán.

There is an attractive castle at Clononey, and Anthony
Trollope first started writing novels whilst living at Banager, a
pretty little village on the canal. At Birr, the gardens of the castle
are open to the public, and in Portarlington, built on the canal,
the gardens of the old town houses run down to the river.

BIRR

Minnocks' Farmhouse
Roscrea Road, Birr, Co. Offaly
Tel: 0509 20591 Fax: 0509 21694
Email: Minnocksfarmhouse@eircom.net

This Georgian-style house with colonnades, Georgian doors,
windows, ceiling rose and cornices was cleverly converted from
a farmhouse in 1991. It is part of a 40-hectare working dairy
farm. There are two ground floor bedrooms, which have firm
beds and are individually decorated with matching fabrics and
curtains. All rooms include telephone. Breakfasts include freshly
made scones, potato bread, eggs, bacon, cream and milk from the
farm; special diets catered for at breakfast by arrangement. There
are some good value restaurants close by, which Veronica will be
happy to give you information on. Smoking is allowed in the
lounge, if other guests do not object.

Veronica Minnock is a gracious host and has been awarded the
Golden Thoughts Tourist Award, an accolade for "service above
and beyond the call of duty." A cup of tea is offered upon arrival
– in fact, at Minnocks' farm, the kettle is rarely off the boil! Visa
accepted. The farm is close to the new Telescope and Science
Centre. Directions from Birr town: N62 heading south, situated
on left side of the road, 3km from Birr.

OWNER Veronica Minnock OPEN All year ROOMS 1 double, 2
twin, 2 family, 1 single/double; all en suite. TERMS €25.50;
reduction for children; single supplement €8.50 MEALS dinner

Parkmoor Farm

Fivevalley, Birr, Co. Offaly
Tel: 0509 33014

A 200 year-old impressive farmhouse, nestled in a peaceful valley, approached via a tree-lined drive, set on a 300-acre working farm of suckler cows. The entry has Victorian hand-made tile, the house is furnished with antiques, and both bathrooms have the original Victorian baths. Tea makers and hairdryer available in rooms. The large bedrooms, off the galleried landing, all have hand painted pitch pine. The house has a wonderful informal and friendly ambience, enhanced the bubbly and helpful owner, Grace Grennan. Non-smokers preferred.

   Breakfast is a banquet, featuring home made brown scones, croissants, preserves and marmalade, followed by a traditional cooked choice hot off the Aga; special diets can be catered for at breakfast. Of special interest is the Famine Hutch in the kitchen and the Italian consul table and matching mirror. There is a sitting room for guests, but they are often found in the cosy kitchen chatting to the owners. There are three lovely children who enjoy meeting people. Guests may wander around the farm. The Glendine Bistro is close by for evening meals. Situated off the N52 near Birr, sign-posted.

OWNER Padraig & Grace Grennan OPEN All year except for Christmas ROOMS 3 double; 1 en suite. TERMS €35.50–38; reduction for children; single supplement €6.50

RAHAN

Canal View Country House

Rahan, Tullamore, Co. Offaly
Tel: 0506 55868 Fax: 0506 55034
Email: canalview@eircom.net

Canal View is an attractive, modern dormer bungalow in a peaceful position backing onto the Grand Canal. Guests can fish from the back garden for bream, rudd, tench and perch, or walk along the canal bank and watch the cruisers pass by. Angling maps are available. A 10-minute stroll brings you to the ancient Rahan Church. A patio, picnic and play area and rowing boats, as well as a sauna, steam room and jacuzzi, are all available at no extra charge. Breakfast and evening meals are served in the pretty dining room, which overlooks the canal. Smoking is permitted in the lounge only. The bedrooms are tastefully decorated with matching fabrics and wallpapers. Canal View offers extremely high standards and guests are assured of a warm welcome and attention to detail in this pleasant house. Guests often have the opportunity of watching the local farmer's cows swimming from one yard to another across the canal, which occurs in the morning and the evening. Guided bog tours, horseback riding and a 9-hole golf course are all available close by. A Treatment Room has been added to the house, featuring a sauna, steam room, massage, reiki, and beauty treatments. Guests can also partake of pedal row boating in the canal. Visa, Access, Barclaycard accepted. Take N52 towards Birr from Tullamore for 2 1/2 miles. As you reach speed limit sign in Muckleagh Village, turn right at the Fox. The house is sign-posted from there, 2 1/2 miles on the right.

OWNER Bernadette & Anthony Keyes OPEN April 1 – October 31 ROOMS 1 double, 2 family, 1 single; 3 en suite. TERMS €20.50–23; reduction for children; single supplement €6.50 MEALS dinner

Pine Lodge
Tullamore, Co. Offaly
Tel: 0506 51927 Fax: 0506 51927

This exceptionally well-maintained house with high standards is delightful in every way. It is set in almost one hectare of lawned gardens with outstanding views of the surrounding countryside, providing the ultimate in relaxation. All but one of the well-appointed bedrooms have pine furnishings.

There is a sitting room with TV, where smoking is permitted, and a separate dining room, where excellent wholesome breakfasts are served at separate tables. Claudia Krygel, who is from Germany, prides herself on the wholesome food served. Breakfast consists of smoked salmon, eggs and pancakes as well as traditional fare. Little wonder that Claudia has been the recipient of the National Irish Breakfast Award. Imaginative evening meals are also served (advance notice is required). Vegetarian and special diets can also be catered for. There are some enjoyable countryside walks, and golf and fishing are close by. There is a log cabin, which houses a large, heated indoor pool, sauna and steam room and sun bed. Massage and reflexology are also available. There is a charge for the pool, sauna and steam room per session. Not suitable for children under 12. From Tullamore, take the N52 to Birr, after two miles, take right fork, approximately 1 mile from there turn left. Sign-posted from here.

OWNER Claudia Krygel OPEN March – October ROOMS 2 double, 2 twin; all en suite. TERMS €29; single supplement €6.50 MEALS dinner

Castletown House
Donaghmore, Co. Laois
Tel: 0505 46415 Fax: 0505 46788
Email: castletown@eircom.net
Website: www.castletownguesthouse.com

Castletown House has been awarded for the third time the prestigious Agri-Tourism Provincial Award. This warm and welcoming nineteenth-century farmhouse stands in scenic countryside surrounding an 80-hectare beef and sheep farm, on which the ruins of a Norman castle remain. It is approached via a private drive through open fields full of grazing sheep. The house is spotlessly clean, with a comfortable and relaxed atmosphere. Improvements are ongoing; the hallway, kitchen and dining rooms have newly tiled floors, and TV and hairdryer are available in all bedrooms.

This must be one of the best value accommodations in Ireland; the bedrooms are all a good size, and there are several pieces of antique furniture. Fresh farmhouse breakfasts and pre-arranged light evening meals are served in the dining room, which has a marble fireplace; there is also a sitting room with TV and information on what to see and do in the area. Smoking is only permitted in the lounge. Guests enjoy gathering in the family kitchen for a cup of tea and a chat with the friendly owners. A conservatory games room is available to guests and there is an open farm on the property with star billing going to the three donkeys Mollie, Donna and Wilkie.

The nearby Donaghmore Famine Museum is undergoing restoration, and is well-worth a visit. Donaghmore was the setting for the film "All Things Bright and Beautiful", starring Gabriel Byrne. Access, Mastercard, Eurocard, J.C.B. accepted.

OWNER Moira Phelan OPEN March 1 – November (other dates may be arranged) ROOMS 2 double, 1 family, 1 triple/ twin; all en suite. TERMS €21.50; reduction for children MEALS light meals

Chez Nous
Kilminchy, Co. Laois
Tel: 0502 21251

Chez Nous is a classic Irish vernacular design residence, situated in a quiet spot in a peaceful cul-de-sac. Guests who book in here are treated as friends and enjoy first-class accommodation. The luxuriously appointed bedrooms are very tasteful, the sunshine suite has a half tester canopied bed, and all are tastefully decorated in soft pastels of pink sorbet, peach blossom, and lavender blue. The family suite has two double rooms and a separate single, ideal for families or friends travelling together. Just about everywhere you look is decorated with bows, ribbons and pretty curtains. Breakfasts are a banquet, and include sugar-rimmed orange juice, edible flowers, potato cakes, pan-fried trout, home-baked brown bread, home-made preserves and marmalade, or for those who prefer, a traditional Irish breakfast. There is a conservatory with a blue and yellow décor, where guests may help themselves to tea and coffee, and cosy log fires in the sitting room. Evening meals are served, if arranged in advance, but there are options for eating out at several venues close by. The house was featured in Select, a yearly magazine which features houses and furnishings of special interest. Not suitable for children under 10.

OWNER Audrey & Tony Canavan OPEN All year ROOMS 2 double, 2 twin, 2 family; all en suite. TERMS €23.50–25.50; reduction for children; single supplement €6.50 MEALS dinner

Ballaghmore House
Borris-in-Ossory, Co. Laois
Tel: 0505 21366
Email: ballaghmorehse@eircom.net

This modern cream-and-green shuttered farmhouse sits way back off the road in a large landscaped garden with a pond and a small waterfall. It is part of a 30-hectare mixed farm and there is new coarse fishing lake on the property; the land runs adjacent to an 18-hole golf course. Beautifully maintained with tasteful décor, the bedrooms are reached by a split mahogany staircase, and have cast-iron beds, lace canopies, and restful pastels of peach, cream, lemon and grey. Excellent breakfasts and pre-arranged high tea or evening meals are served in the inviting dining room and there is a turf fire in the lounge, the only smoking room in the house.

The warm hospitality shown to guests and the extremely high standards found at Ballaghmore House make this an excellent choice for touring this unspoiled area. Specialist in package activity holidays: fishing, golfing, walking and cycling. American Express, Visa, Mastercard, Access accepted. On N7 half-way between Limerick and Dublin, between Roscrea and Borris-in-Ossory.

OWNER Carole England OPEN All year ROOMS 1 double, 2 twin, 1 family; all en suite. TERMS €25.50–30.50; reduction for children; single supplement €8.50 MEALS dinner

STRADBALLY

Tullamoy House
Stradbally, Co. Laois
Tel: 0507 27111 Fax: 0507 27111

This impressive stone built house, part of a working sheep and cattle farm, stands in tranquil surroundings, 5km from Stradbally. Families are welcome, baby-sitting can be provided, and there is cot and high chair available. The rooms are quite large and are furnished in keeping with the character of the house. Breakfast and home-cooked dinners are available, by prior arrangement; children's meals can also be provided. Special diets can be catered for if pre-arranged. The ambience is friendly, your hosts, very helpful and they are happy to give advice on activities in the area.

This is a good location from which to visit this scenic region, and there is fishing, horse riding, a forest park, pitch and putt course, golf and the Curragh race course close by. Guests are welcome to explore the farm and make use of the pleasant garden. There is a sitting room and separate dining room. Smoking lounge only. Directions 5km off the N80, 20km north of Carlow.

OWNER Pat & Caroline Farrell OPEN March – October ROOMS 4 double/ family; all en suite. TERMS from €29; reduction for children; single supplement €6.50 MEALS dinner

COUNTY ROSCOMMON

County Roscommon is an island county 60 km in length. Two-thirds of the county is surrounded by water. In the north are the largest lakes: Lough Key, Lough Gara and Lough Boderg. The great Lough Ree is in the east. The limestone foundation of the whole county and the numerous lakes make it a fisherman's paradise.

Large areas of arable land are to be found in the centre of the county, and the principal occupation of the people is raising cattle and sheep.

Roscommon is a county of abbeys and castles. You can visit Clonalis House, Castlerea, once the home of two of Ireland's high kings in the twelfth century; Strokestown Park House, with its records of Famine-ridden Ireland; prehistoric Rathcroghan; St John's Interpretative Centre; medieval Boyle and picturesque Lough Key with its forest park.

For those interested in contemporary art, the Glebe House Gallery is situated midway between Boyle and Carrick-on-Shannon at Crossna, Knockvicar.

CARRICK-ON-SHANNON

Avondale House
Roosky, Carrick-on-Shannon, Co. Roscommon
Tel: 078 38095

This attractive house stands in its own grounds 500 m from the River Shannon. This friendly, family-run establishment has a relaxing, cosy atmosphere. Carmel Davis was formerly in the hotel trade but missed the personal contact with people and decided to open her own bed & breakfast establishment. Carmel and her husband were successful from the beginning and soon added on additional bedrooms. The bedrooms are clean and comfortable and have orthopaedic beds. The cosy TV lounge has a turf fire, and smoking is permitted here only. Excellent home-cooked evening meals are available if ordered in advance, and there is a new hotel within walking distance which has an excellent restaurant and bar food. Avondale is a good base for anglers; there is a tackle room with fridges and drying facilities are also available. For people who enjoy walking there is a pleasant river walk close by. Guests are well taken care of at Avondale and are assured of personal attention from the pleasant owners. Visa, American Express accepted.

OWNER Carmel Davis OPEN All year ROOMS 2 double, 2 twin, 1 family; all en suite. TERMS €31.50; reduction for children; single supplement €6.50 MEALS dinner

Glencarne House
Ardcarne, Carrick-on-Shannon, Co. Roscommon
Tel: 079 67013

This charming Georgian house, approached up a private drive, is located in scenic countryside with lovely views overlooking green fields and grazing sheep. A very warm welcome awaits you at Glencarne House. Agnes Harrington has won several awards, including the Galtee Breakfast Award and the Agri-Tourism National Award. Special diets may be catered for if pre-arranged. The house is well maintained and freshly decorated. It is warm and relaxed, and the bedrooms have every comfort, including armchairs, hot water bottles and electric blankets, and some have antique brass beds. There is a peaceful, old-fashioned lounge with a marble fireplace which, along with the dining room, has a real fire on chilly days. Smoking is allowed in TV lounge only. Agnes Harrington is an excellent cook; if pre-booked, evening meals are prepared fresh daily and desserts feature some of the best pastry in Ireland. There is a golf course within 1 km and lots of outdoor activities and wildlife walks in the nearby 325-hectare Lough Key Park. Many guests have been returning to this special place over the years and early reservations are recommended. On N4 between Boyle and Carrick on Shannon.

OWNER Agnes Harrington OPEN March 1 – October 15 ROOMS 3 double, 1 twin, 1 family, 1 single; all en suite. TERMS €31.50; 25% reduction for children; single supplement €6.50 MEALS dinner

CASTLEREA

Clonalis House
Castlerea, Co. Roscommon
Tel: 907 20014 Fax: 907 20014
Email: Clonalis@iol.ie
Website: http://www.hidden-ireland.com/clonalis/

Clonalis House is an impressive Victorian Italianate mansion, built on a 700-acre wooded estate. It was the home of the O'Conors of Connacht, descendants of Ireland's last High Kings and traditional Kings of Connacht. The house is furnished in keeping with its character; the bedrooms have half tester and or four poster beds, all have their own bathroom. Guests are welcome to browse through the archive and library, dating from the 16th century, and of special interest are the heirlooms, such as Carolan's Harp and the O'Conor Coronation Stone.
Dinners are served, with vegetarian and special diets, if pre-arranged, and for guests staying three or more nights there is a reduction. Clonalis House is a non-smoking establishment. The

house is not suitable for children under 14. Guests are welcome to take walks on the estate, and Galway, Sligo and Mayo are within an hour's drive. Visa, Mastercard, Access accepted. On the west side of Castlerea on the N60.

OWNER Pyers and Marguerite O'Conor-Nash OPEN April 15 – September 30 ROOMS 3 double, 1 twin; all en suite. TERMS €73.50; single supplement €12.50 MEALS dinner

STROKESTOWN

Church View House
Strokestown, Co. Roscommon
Tel: 078 33047 Fax: 078 33047
Email: churchviewhouse@eircom.net

This spacious, 200-year-old, rambling country house stands in a scenic location. It has been in the Cox family for four generations and is part of a 100-hectare working farm. The original structure of a Famine fever hospital is found on the grounds. The house continues to be well maintained, and the good-sized bedrooms are simply furnished. One of the lounges has the original marble fireplace. Evening meals are available, but must be ordered in advance, and include tasty home-made dishes and desserts. Church View House is not licensed, but guests may bring their own wine. Strokestown Park House, the Famine Museum and gardens are 6 km away. On N4 west from Dublin to Rooskey turn left onto 371 to Strokestown, house is sign-posted on this road.

OWNER Harriet Cox OPEN All year (advance booking required during winter months) ROOMS 2 double, 2 twin, 2 family; 3 en suite. TERMS €25.50–31.50; 25% reduction for children; single supplement peak season only MEALS dinner

COUNTY TIPPERARY
Located in the centre of the southern part of Ireland, Tipperary is a beautiful county of rich farmland. From the top of Slievenamon there is a splendid view. To the north you can see the Rock of Cashel, a steep outcrop of limestone topped by impressive ruins – a truly spectacular sight, particularly during the summer when it is floodlit at night. From early times the rock was a fortress and seat of chieftains, and later it became an important religious site.

Today you can see the vast ruins of the gothic cathedral, which dates from the thirteenth century; the tower of the Castle; the cross of St Patrick, the massive base of which is said to be the coronation stone of the Munster kings; and Cormac's

Chapel, which dates back to 1130.

The Cashel Palace Hotel is a very fine Queen Anne-style house, formerly the residence of Church of Ireland bishops, located in the busy town of Cashel.

A fine collection of sixteenth-century and seventeenth-century books can be found in the Diocesan Library in the precincts of St John the Baptist Cathedral. There's a good craft shop where you can buy Shanagarry tweed. Situated between Thurles and Cashel, Holy Cross Abbey was built in 1110, to house a part of the True Cross, and later became a popular place of pilgrimage.

Cahir, a most pleasant town on the River Suir, has a beautifully restored fifteenth-century castle on an island in the river, and now houses the tourist office. Tipperary, famous for the song "It's a Long Way to Tipperary," is a great farming centre. The mountains between Nenagh and Toomvara were the home of Ned of the Hill, the local Robin Hood. Nearby is Nenagh Round, all that remains of a castle built in 1200.

Kilcooly Abbey, the Abbey of the Holy Cross and the attractive old church at Fethard are all worth seeing. At Ahenny are two elaborately carved eighth-century stone crosses, and at Carrick-on-Suir, there is a fine example of a Tudor mansion, which can be visited by request.

BANSHA

Bansha House
Bansha, Co. Tipperary
Tel: 062 54194 Fax: 062 54215

This impressive Georgian residence is approached by an avenue of beech trees, set in 40 hectares of land. The house is furnished in keeping with its character and there are several pieces of antique furniture. The bedrooms are large, and two are on the ground floor. The charming lounge has a log fire and leads out onto the gardens. A relaxed and comfortable atmosphere

pervades this non-smoking house, and guests can often be found in the kitchen with Mary, chatting about what to see and do in the area.

John and Mary breed racehorses, and their stables-registered Equestrian Centre offers horseback riding. There is an all-weather 1km track on the farm. Cooking is of a very high standard, with home-made breads, tarts and pies. Glorious scenic tours can be taken from here. This is superb place for guests wanting some peace and tranquillity. A self-catering cottage is also available. Visa, Mastercard accepted. 1km off the main Limerick–Waterford Road. N24 at Bansha. 5 miles from Tipperary town.

OWNER John & Mary Marnane OPEN All year except for Christmas ROOMS 4 double, 3 twin, 1 single; 5 en suite. TERMS €35.50; reduction for children; single supplement €7.50. MEALS dinner from €21.50 (booking required)

Lismacue House

Bansha, Co. Tipperary
Tel: 062 54106 Fax: 062 54126
Email: lismac@indigo.ie
Website: www.lismacue.com

Lismacue House has been in Kate Nicholson's family since it was built in 1813. It is a classic, beautifully proportioned Irish country house, set in its own extensive grounds at the foot of the magnificent Galtee Mountains. The approach to the house is via one of the most impressive lime-tree avenues in Ireland. The spacious drawing room and library have their original wallpaper.

Breakfasts and dinners are served in the imposing dining room; special diets can be catered for if pre-arranged. Traditional log fires burn in the warm and welcoming reception rooms. Special interest holidays are available, such as pony trekking for adults and children and, from November to February, hosted hunting holidays. There is also trout fishing on the estate's own river (tuition available). There are three golf courses and tennis courts close by and the Rock of Cashel and Cahir Castle are just a short drive away. French is spoken here. Visa, Mastercard, American Express accepted. Take N24 from Tipperary through Bansha towards Cahir, entrance is just outside Bansha on the left.

OWNER Kate Nicholson OPEN March 17 – October 31 ROOMS 2 double, 1 twin, 2 family; 3 en suite. TERMS €57–70; reduction for children; single supplement €14 MEALS Dinner €33 (except Sunday)

Ashling
Cashel Road, Cahir, Co. Tipperary
Tel: 052 41601

This pink-washed low building is situated 2 km outside Cahir, and has lovely views from the front of the house. Breda Fitzgerald is a very friendly, chatty lady who keeps an immaculately clean and tidy house. The rooms are on the small side, but are comfortably furnished, and there is a large sitting room off the dining room. Non-smoking house.

OWNER Breda Fitzgerald OPEN All year ROOMS 2 double, 2 twin; 3 en suite TERMS. €25.50; reduction for children; single supplement €12.50

Ardmayle House
Cashel, Co. Tipperary
Tel: 0504 42399 Fax: 0504 42420
 E-mail: ardmayle@iol.ie

Ardmayle House is a spacious, creeper-covered, unpretentious farmhouse surrounded by an 80-hectare working farm. The bedrooms, furnished with solid old-fashioned and antique furniture, are large and comfortable. The open log fire in the sitting room is the ideal place for making friends and enjoying a hot drink and some delicious homemade scones. Guests are welcome to explore the dairy farm; sheep and horses are also kept. Annette is a warm, kindly host who likes guests to enjoy the best of rural living. They are welcome to fish both banks on the 2.5-km-long private stretch of the River Suir that runs through the property. A ghillie is also available by arrangement. Golf, forest walks and horseback riding can be arranged locally. Evening meals by advance arrangement only. There are also two four-star self-catering cottages on the farm.

OWNER Annette Hunt OPEN April 1 – October 1 ROOMS 1 double, 1 twin, 3 family, 1 single; 4 en suite. TERMS €25.50; reduction for children; single supplement €8.50

Knock-Saint-Lour House
Cashel, Co. Tipperary
Tel: 062 61172

A circular driveway leads to this large, square, modern whitewashed house with its stone pillared porch, surrounded by 13 hectares of beef and tillage farming. There is a formal drawing room, but the TV lounge has comfortable chairs, a piano and a fireplace. The rooms are large and comfortable, and the house has good views of the Rock of Cashel. There is a good supply of information on the area, and Eileen O'Brien is happy to advise guests on what to see and do in the area.

OWNER Eileen O'Brien OPEN April 1 – November 1 ROOMS 2 double, 3 twin, 2 family, single; all en suite TERMS €23; reduction for children; single supplement €8.50. MEALS dinner

Rahard Lodge
Dualla Road, Cashel, Co. Tipperary
Tel: 062 61052

Rahard Lodge is approached up a tree-lined driveway and set amidst glorious landscaped gardens with superb views of the Rock of Cashel, which is floodlit at night. Built by the owners 30 years ago, this long, low, whitewashed house is surrounded by a 52-hectare beef and sheep farm. The bedrooms, all on the ground floor, are large and comfortable. An additional bonus are the delightful owners, Mr and Mrs Foley, who are interested in antiques; there are some excellent pieces about. Guests are greeted with a hot drink on arrival and very often a slice of delicious home-baked cake or some scones. The house is impeccably maintained; there are rich carpets and the spacious lounge has an open fireplace. Smoking is allowed only in the lounge.
  Freshly prepared breakfasts only are served, but there is no shortage of venues for evening meals in the Heritage town of Cashel. Guests are welcome to sit in the lovely award-winning gardens, which were awarded first prize in County Tipperary and third place in the All-Ireland competition. Visa, Mastercard accepted. Take R691 from Cashel.

OWNER Moira Foley OPEN March 1 – November 30 ROOMS 2 twin, 4 family; all en suite. TERMS €34.50; reduction for children; single supplement €9. MEALS light meals on request

Ros Guill House
Dualla Road, Cashel, Co. Tipperary
Tel: 062 61507 Fax: 062 61507

This small, neat-looking house was built by the owners 28 years ago, and Mrs Moloney has been running a bed & breakfast here for 26 years. Ros Guill House is well shielded from the road by evergreen trees and a small front garden, which has been a winner in the Bord Fáilte National Garden Competition. Evelyn Moloney is also a proud recipient of the Galtee Breakfast Award. The house has been freshly decorated and new carpets have been fitted; double-glazing has been added to this well-maintained property. The rooms are a little on the small side, but immaculately clean, and the dining room has views of the castle and the Galtee Mountains. Evelyn is a very friendly lady who takes excellent care of her guests. Visa, Mastercard, Eurocard accepted.

OWNER Evelyn Moloney OPEN May 1 – October 20 ROOMS 2 double, 2 twin, 2 family; 3 en suite. TERMS €31.50; reduction for children; single supplement €12.50

CLONMEL

Woodruffe House
Cahir Road, Clonmel, Co. Tipperary
Tel: 052 35243

This spacious and elegant house, set on 110 hectares of mixed farming, is surrounded by a lovely garden full of mature trees and flowers. This is a warm and inviting house, and even though it was only built in 1977, it has the ambience of a bygone era. The four spacious bedrooms are beautifully decorated with matching Sanderson wallpapers and fabrics. Guests enjoy the log fires on chilly evenings. Owner Anne O'Donnell is a gracious host who offers complimentary refreshments on arrival. Evening meals are available, if pre-arranged. Anne is an excellent cook; a favourite dish with guests is her baked fish with its delicious sauce, and her mouth-watering desserts, such as pavlova with fresh fruit, are equally popular. There are walks through the farm, and Cahir, Cashel and Clonmel are within driving distance.

OWNER Anne O'Donnell OPEN April 4 – September 30 ROOMS 3 double, 1 twin; 2 en suite. TERMS €19–21.50; reduction for children; single supplement €6.50 MEALS dinner

CLOUGHJORDAN

Modreeny, Charlie Swan Equestrian Centre
Cloughjordan, Co. Tipperary
Tel: 0505 42221 Fax: 0505 42128
Email: cswan@iol.ie

This impressive Georgian residence stands on a 200 acre estate of peaceful farm and parkland. As the name indicates, this a very popular choice for folks who love outdoor activities. In addition to horse riding, there is an outdoor swimming pool, rough shooting in season, an 18 hole golf course with a ten minute drive, and for fishing enthusiasts Lough Derg and the Shannon are also within reach. A games room and sauna is provided for guests. Excellent, freshly prepared breakfasts are served in the elegant dining-room at separate tables. Special diets can be catered for if notice given. Dinners can also be booked and there is a full license. The Cellar Bar has bar food. The house is furnished with family heirlooms and antiques, the ambience is informal and welcoming. The bedrooms, all with their own bathrooms, are tastefully co-ordinated, are spacious, bright and comfortable. The Ormond and North Tipperary Hunts take place in Modreeny, and the hounds are kennelled on the estate. Hunting takes place November to March, arrangements can be made for guests to ride out with the hounds. Mastercard, Visa accepted. Situated 9 miles from Nenagh on the Borrisokane–Cloughjordan Road.

OWNER Theresa & Donald Swan OPEN February – December 20 ROOMS 4 double; all en suite. TERMS from €38; reduction for children; single supplement €7.50 MEALS dinner (if pre-booked)

MULLINAHONE

Killaghy Castle
Mullinahone, Co. Tipperary
Tel: 052 53112 Fax: 052 53561
Email: c.killaghycastle@eircom.net

This Norman castle, whose original owners were Cromwellian planters, has been added on to and extended over the years. Originally it was just a Motte and Bailey, still visible to the left of the castle. During Tudor times a long house was added to the rear of the property, and in 1800 two other buildings were added, making Killaghy the castle we see today. It is part of a 96-hectare dairy and tillage farm. The present owners, the Collins family, moved here in 1995 from Cork.

Moira Collins is a down-to-earth and friendly lady, who has created an informal, welcoming atmosphere, adding her personal touch by redecorating and installing new curtains and orthopaedic beds. The house is full of antiques purchased specifically for the house to enhance the old-world ambience. This well-maintained property is non-smoking. The bedrooms are enormous and some have original fireplaces, as do the dining room and the drawing room; the latter is a wonderful spot to relax in and help yourself to tea or coffee.

The drawing room has interesting coving and a terra-cotta border. The house has glorious views all round. There is a nature trail and walled garden, as well as games and two tennis courts for guests' use. Visa, Mastercard accepted.

OWNER Moira Collins OPEN All year ROOMS 2 double, 1 twin, 1 double/single; 3 en suite. TERMS €31.50–44.50; reduction for children; single supplement €12.50 MEALS dinner €25.50–44.50

Otway Lodge Guest House

Dromineer, Nenagh, Co. Tipperary
Tel: 067 24133 / 24273

Otway Lodge is in a lovely position overlooking Lough Derg.
Parts of the house, which was formerly part of a barracks, are
over 100 years old. It has been extended and tastefully
modernised since that time. The modestly furnished bedrooms
are a good size, as are the bathrooms. There is a spacious guest
lounge with a peat fire, TV, harp and piano. Frank and Ann work
as a team and enjoy their business, and always have a pot of tea
on the hob. There is a small shop on the premises offering
sweets, lemonade and other snacks. This is an ideal spot for
families and water sports enthusiasts as there is windsurfing,
sailing, water-skiing and trout and coarse fishing available. There
are also boats for hire.

OWNER Ann & Frank Flannery OPEN All year ROOMS 2 double,
4 twin; all en suite. TERMS €23; reduction for children; single
supplement €7.50

Gurtalougha House

Ballinderry, nr. Nenagh, Co. Tipperary
Tel: 067 22080 Fax: 067 22154

Bessie and Michael Wilkinson have retired and this beautiful
home has been taken over by the Pettits, who have been busy
refurbishing and improving on the high standards already established. Gurtalougha is approached via a peaceful avenue that
winds for 1.5 km through 60 hectares of mature forest. Built in
the nineteenth century, the house is in an ideal location on the
banks of the River Shannon; in the distance can be seen the
mountains of Clare and Galway. This is an informal and relaxed
house – the emphasis here is on relaxation, and there are log
fires and antique furnishings. The spacious and elegant bedrooms
have wooden floors and comfortable beds. One has a balcony
overlooking the lake. Breakfasts are served in the dining room,
which has a view, as do the drawing room and library. The Pettits
have introduced an imaginative and extensive menu, featuring the
finest ingredients, fresh produce and splendid tasty sauces. There
are lovely woodland walks available with a great variety of
wildlife such as red squirrels, badgers, otters and kingfishers.
Boats and windsurfing boards are available at no extra charge,
and there is swimming from the jetty and croquet on the lawn.
There are four golf courses, pony trekking, two hard tennis
courts and a sailing school close by.

OWNER Ann Pettit OPEN All year ROOMS 8 double, 2 twin; 8
en suite. TERMS €63.50; reduction for children MEALS dinner

Riverrun House

Terryglass, Co. Tipperary
Tel: 067 22125 Fax: 067 22187

Riverrun House stands in its own beautifully landscaped grounds of 0.5 hectares in the centre of Terryglass, the recipient of the famous Tidy Village Award. Tom and Lucy Sanders have been running their bed & breakfast very successfully since 1991 and are as enthusiastic as ever. Three of the well-appointed bedrooms are located on the ground floor, tastefully decorated in pretty pastel floral colours with matching fabrics and pine furniture. Two have lake views. This house of character is very comfortable and full of interesting antiques. A pleasant five-minute stroll away is the busy harbour set on the north east shore of Lough Derg – the largest of the lakes on the Shannon system. Riverrun House has a hard tennis court, bicycles for guests' use, and fishing boats for hire. There is an 18-hole golf course close by. Excellent breakfasts are served, including freshly squeezed orange juice, home-baked soda bread and yoghurts, as well as traditional fare. Vegetarian breakfasts are available on request. Evening meals are not available, but Tom and Lucy Sanders would be happy to make recommendations on where to eat. Visa, Mastercard, American Ex-press accepted.

OWNER Lucy Sanders OPEN All year ROOMS 2 double, 2 twin, 2 family; all en suite. TERMS €31.50; reduction for children; single supplement €6.50

Clonmore House

Galbally Road, Tipperary, Co. Tipperary
Tel: 062 51637

Guests continue to enjoy this immaculate, detached house set back from the main road on the edge of town. The bedrooms are tastefully decorated and colour-co-ordinated with modern fitted wardrobes.

Breakfasts only are served in the attractive dining room with its pretty lace tablecloths. The spacious lounge overlooks the garden – both are available to guests. A fire is lit in the lounge on chilly days, and guests may enjoy a hot drink in the evening; it is a pleasant spot to unwind after a busy day of sightseeing. On fine days the sun lounge is a popular place to sit; it is also the only smoking area in the house. Mary Quinn is a delightful hostess who prides herself on personal service. She is pleased to advise on good local restaurants. The town centre is just a five-minute walk away.

OWNER Mrs Mary Quinn OPEN March – October ROOMS 2 double, 3 twin, 1 family; all en suite. TERMS €25.50; reduction for children; single supplement €6.50

Woodlawn
Galbally Road, Tipperary, Co. Tipperary
Tel: 062 51272
Email: Woodlawn_tipp@hotmail.com

This traditional-style house, with an English russet brick exterior, stands a good distance off the road in a quiet spot behind a large, landscaped garden. It was built as a family home 12 years ago, and when the two sons left home, the owners used the excess space for a bed & breakfast. It is beautifully maintained, has a tranquil ambience and the rooms to the rear of the house overlook horses grazing in the fields. The bedrooms are individually decorated with restful pastel colours and have plenty of wardrobe space. Nuala O'Sullivan is extremely hospitable, and goes out of her way to ensure her guests are well taken care of. Smoking allowed in lounge only. Excellent breakfasts are served and include a wide cereal choice and fresh fruit, followed by a traditional Irish breakfast. One and a half miles from Tipperary on the B662 Galbally Road.

OWNER Nuala O'Sullivan OPEN April – October ROOMS 2 double, 1 twin, 1 double/single; all en suite. TERMS €25; reduction for children; single supplement €6.50

COUNTY WESTMEATH
Centrally located, this county offers a peaceful and beautiful landscape, excellent fishing and lots of history.

The main attractions are its lakes. The four largest are Loughs Owel, Ennell, Derravaragh and Lene. Beautiful Lough Sheelin is farther north and there are a number of small lakes too, as well as Lough Ree, an expansion of the Shannon, which is now popular for sailing, cruising and coarse fishing. On many of the islands that dot the lakes are remains of early Christian churches.

Mullingar, the county town, is a thriving commercial centre and attractive market town. It is in one of the best cattle-raising districts of Ireland, and is also a great centre for hunting, shooting and fishing.

Athlone is the largest town in the country. Originally a fording point of the Shannon, Athlone is now a busy market town, major road and rail terminus, and harbour on the inland waterways system. Athlone Castle, now housing a museum dealing with local history, is a strongly fortified building with many interesting features. It has been a famous military post since its original construction in the thirteenth century.

Lough Derravaragh, one of the most beautiful in County Westmeath, is associated with the most tragic of Irish legends, when the Children of Lir were changed into swans by their jealous stepmother and spent 300 years on dark waters. Tullynally Castle is near Castlepollard. Seat of the Earls of Longford, the castle has a spectacular façade of turrets and towers. Fore is the most historic Christian site in Westmeath. There are several ruins to see, dating from the tenth century, among them St Fechin's Church, an unusual feature of which is the massive cross-inscribed lintel stone.

ATHLONE

Cluain-Innis
Summerhill, Galway Road, Athlone, Co. Westmeath
Tel: 0902 994202

Cluain-Innis is a friendly, cosy bungalow situated 4km from Athlone. The bedrooms are fresh and bright, prettily decorated and are all on the ground floor. Improvements are ongoing and TV and hairdryers have been added to the rooms. Kathleen is friendly and helpful, she enjoys having people stay, "a real home from home experience". The lounge is tastefully decorated with matching pink and red fabrics, attractive lights and wall lamps, and tea and coffee makers. Smoking is permitted in the lounge. Breakfast only is served but there is a good choice of restaurants and pubs in Athlone for evening meals. This is an ideal location for touring Clonmacnois and Deer Park. Fishing and golf are close by. Visa, Mastercard accepted. Situated in a cul de sac on the N6 Galway Road, 3 miles from Athlone town centre. Left hand side of the road 500 yards, at the end of the dual carriageway.

OWNER Kathleen Shaw OPEN April – October ROOMS 1 double, 1 twin, 1 family; 1 en suite. TERMS €21.50–24; reduction for children; single supplement €4

Shelmalier House
Cartrontroy, Athlone, Co. Westmeath
Tel: 0902 72145 Fax: 0902 73190
Email: shelmal@iol.ie

Shelmalier House is a spacious, modern house standing in its own grounds with an attractive front garden. The bedrooms, two of which are on the ground floor, are beautifully appointed, recently upgraded, and have firm, comfortable beds. This is very much a family-run establishment, with considerate hosts who extend a very personal service to ensure their guests' comfort. The TV lounge is spacious, and there is a sun porch where guests may help themselves to complimentary tea or coffee at any time. Smoking is allowed in lounge and bedrooms.

Jim and Nancy specialise in coarse fishing holidays, but a warm welcome is extended to all visitors. Evening meals are served with the emphasis on fresh food and home-baking, but they must be ordered in advance. There is an 18-hole golf course on the shores of Lough Ree, trail walks and a heated swimming pool within 10 minutes' walk. This is a delightful house with most hospitable hosts. All major credit cards are accepted. Situated on Retreat Road (Cartrontroy), sign-posted off R446 and R55.

OWNER Jim & Nancy Denby OPEN January 7 – December 20 ROOMS 3 double, 2 twin, 2 family; all en suite TERMS €25.50; reduction for children; single supplement €7.50

CASTLEPOLLARD

Whitehall Farm House
Castlepollard, Co. Westmeath
Tel: 044 61140

This creeper–covered, nineteenth-century farmhouse is approached up a private drive. It is set among mature trees and a garden, part of a working cattle, sheep and tillage farm. The house is furnished in keeping with its character and retains the original casement shutters. The bedrooms are warm and cosy with attractive bed linens and comfortable beds. There is a good-size TV lounge and a separate dining room where freshly prepared breakfasts and home-cooked, four-course evening meals are served. Abigail, a friendly, outgoing lady, has been running her bed & breakfast establishment for over eight years. Guests enjoy the special warmth and hospitality here and many folks are happy repeat visitors. Guests are welcome to wander around the farm and watch the animals. The ancient monastic village of Fore nearby contains an interesting seventh-century church. Traditional Irish music can be heard at local pubs and perhaps, too, some of the folklore tales of the area.

OWNER Donagh & Abigail Smyth OPEN April 1 – November 1 ROOMS 1 double, 2 twin; all en suite. TERMS €19–22; reduction for children 33%; single supplement €6.50 MEALS dinner

HORSELEAP

Woodlands Farm Guest House
Streamstown, nr. Horseleap, Mullingar, Co. Westmeath
Tel: 044 26414

This charming 200-year-old farmhouse, surrounded by ornamental trees, is part of a 50-hectare cattle farm, and is a marvellous spot for families. Mary Maxwell has created a wonderful, informal, welcoming atmosphere. Guests are encouraged to explore the farm and there are free pony rides for children. The bed-

rooms are spacious and there are lots of antique furnishings,
including a chaise-longue and a lovely dresser. Guests enjoy sitting around in the spacious lounge, which has a grand piano, and
musical evenings are encouraged. Smoking is permitted only in
the lounge. Four of the bedrooms are on the ground floor.
Breakfast and pre-arranged dinners are served in the very large
dining room; when possible, meals feature fresh, home-grown
produce. Vegetarians can be catered for with advance notice.
Take N4 from Dublin, onto N6 going west. At Horseleap turn
right at the filling station, watch for "Woodlands Farm" sign.

OWNER Mary Maxwell OPEN March 1 – October 1 ROOMS 2
double, 2 twin, 1 family, 1 single; 4 en suite. TERMS €25; reduction
for children; single supplement €8 MEALS dinner

MOATE

Cooleen
Moate, Co. Westmeath
Tel: 0902 81044

This well maintained, attractive bungalow with hanging baskets
and flower tubs is situated in a country setting of 0.5 hectares.
Ethna Kelly is a considerate host and guests are greeted with a
hot drink upon arrival. The good-sized rooms are tastefully
furnished and decorated, and have comfortable beds. Cooleen is
a non-smoking house. Breakfasts are excellent and include fresh,
home-baked scones, and are served in the lush conservatory on
warm days. There is a lounge where turf fires burn in the
evening. Bicycles are available and there are some lovely walks
winding past the bog. This is perfect for folks who are looking
for an informal, home-away-from-home atmosphere.
2km off N6 on Ballymore Road.

OWNER Ethna Kelly OPEN All year except for Christmas
ROOMS 1 double, 1 family; both en suite. TERMS €25.50;
reduction for children; single supplement €5.50

Temple Country House
Horseleap, Moate, Co. Westmeath
Tel: 0506 35118 Fax: 0506 35118
Email: templespa@spiders.ie

This lovely, 200-year-old country house sits in a secluded position amidst mature trees and gardens on a 57-hectare cattle farm. It was built on the site of a sixth-century monastery – hence the name. The house has been in the same family for three generations and is full of old-world charm; there are marble washstands and fireplaces, and brass beds. Bernadette is an excellent cook; dinners are served in the large dining room and feature tasty, healthy foods, fresh vegetables, local meats and delicious home-made desserts. After dinner, guests gather round the open fire in the lounge, often joined by Bernadette and Declan. A games room and a library were added in the mid-1990s.

Temple House is becoming well-known for its health and leisure facilities. Special packages are offered for individual or small groups in the "Temple Spa", with sauna, steamroom, beauty salon, yoga room, aromatherapy and reflexology. Guided walks are also organised. Fishing and golfing holidays at championship courses can also be arranged. Reservations should be made as far ahead as possible.

Temple House is a haven of peace and tranquillity, the food is excellent and Bernadette and Declan are the perfect hosts. Vegetarian and special diets can be catered for with advance notice. Visa, Mastercard accepted.

OWNER Declan & Bernadette Fagan OPEN January 15 – November 30 ROOMS 2 double, 4 twin, 1 family, 1 single, 5 new in courtyard; all en suite. TERMS €51–76; reduction for children; single supplement €19 MEALS dinner

MULLINGAR

Hilltop Country House
Delvin Road, Rathconnell, Mullingar, Co. Westmeath
Tel: 044 48958 Fax: 044 48013
Email: hilltopcountryhouse@eircom.net

This exceptionally well maintained, spacious, split-level house is approached by a private gravel drive. The house sits in an elevated position with views of Sheever Lough in the distance and the city at night. The house was specifically designed for bed & breakfast; the bedrooms are all large, with a high standard of décor, and have comfortable firm beds and TV. One of the bedrooms is on the ground floor and has its own entrance. New carpeting has been installed, and a conservatory has been added. Freshly prepared breakfasts are served in the bright dining room overlooking pretty countryside. Dympna and Sean are extremely hospital and helpful, and are happy to assist with itinerary planning. Hilltop has facilities for the angler, including a tackler with drying facilities. Boat hire can be arranged. Tea-makers are available in the hallway. There are several options in the area for evening meals. Access, Visa accepted.

OWNER Sean & Dympna Casey OPEN February 1 – November 30 ROOMS 2 double, 3 twin; all en suite. TERMS €28; single supplement €7.50

Keadeen
Irishtown, Mullingar, Co. Westmeath
Tel: 044 48440

There is a comfortable, easy-going atmosphere at this well maintained, extensively refurbished bungalow, situated in a peaceful location on the edge of town. To quote Madge Nolan, "I have never met a guest I didn't like," which could have something to do with her friendly and welcoming personality.

The bedrooms are spotlessly clean and are individually decorated in bright colours, with warm duvets and rich carpets. There is a TV lounge where smoking is permitted.

Breakfasts are served from 7 a.m. to 10:30 a.m. and consist of home-made marmalades, preserves and freshly baked bread. Dinners are no longer available, but Madge Nolan will be happy to recommend local establishments for evening meals. Local amenities include golf, swimming, fishing and boating. On the N4 from Dublin take third exit for Castlepollard, turn left, continue to mini roundabout, second exit, sign-posted from there.

OWNER Madge Nolan OPEN March - October ROOMS 1 double, 1 twin, 1 family; 2 en suite. TERMS €24; reduction for children; single supplement €2.50

Lough Owel Lodge
Cullion, Mullingar, Co. Westmeath
Tel: 044 48714 Fax: 044 48714

Lough Owel Lodge is a delightful country house approached by a long private drive. It has panoramic views of Lough Owel and the surrounding countryside. There are 20 hectares of fertile farmland, and the property extends down to the lake. Lough Owel is one of the best known trout lakes in Europe. Ghillie service is available, boat engines can be hired, and fuel supplied. The house is well maintained and appointed, and the spacious lounge overlooks the gardens and hard tennis court. There are

several interesting pieces of antique furniture about. The bedrooms are individually furnished; two have four-poster beds, and all rooms have had TV installed. Smoking is allowed in the lounge only. Special diets can be catered for if prearranged. Guests looking for the perfect place to unwind will be well satisfied with this charming house situated in this secluded, tranquil setting. Wind-surfing and golf are available close by.
Visa, Mastercard accepted. N4 north from Mullingar, sign-posted just before the road on left.

OWNER Martin & Aideen Ginnell OPEN March 1 – December 1 ROOMS 3 double, 1 twin, 1 family; all en suite. TERMS €25.50–29; reduction for children; single supplement €7.50 MEALS dinner

Mearescourt House
Rathconrath, Mullingar, Co. Westmeath
Tel: 044 55112 Fax: 044 55112

This Georgian House, part of a working farm, stands in a well maintained garden, 200 acres of land, with a private lake. The spacious en-suite bedrooms have TV and tea-making facilities, and are tastefully decorated and furnished with antiques. Although retaining its old world charm, the house has all modern amenities, skilfully combined, with many original features. The elegant drawing room has log fires, where guests can relax and enjoy a drink after a busy day. (The house has a wine license). Smoking is permitted in designated areas.

Breakfasts are served in the bright dining room, there is an excellent choice of starters on the buffet, and a freshly prepared cooked breakfast is also on offer. Eithne Pendred is a warm and informal host, guests feel very much at home in this comfortable and gracious house. There are some wonderful walks to be taken on the grounds, which is full of birds, squirrels and other wild life. Dinners are not served, but there is a wide choice of establishments for evening meals within a short drive. Golf, Angling, and Horse riding are all close by. Take the Bally Road for 9 miles, turn right at sign for Ballynacargy, left for Moyvore, house sign-posted from there.

OWNER Eithne Pendred OPEN All year except for Christmas.

ROOMS 4 double/twin; all en suite. TERMS €40.50; reduction for children; single supplement €12.50

Mornington House

Multyfarnham, Co. Westmeath
Tel: 044 72191 Fax: 044 72338
Email: info@mornington@ie
Website: www.mornington.ie

Mornington House, a gracious family home, was built in 1854 and extended in 1896. It is surrounded by beautiful trees – the Mornington Oak is over 200 years old. It is within easy walking distance of Lough Derravarragh – the Lake of the Oaks – one of the three lakes where the children of Lir spent 300 years of their 900-year exile. The grounds are inhabited by foxes, badgers, storks among a wealth of flora and fauna. The house is furnished with much of the original furniture and many family portraits, and retains the ambience of a bygone era, lovingly combined with all-modern comforts. Smoking is permitted only in the drawing room. Mornington is an oasis of peace and tranquillity, an ideal location in which to explore the Midlands and the surrounding scenic area; Dublin is within a 90-minute drive. The reception rooms have open log and turf fires.

Anne and Warwick are charming hosts; Anne is an excellent cook, and wonderful dinners are served by candlelight in the Victorian dining room, featuring fresh fruit, vegetables and herbs from the walled garden. Vegetarians can be catered for with advance notice. The bedrooms are large; two have brass beds. Children are welcome by arrangement. Canoes, boats and bicycles are available for hire. All major credit cards accepted. N4 from Mullingar bypass take R394 for 8km to Crookedwood, left at Wood Pub, 2km to first junction turn right; house is 1km on the right.

OWNER Warwick & Anne O'Hara OPEN April 1 – October 31
ROOMS 3 double, 1 twin, 1 single; 2 en suite. TERMS €50 sharing; reduction for children; single supplement €10 MEALS dinner

Northern Ireland

COUNTY ANTRIM

County Antrim's attractions are many. The city of Belfast lies on the shores of Belfast Lough, in a most attractive setting, surrounded by hills that can be seen from most parts of the city. It became a thriving commercial centre and port in the nine-teenth century, and now has a population of 300,000, about a quarter of the population of Northern Ireland. Among the many sights in Belfast are the grand City Hall, the ornate Crown Liquor Saloon, St Anne's Cathedral, W5 at the huge Odyssey complex and the Ulster Museum, which contains the treasures from the wreck of the Spanish Armada vessel, the 'Girona'.

The town of Antrim is set back from Lough Neagh, the largest expanse of inland water in the British Isles, and famous for its eels. The main fishery is in Toomebridge.

The Country Antrim stretch of coastline is among the most spectacular and scenic in Europe. Carrickfergus to the south, the oldest town in Ireland, is dominated by its castle. Farther north lies Larne, an important port, only a two-and-a-half hour ferry ride from Scotland. Beyond Larne, the coast road built in the 1830s affords breathtaking views of the coast and cliffs. Along this road, it is possible to see the formation of the earth's outer crust.

The coast road connects each of the nine famous Glens of Antrim: green valleys running down to the sea, with rivers, waterfalls, wildflowers and birds. From south to north they are: Glenarm, Glencloy, Glenariff, Glenballyeamon, Glenaan, Glencorp, Glendun, Glenshesk and Glentaisie, which are said to mean: glen of the army, glen of the hedges, ploughman's glen, Edwardstown glen, glen of the rush lights, glen of the slaughter, brown glen, sedgy glen, and Taisie's Glen (referring to the legendary princess of Rathlin Island).

The resort town of Ballycastle is famous for its "Oul Lammas Fair," which once lasted a week and now takes place over two hectic days at the end of August. Ballintoy, a pictur-esque, Mediterranean-looking fishing village, is one of the pretti-est towns on the coast. Beyond the town is one of the word's most amazing natural wonders, the Giant's Causeway. This is made up of a mass of basalt columns, altogether some 40,000, which are all tightly packed together, reaching heights of 12 m, and which disappear into the sea. They appear at Staffa Island on the Scottish coast, and there are many legends attached to this natural phenomenon.

AHOGHILL

Neelsgrove Farm

51 Carnearney Road, Ahoghill, Ballymena, Co. Antrim BT42 2PL
Tel: 028 2587 1225 Fax: 028 2587 8704
Email: msneely@btinternet.com
Website: www.neelsgrove.freeserve.co.uk

In a very rural location surrounded by farmland and an acre of garden, Neelsgrove Farm is a neat, well kept farmhouse with friendly owners. It offers simple, comfortable accommodation. One of the bedrooms is on the ground floor, and they all have TV and tea- and coffee-making facilities. It is convenient for the Glens of Antrim, and golf, fishing, forest and river walks are near-by. From Ahoghill take the B93 Randalstown road for one quarter mile, first road on right for two miles.

OWNER Margaret & Andrew Neely OPEN All year ROOMS 3 double/twins, 2 en suite. TERMS from £16; reductions for children MEALS evening/light meals

BALLINTOY

Whitepark House

Whitepark Bay, Ballintoy, Co. Antrim BT54 6NH
Tel: 028 2073 1482
Email: bob.isles@virgin.net
Website: www.whiteparkhouse.com

Just off the coast road between the Giant's Causeway and Carrick-a-Rede Rope Bridge, Whitepark is a most interesting house. Dating from the 18th century, with later additions, it used to own the beach. Now, across the road, there's a path that leads to lovely, sandy Whitepark beach. The central room of the house with a lovely bowed end is where breakfast is served, and guests like to gather around the fire in the long drawing room, which overlooks the gardens that surround the house. Of the three upstairs bedrooms, one is particularly large with windows all around, and they all share one large bathroom. The house is full of bits and pieces acquired from Sri Lanka, where Bob and Siobhan like to escape to in the winter. House is not suitable for children. No smoking in bedrooms, pets outside. Major credit cards accepted.

OWNER Bob & Siobhan Isles OPEN All year ROOMS 2 doubles, 1 twin, one public bathroom TERMS £25; single supplement £5

Colliers Hall

50 Cushendall Road Ballycastle, Co. Antrim BT54 6QR
Tel: 028 20762531

This eighteenth century pebble-dashed farmhouse lies just off the main road 3 kilometres south of Ballycastle. The bedrooms are spacious, with the washbasins cleverly incorporated into marble washstands, and all have tea- and coffee-making facilities and hairdryers. The house is furnished with a mixture of traditional and antique furniture, and one room has a four-poster bed. The large TV lounge has an original marble fireplace, and dinner, if booked in advance, is served in the dining room. Recently opened is the hostel, a renovated barn, offering simple, bright small rooms, all en suite, with an upstairs lounge/kitchen. These rooms are available for bed & breakfast guests at the bargain price of 15 per person There are lovely walks through the woods, with views of the Knocklayde Mountains and Glenshesk Valley. An 18 hole golf course is close by, and it is 3 kilometres to the ferry terminal serving Ballycastle to Campbelltown in Scotland. Colliers Hall offers comfort, excellent value and a warm atmosphere. No pets, smoking in TV lounge only. Visa and Mastercard accepted.

OWNER Gerard & Maureen McCarry OPEN April – October ROOMS 3 double or twin; all en suite. TERMS £20; single supplement £5; reductions for children MEALS dinner £12.50

Kitchen Bar B&B

16-18 Victoria Square, Belfast BT1 4QA
Tel: 028 9032 4901

Since 1850 this centre of the city atmospheric pub has been in the Catney family. A very popular lunchtime venue, it is also known for its traditional music nights. Recently the upstairs bed-rooms, which had been dormant for years, were converted into updated sleeping accommodation. The rooms are enormous, with a bedroom area at one end, a sitting area, and fully equipped kitchen, including even a washing machine. For just over £20 per person, this is incredible value. Breakfast, served in the bar, can be substituted for dinner, if preferred.

OWNER Pat Catney OPEN All year. ROOMS 6 double/twin. TERMS £22.50; single supplement £5; MEALS lunch & dinner

Roseleigh House
19 Rosetta Park Belfast BT6 ODL
Tel: 028 90 644414 Fax: 028 90 64298
Email: roseleighhouse@ukonline.co.uk

This restored Victorian-style, brick-built house is surrounded by
a small garden. It is in a residential area of south Belfast,
conveniently located for bus routes leading into the city centre.
Roseleigh House was taken over by Helen Hunter, who is a
friendly, competent lady, in 1999, and starting with the bedrooms,
is in the process of refurbishing the property. The bedrooms all
have TV, hairdryer and tea- and coffee-making facilities. A laundry
service is available, and both lunch and dinner are served if
arranged in advance. No pets. There is a car park to the rear of
the house. Major credit cards accepted.

OWNER Helen Hunter OPEN All year ROOMS 3 double, 2 twin,
1 family, 2 single, all en suite. TERMS from £27 MEALS lunch,
dinner

Greenwood Guest House
25 Park Road Belfast BT7 2FW
Tel: 028 9020 2525 Fax: 028 9020 2530
Email: info@greenwoodguesthouse.com
Website: www.greenwoodguesthouse.com

Run by a friendly, young couple with two small children,
Greenwood is a modest Victorian terraced house overlooking
Ormeau Park. The rooms are simply and stylishly furnished, and
there is a pleasant lounge and bright breakfast room, where an
interesting menu is offered. Greenwood is well placed for the
centre of Belfast, and offers an informal atmosphere with very
helpful owners.

OWNER Jason & Mary Harris OPEN All year ROOMS 7 doubles
or twins; all en suite. TERMS £27.50; single supplement £10

Oakdene Lodge
16 Annadale Avenue Belfast BT7 3JH
Tel: 028 9049 2626 Fax: 028 9049 2070
Email: booking@oakdenelodge.com
Website: www.oakdenelodge.com

This substantial detached Victorian house is located two and a
half miles from the city centre, and is popular with business
visitors. It offers good, simple accommodation without a lot of

atmosphere. Peter Stephens, who runs Oakdene efficiently, took over the business from his father six years ago. Five of the bedrooms are in the original part of the house, which has high ceilings, old fireplaces and tiny bathrooms, and the remaining 12 rooms are in the newer additions. One of these rooms is suitable for wheelchairs. There is a smoking and non-smoking lounge as well as breakfast room. Major credit cards are accepted.

OWNER Peter Stephens OPEN All year ROOMS 17 doubles or twins all en suite. TERMS £27.50; single supplement £11

Tara Lodge
36 Cromwell Road, Belfast BT7 1JW
Tel: 028 90590900 Fax: 028 9059 0901
Email: info@taralodge.com
Website: www.taralodge.com

A purpose-built, small hotel/guest house, Tara Lodge was opened in 1998. It is situated on a quiet residential street, close to the University and within easy access of the city centre. It offers well planned, functional, bright bedrooms, simply and attractively furnished with all amenities including hairdryers, trouser presses, telephones, TV and tea- and coffee-making facilities. One bedroom is suitable for disabled guests. There is a small TV lounge on the first floor and a quite extensive dining room, where breakfast, lunch and dinner are available. There is a large off-street parking area. Tara Lodge is particularly suited to business people. No pets. Some designated smoking rooms. Most major credit cards accepted.

OWNER Conor O'Donnell OPEN All year except for Christmas ROOMS 19 double/twin/single/family; all en suite. TERMS £29–39; single supplement £15–25 MEALS lunch £5–6, dinner £14–19

BELFAST BT9

Ash-Rowan Town House
12 Windsor Avenue, Belfast BT9 6EE
Tel: 02890 661758 Fax: 02890 663227
Email: ashrowan@hotmail.com

This late Victorian house stands in its own garden in a quiet, tree-lined avenue in south Belfast, and was one time the home of Thomas Andrews, the designer of the 'Titanic'. He left from here for the ship's maiden voyage. Ash-Rowan is a most attractive house of character, with some original fireplaces, interesting colours and furnishings, antiques and all kinds of knick-knacks. It is a cosy place with a friendly atmosphere, and Sam and Evelyn have thought of just about everything for their guests, combining all the facilities of a hotel with personal service at a reasonable price. There are flowers and newspapers, and a laundry service is available. The bedrooms all have TV, hairdryers, trouser presses, information packs, bathrobes, linen sheets and tea- and coffee-making facilities. A popular place to sit is the new conservatory, and Ash-Rowan's renowned breakfasts, which include freshly squeezed orange juice and home baked bread are served in the breakfast room. Pets in cars only. Visa and Mastercard accepted, and there is secure off street parking. The house is ten minutes from the city centre and five minutes from the M1 and M2, and is found between the Malone and Lisburn Roads.

OWNER Evelyn & Sam Hazlett OPEN All year except for Christmas ROOMS 5 double, twin, single; all en suite. TERMS £36 43

Avenue House
23 Eglantine Avenue, Lisburn Road, Belfast, Co. Antrim BT9 6DW
Tel: 028 9066 5904 Fax: 028 9029 1810
Email: stephe.kelly6@ntlworld.com

This late Victorian terraced brick built house, which stands on a fairly busy residential tree lined street has been totally renovated. The rooms are spacious and light and furnished with elegant simplicity. The bedrooms vary in size and all have TV, telephones, hairdryers, trouser presses and tea- and coffee-making facilities. Both the breakfast room and drawing room have their attractive, original marble fireplaces, and the rooms are separated from each other by a pull-up wall. No pets, smoking restricted to some areas. Avenue House is located between the Malone and Lisburn roads. It is conveniently placed for the University and centre of town, which can easily be reached by bus.

OWNER Stephen Kelly OPEN All year ROOMS 2 double, 2 twin, 1 family; all en suite. TERMS £22.50; single supplement £12.50 MEALS dinner £20

Camera House
44 Wellington Park Belfast BT9 6DP Co. Antrim
Tel: 028 9066 0026 Fax: 028 9066 7856
Email: malonedrumm@hotmail.com

Paul Drumm took over this attractive Victorian townhouse from his aunt five years ago. It is very charmingly and simply furnished in muted tones with pretty pottery in the dining room. Camera House is on a quiet tree-lined street close to Queen's University and within easy range of the centre of Belfast. No pets, smoking in bedrooms only. Major credit cards accepted.

OWNER Paul Drumm & Caroline Malone Drumm OPEN All year
ROOMS 12 – double/twin/single/triple; 2 en suite. TERMS £24

The Old Rectory
148 Malone Road Belfast Co. Antrim BT9 5LH
Tel: 028 9066 7882 Fax: 028 9068 375
Email: info@anoldrectory.co.uk

When the Old Rectory was built in 1896, it was out in the
countryside. Now it is within a comfortable distance of the city
centre – three kilometres – and still has views of the Belfast
mountains. It was designed by the architect Henry Seaver, who
was also responsible for the neighbouring Church of St John's
(he was the brother of the then minister, Rev. Richard Seaver).
Later in life it became a nursing home, before becoming the
family home of the Callans. It is furnished and decorated with
individual taste and has some interesting pieces whilst retaining
the feel of a family home. Books and newspapers can be found in
the sitting room, and a complimentary "hot Irish whiskey" is
served each evening. The bedrooms each have TV, hairdryer,
trouser press and tea- and coffee-making facilities. Guests have
use of a croquet lawn. Malone Road is one of the principal
streets leading into the centre of town and is right on the bus
route. Pets in cars only, smoking permitted on front porch.

OWNER Mary Callan OPEN All year except for Christmas
ROOMS 5 double/twin/family/single; 3 en suite, 2 private
bathrooms. TERMS £25–30; single supplement £11; reductions for
children

BROUGHSHANE

Dunaird House
15 Buckna Road Broughshane Co. Antrim BT42 4NJ
Tel: 02825 862117

Built in 1920, this substantial house stands just outside
Broughshane. The Grahams bought the house, partly to do bed
and breakfast, and partly because 20 hectares went with the
house, which extended John Graham's existing farm. The house
provides luxury accommodation, with carpets and wallpapers of
all types and varieties. Some of the rooms have their original
fireplaces, and two of the bedrooms are front facing with lots of
windows and lovely views. All rooms have telephones, TV,
hairdryers and tea- and coffee-making facilities. John and Sylvia
are a friendly young couple who do everything they can to make
their guests' stay comfortable.

OWNER John & Sylvia Graham OPEN All year. ROOMS 2 double,
1 twin; all en suite. TERMS £22.50; single supplement £7.50;
reductions for children

Craig Park

Bushmills Co. Antrim BT57 8YF
Tel: 028207 32496 Fax: 028207 32479
Email: jan@craigpark.co.uk
Website: www.craigpark.co.uk

Craig Park, situated in open countryside, has views of the
Donegal and Antrim hills, and is three kilometres inland from
Bushmills. The original house has had a new piece added to it,
built in the Georgian style, giving it an imposing look. This new
part of the house accommodates the guests with three good
sized bedrooms, a large sitting room and a dining room, where
breakfast only is served. There are great walks, cycling and golf,
and the Giant's Causeway is nearby. Visa and Mastercard accepted.

OWNER Jan Cheal OPEN All year except for Christmas ROOMS
1 double, 1 twin, 1 family, all en suite. TERMS £27.50; single
supplement £7.50

Killen's Restaurant

28 Ballyclough Road, Bushmills, Co. Antrim BT57 8UZ
Tel: 028207 41536 Fax: 028 2074 1070
Email: peter@killens.com
Website: www.killens.com

Once an old schoolhouse, the building was extended and
recently refurbished, and it has pleasant views. The bedrooms are
light and attractively decorated in bright colours, with refitted en
suite bathrooms. All the rooms have TV, hairdryers and tea- and
coffee-making facilities, and one is a suite with a four poster bed
and jacuzzi bath. Families are very welcome and there is a
children's play area. There's also an indoor swimming pool, sauna,
sun bed and sun lounge. Peter Lafferty, who's from Scotland and
is an award winning chef, runs the restaurant, featuring local,
international and vegetarian cuisines. Killen's is close to the scenic Antrim coast and the Bushmills Distillery. No smoking in the
restaurant. All major credit cards accepted

OWNER Peter Lafferty OPEN All year except for Christmas.
ROOMS 5 double, 1 suite; all en suite. TERMS £25; single supplement £10; reductions for children. MEALS dinner from £12

Valley View

6a Ballyclough Road, Bushmills, Co. Antrim BT57 8TU
Tel: 028 207 41608 Fax: 028 207 42739
Email: valerie.mcfall@btinternet.com
Website: www.irish-bnb.com/valleyview

This whitewashed, modern house was built by the McFalls and extended recently to provide more guest accommodation. It is surrounded by its own 24 hectares of farmland, supporting beef and sheep, and is six kilometres inland from Bushmills. Mrs. McFall is a cheerful, friendly host with young children, and is welcoming to families; there is a children's play area. The accommodation is simple and bright. Guests have use of a comfortable sitting room and breakfast only is served at separate tables in the dining room. One room is suitable for the disabled, and they all have TV, hairdryers and tea- and coffee-making facilities. The attractions of the north Antrim coast are within easy reach, including the Giant's Causeway, Carrick-A-Rede Rope Bridge, Bushmills Distillery, Dunluce Castle and Rathlin Island. There is a large self catering unit sleeping 8 people. Pets OK in cars. No smoking. Visa and Access accepted. Valley View is sign-posted off the B67 and B17.

OWNER Mrs. Valerie McFall. OPEN All year except for Christmas
ROOMS 3 double, 2 family, 2 twin; all en suite. TERMS £20; single supplement £5; reductions for children

CRUMLIN

Caldhame Lodge

102 Moira Road, Nutts Corner, Crumlin, Co. Antrim BT29 4HG
Tel: 028 94 423099 Fax: 028 94 423099
Email: info@caldhamelodge.co.uk
Website: www.caldhamelodge.co.uk

Caldhame Lodge is just off the main Moira Road, in its own grounds and just five minutes from the airport. It was built in the early 1990s as the McKavanaghs' family home. Since then it has been adapted to accommodate guests and is comfortable, very well furnished with new furniture, and is meticulously maintained. The rooms have every possible amenity, some bedrooms have jacuzzi baths and four poster beds and one room has a steam/sauna room. The bedrooms all have hairdryers, trouser presses, telephones and irons. Breakfast and evening meals by arrangement are served in the dining room/sun lounge, and guests have use of two further lounges, one with TV. Anne Kavanagh runs a very professional business-like establishment and has won accolades for being the best guest house. Pets can be accommodated in the garage, one room is allocated for smoking. Major credit cards accepted. Caldhame Lodge can be found on the A26 ten and a half miles from Junction 9 on the M1.

OWNER Anne McKavanagh OPEN All year ROOMS 2 double, 2 twin, 2 family; all en suite. TERMS £22.50; single supplement £7.50; reductions for children MEALS dinner from 12

Keef Halla
20 Tully Road, Nutts Corner, Crumlin, Co. Antrim BT29 4SW
Tel: 028 9082 5491 Fax: 028 9082 5940
Email: info@keefhalla.com
Website: www.keefhalla.com

Keef Halla, meaning 'welcome' in Arabic, acquired its name because Charles Kelly used to work in Saudi Arabia and bought the house with the money he earned there. It is an old country house that has been renovated and recently extended. Charles Kelly, who runs the guest house (Siobhan is a teacher in Belfast), has earned a reputation for the level of comfort and service he provides – borne out by being awarded accolades for the best guest house. The bedrooms all have telephones, hairdryers, trouser presses, TV and tea and coffee-making facilities. The comfortable sitting room has an open fire, leather sofa and chairs, and leads into the dining room, where meals are available all day long if arranged in advance. Packed lunches can also be provided. One guest arriving by helicopter landed in the garden, and Keef Halla claims to be the nearest guest house to the airport. A free email service is available. Pets can be accommodated in outbuildings. Some rooms are available for smokers. Major credit cards accepted. The house stands just off the main A26 road, five minutes from Belfast International Airport.

OWNER Mr & Mrs Charles Kelly OPEN All year ROOMS 2 doubles, 5 family; all en suite. TERMS £25; single supplement £15; reductions for children. MEALS lunch £5–8, dinner £10–15

CUSHENDALL

Glendale Bed & Breakfast
46 Coast Road, Cushendall, Co. Antrim BT44 ORX
Tel: 028 2177 1495

This attractive white, pebble dashed house is down a private driveway off the main A2 road in the village of Cushendall. It enjoys lovely views of the Antrim plateau and sea. The O'Neills are friendly and welcoming hosts, attracting a lot of repeat visitors. Mr. O'Neill works on the Larne – Cairnryan ferry, and enjoys outlining sightseeing itineraries for guests. The house is well maintained and comfortably furnished and the bedrooms have hairdryers and tea- and coffee-making facilities. Glendale is within walking distance of the beach and golf course. Visa, Eurocard and Mastercard accepted.

OWNER Mrs. Mary O'Neill OPEN All year ROOMS 1 double, 5 family; all en suite. TERMS £17; reductions for children

CUSHENDUN

The Villa Farmhouse
185 Torr Road, Cushendun, Co. Antrim BT44 0PU
Tel: 028 2176 1252 Fax: 028 2176 1252

Catherine Scally is in her nineties and has lived at the Villa since she married, opening her bed and breakfast business some 40 years ago. Now she is ably assisted by Maggie, who does everything, including the provision and supervision of not only breakfast, but lunch, afternoon tea and dinner. The house is situated way up above the delightful little village of Cushendun, which is owned by the National Trust and contains the smallest pub in Ireland. It has fantastic views of the spectacular coastline, the sea, and is on the Ulster Way. Both house and garden are immaculately kept and guests have use of a charming sitting room full of photographs. This arrangement of family photos and the home was featured in the Australian TV show "Good Morning Australia". The bedrooms have tea- and coffee-making facilities, two have sea views, and the other has views of the hills behind. For the infirm there is a chair lift, and the Coach House is available for self catering. Pets by arrangement. From Cushendun take Torr Road, at T-junction turn right, after half a mile the Villa is the third road on the left.

OWNER Catherine Scally OPEN February – October. ROOMS 1 family, 1 single, 1 double; all en suite. TERMS £18–20; single supplement £2–4; reductions for children MEALS lunch, afternoon tea, dinner

MUCKAMORE

The Beeches Country House
10 Dunadry Road Muckamore Co. Antrim BT41 2RR
Tel: 028 9443 3161 Fax: 028 9443 2227
Email: reception@thebeeches.org
Website: www.thebeeches.org

This Edwardian country house stands in a large, pleasant garden just off the A6 between Templepatrick and Antrim and only eight kilometres from Belfast airport. The Allens, a very friendly couple, offer comfortable accommodation and hold a Taste of

Ulster cooking award. The bedrooms have every possible amenity, including hairdryers, trouser presses, telephones, TV, irons and ironing boards and tea- and coffee-making facilities. There is a snack menu and evening meals are available if booked in advance. Pets OK in cars, no smoking. Visa, Access, Mastercard and American Express accepted. The Beeches is one mile from the Hilton Hotel and golf course.

OWNER Mrs Marigold Allen OPEN All year ROOMS 3 double, 2 single; all en suite. TERMS £30; single supplement £5 reductions for children. MEALS snack menu, dinner £15

PORTRUSH

Glenkeen Guest House
59 Coleraine Road Portrush Co. Antrim BT56 8HR
Tel: 028 7082 2279
Email: glenkeen@btinternet.com

Glenkeen is a well maintained, clean guest house located on the edge of Portrush. It is set back a little, by its car park, from the busy main A29 road. Mrs. Little is a friendly and efficient lady who has been in the bed & breakfast business for a number of years, and is most particular about keeping the house in good decorative order. The large comfortable rooms have TV, telephone and tea- and coffee-making facilities. Breakfast is served in the dining room, and the pleasant sitting room has comfortable chairs and sofas. There is a chair lift on the stairs for infirm or disabled guests. Some bedrooms are non-smoking. Pets outside only. Visa and Mastercard accepted.

OWNER Mrs. Roberta Little. OPEN All year ROOMS 10 double/twin, all en suite. TERMS £22; single supplement £5–7; reductions for children

Maddybenny Farm House

18 Maddybenny Park, Longuestown Road Portrush Co. Antrim
BT52 2PT
Tel: 028 7082 3394 Fax: 028 7082 3394
Email: accommodation@maddybenny22.freeserve.co.uk
Website: www.maddybenny.freeserve.co.uk

Maddybenny Farm, meaning "sanctified or holy post", dates from
the 1600s. It was built as a plantation house on lands belonging
to the Earl of Antrim. The first Presbyterian minister, Rev. Gabriel
Cornwall, lived here. Added on to over the years, the house
floor plan is unusual in allowing one to walk completely around
the house from the inside. It is approached up a long track and
stands in a wonderful, rural location. It is part of a big complex
of buildings consisting of the farm, stables and six self catering
cottages. The riding school is run by Rosemary White's son, and
offers tuition to guests by an international rider. Maddybenny
Farm is a comfortable, relaxed place. It is a bright and spacious
house with a comfortable drawing room, games room and dining
room where breakfast only is served. The bedrooms are very
large, and have hairdryers, TV and tea- and coffee-making
facilities. There is a fridge for guests' use and laundry facilities.
Rosemary White is a marvellous host with a wonderful sense of
humour. Her breakfasts are copious and include home baking
and fresh trout. Maddybenny is very near the Royal Portrush
Golf Club, the Giant's Causeway, the University and beaches. The
self catering cottages are equipped to a high standard and sleep
six to eight people. Pets OK in cars, no smoking in the dining
room. Visa and Mastercard accepted. The farm is sign-posted on
the A29 Portrush to Coleraine road.

OWNER Rosemary White OPEN All year except for Christmas
ROOMS 1 double, 1 twin, 1 family; all en suite. TERMS £25–27.50;
single supplement £5–10; reductions for children

The Moat Inn
Donegore Hill Templepatrick Co. Antrim BT41 2HW
Tel: 028 9443 3659 Fax: 028 9443 3726
Email: themoatinn@talk21.com

Set in pretty countryside with pleasant rural views this old coaching inn is located in an improbable position (for a coaching inn) on the side of a hill away from any urban centre. Yet this building dating from 1740, part of the Earls of Donegal estates, has been a farmhouse, a coaching inn and a public house. The Thompsons have done an incredible job renovating this very interesting house. They are both musicians and are a delightful, interesting young couple. The house has some unique features, like the original wood ceiling on the upper floor, which is exposed in one of the bedrooms, and the high bannisters around the top of the stairs. The rooms are furnished with a lot of thought, and as a family home. The dining room has an old French dining table, there's a cosy sitting room dominated by a grand piano, and the upstairs library has a built in organ. The Moat Inn is cosy and friendly, has a great atmosphere and offers excellent food. It is only a twenty minute drive into central Belfast and closer still to the airport. Free airport transfers are provided. No pets, no smoking in the bedrooms. Visa and Mastercard are accepted. It is wise to get directions to the property.

OWNER Rachel Thompson OPEN All year ROOMS 3 doubles or twins; all en suite. TERMS £30 MEALS dinner £18

COUNTY ARMAGH

County Armagh is the smallest and most varied county in Northern Ireland, ranging from magnificent mountain scenery in the south to rich fruit-growing land in the north, interspersed with small lakes and dairy farms.

Armagh, the ancient capital of Ulster and former great centre of learning, has been the spiritual capital of Ireland for 1,500 years and is the seat of both Catholic and Protestant archbishops. The two cathedral churches are prominent features in the city. The Church of Ireland cathedral stands on the hill where St Patrick built his stone church, and the twin spires of the Catholic cathedral, which was finished in 1873, rise from the opposite hill.

In the south of Armagh the mountains of Slieve Gullion contain an unspoilt area of small villages and beautiful scenery. Crossmaglen has the largest market square in Europe and has become the centre of the recently revived lace-making industry.

There is an enormous open-air market every Sunday at Jonesborough.

Whilst driving down a country lane, you might come across the great Armagh game; roads bowls, which is shared with County Cork. The object is to hurl a metal bowl weighing 1 kg as far as possible, covering several miles in the shortest number of shots. Children are sent ahead to warn motorists.

The orchard of Ireland, rich, fruit-growing country in the northeast, is at its best in May. Apple Blossom Sunday takes place in late May.

ARMAGH

Hillview Lodge
33 Newtownhamilton Road, Armagh, Co. Armagh BT60 2PL
Tel: 028 3752 2000 Fax: 028 3752 8276
Email: alice@hillviewlodge.com
Website: www.hillviewlodge.com

Hillview is a modern building about two kilometres outside Armagh, set just back from the road beside a golf driving range, which is under the same ownership. The accommodation is functional and well designed, and the entire house has plain wood-type floors, without any rugs. The bedrooms all have hairdryers, telephones, TV and tea and coffee making facilities. One ground floor room is suitable for the disabled. The dining room, where breakfast only is served, has a sitting area, and there is a further place to sit in the entrance/reception room. Hillview is well suited to business people, or those who want to practise their golf swing. The driving range is floodlit for night use. Pets in owners' cars and smoking is permitted in the conservatory. Visa, Mastercard, Delta and Switch are accepted. Hillview is located on the B31 Newtownhamilton road.

OWNER Mr & Mrs McBridge OPEN All year. ROOMS 1 double, 1 single, 1 twin, 1 triple, 2 family; all en suite. TERMS £25; single supplement £5; reductions for children

Padua House
63 Cathedral Road, Armagh, Co. Armagh BT61 7QX
Tel: 028 3752 2039 0r 028 3752 8888 Fax: 028 3752 3584

Guests are made to feel like part of the family at Padua House. Mr. And Mrs. O'Hagan are a friendly, welcoming couple who thoroughly enjoy their visitors. The family lounge is shared with guests, who are encouraged to join the owners after a busy day's touring. Tea and scones are offered on arrival, a hot drink is almost always available, and the O'Hagans are always happy to assist guests with itineraries and recommendations on places to eat. The house has a lived in family feel to it and a collection of dolls line the staircase. The accommodation is clean and basic, and all bedrooms have a TV, hairdryer and iron. A hearty breakfast is served in the dining room. No pets, smoking permitted in the TV lounge and dining room. Padua House is located within 100 metres of St Patrick's Cathedral.

OWNER Mrs Kathleen O'Hagan OPEN Mid-January – 30 November. ROOMS 1 twin, 1 family; one public bathroom. TERMS £15; reductions for children

RICHILL

Ballinahinch House
Richill, Armagh, Co. Armagh
Tel: 02838 870081 Fax: 02838 870081
Email: ballinahinchhouse@bigfoot.com
Website: www.ballinahinchhouse.com

This early Victorian house is part of a working arable and beef farm of 50 hectares. It has an informal, welcoming atmosphere and Elizabeth Kee is a delightful host. The rooms are spacious and traditionally furnished, the bedrooms comfortable, all with TV and hairdryers, and the dining room has its original black slate fireplace. There is half a hectare of newly landscaped gardens in front of the house, and the setting is peaceful with lovely walks close by. No pets and no smoking. To reach Ballinahinch House, turn off the A3 onto the B131, take the second road on the left and continue over the crossroads – the house is approximately one and a half kilometres down on the left.

OWNER Elizabeth Kee OPEN April 1 – September 1 ROOMS 4 double, twin, single, family; all en suite. TERMS from £18; single supplement; reductions for children MEALS by request

COUNTY DERRY
Derry (or Londonderry) is probably best known for the tune "Derry Air," also known as "Danny Boy." The city of Derry is situated on a hill on the banks of the Foyle. The city acquired the name Londonderry in the seventeenth century when the City of London financed building and resettlement in the city. The seventeenth-century walls, about 1.5-km-round and 5.5-m-thick, have withstood several sieges and are still intact, giving magnificent views of the surrounding countryside. Derry still preserves its ancient layout, and amongst the historic buildings is the 1633 Gothic Cathedral of St Columb.

From the quay behind the Guildhall, hundreds of Irish emigrants left Derry for America during the eighteenth and nineteenth centuries, amongst them the families and ancestors of Davy Crockett and US President James Polk.

The Mussenden Temple, built by the eccentric Earl Bishop of Derry as testimony of his affection for Lady Mussenden, stands on a windswept headland on the coast at Downhill; adjacent, the castle is now in ruins but exudes an aura of romance and grandeur, and is worth visiting.

One of Ulster's finest fortified farmhouses can be seen at Bellaghy, and whiskey is produced at Bushmills near Coleraine, the town which St Patrick is supposed to have founded.

AGHADOWEY

Greenhill House
24 Greenhill Road, Aghadowey, Coleraine, Co. Derry BT51 4EU
Tel: 028 70 868241 Fax: 01265 868365
Email: greenhill@btinternet.com

A nice old Georgian house standing in its own grounds of trees, lawns and shrubs, with lovely views over farmland to distant hills. This is a 60-hectare arable and beef farm and the Hegartys have owned the property for about 17 years. Accommodation has been upgraded, with new furniture, beds and carpets; two of the bathrooms now have baths and showers, and are well-appointed with every convenience. Smoking is only permitted in designated bedrooms.

Mrs Hegarty, formerly a teacher, now devotes her time to running her successful bed and breakfast; she is a most friendly and cheerful lady. There is a spacious lounge which overlooks the fields, and a marble fireplace where fires burn brightly on chilly evenings. Breakfasts are served at separate tables, and there are many venues nearby which serve evening meals. Greenhill House is the recipient of several awards, including the Taste of Ulster and British Airways Awards. Take the A29 from Coleraine to

Garvagh for seven miles, left of B66 (Greenhill Road) towards
Ballymoney for short distance; Greenhill is signed on the right.
Visa, Delta, Mastercard accepted.

OWNER Mrs Elizabeth Hegarty OPEN March 1 – October 31
ROOMS 2 double, 2 twin, 2 family; all en suite. TERMS £25;
reduction for children; single supplement £5

CASTLEROE

Camus House
27 Curragh Road, Castleroe, nr. Coleraine, Co. Derry
Tel: 028 70 342982

Camus House was built on the site of an old monastery, and is a
listed building, dating from 1685, the oldest house in the area.
The house is in a delightful setting, close to the River Bann, and
Mrs King owns 2km of river frontage. This lovely old ivy-covered
house is approached by a private driveway through park-like
grounds, and has a pretty front garden. Mrs King is a most
friendly and accommodating lady who runs a warm and comfortable bed & breakfast, and is also a member of the "Healthy
Eating Circle Galtee Breakfast Awards." Her passion is fishing,
and this is a great fishing family; her daughter has represented
Ireland.

The house has lots of character and is comfortably furnished as
a family home. In winter, guests use Mrs King's cosy sitting room,
which has an open fire. There is another sitting room, and a
dining room where breakfasts only are served. Not suitable for
children. Smoking is permitted in bedrooms. Telephone for
directions to the house.

OWNER Josephine King OPEN All year ROOMS 1 double, 1
family, 1 single; 1 en suite. TERMS £20; single supplement £5
MEALS packed lunches

COLERAINE

Killeague Lodge
157 Drumcroon Road, Coleraine, Co. Derry BT51 3SG
Tel: 028 70 868229

Margaret Moore previously ran her bed & breakfast from the
farm, which is now lived in by her son. Guests are still welcome
to wander around the farm, but the accommodations are now in
a beautiful new property built on the land. Two of the luxurious
bedrooms are on the ground floor and they are all very tastefully decorated: one has a semicircular wall, old pine furniture and a
pastel lemon décor; another has mahogany furniture and pine
décor; the third large upstairs room is blue, with rich mahogany

furnishings. There is a sun lounge and two other lounges for guests' use. Breakfast is a banquet, served on Royal Albert China, in the elegant dining room, and features, fresh fruit, yoghurts, juice, warm scones, home made preserves, home baked bread, and for those with a large appetite a full traditional Irish breakfast follows.

Margaret is the proud recipient of the "hospitality award winner" Bedrooms have TV. radio and tea makers. Margaret's motto "Good food, fun and fellowship". Children are welcome. The house is non-smoking. Horse-riding can be arranged. Killeague Lodge is within 30 minutes of Giants Causeway and the North Antrim Coast. From Coleraine, take A29 south to Garvagh and Cookstown, House is approximately 5 miles on this road on the left.

OWNER Margaret Moore OPEN All year ROOMS I double, I twin, I family; all en suite. TERMS £20; reduction for children; single supplement £3 MEALS dinner, packed lunches

DERRY

The Merchant House
16 Queen Street, Derry, Co. Derry BT48 7EQ
Tel: 028 71 269691 or 264223 Fax: 028 71 266913

This listed Georgian townhouse, situated in a conservation area, was awarded a Gulbenkian/Civic Trust Award for Restoration, and is within walking distance of most amenities. It has an interesting history; it was built originally for a wealthy merchant, and has been used as a bank and a rectory. There are five good size bedrooms, furnished with period furniture, rich white bedspreads, TV, books, and tea makers. Several original features remain, such as polished wood floors, ceiling coving, and a marble fireplace. An elegant drawing room is available to guests. Breakfasts only are served, and special diets can be catered for. There are several establishments for evening meals within walking distance. Non-smokers are preferred. Spanish is spoken, and off street parking can be requested. Visa, Mastercard accepted.

OWNER Joan and Dr Peter Pyne OPEN All year ROOMS 5 double/twin; I en suite. TERMS from £19; reduction for children; single supplement £3

The Saddler's House
36 Great James Street, Derry, Co. Derry BT48 7DB
Tel: 028 71 269691 or 264223 Fax: 028 71 266913
Email: saddlershouse@btinternet.com

A tastefully restored, and immaculately maintained, 19th-century property townhouse, situated in a conservation area in the heart of Derry. It is the most centrally located bed and breakfast in the city, and is within walking distance of restaurants, shops and most amenities. The bedrooms, 3 of which are en-suite, are furnished with period furniture, all have TV, tea makers and books, and overlook a walled garden. Two are ground floor rooms, one of which is a twin en-suite. Breakfasts are plentiful, with fresh brewed coffee, home-made preserves and marmalade, and a cooked variety, served at separate tables on pretty blue china, in the cosy dining-room. Special diets can be catered for at breakfast. A sitting room is available for guests, and guests are welcome to use the garden. This is popular venue, and early reservations are recommended. Non-smokers are preferred. Spanish is spoken. Off street parking is available. Visa and Mastercard accepted.

OWNER Joan Pyne OPEN All year ROOMS 7 double/twin; 3 en suite. TERMS from £23; single supplement £5

EGLINTON

Longfield Farm
132 Clooney Road, Eglinton, Co. Derry BT47 3DX
Tel: 028 71 810210

This spacious old house stands in a pleasant garden with lawn and shrubs. Improvements have been ongoing, and en suite facilities added to one of the bedrooms The farmyard, which serves the 80-hectare farm of potatoes, beef and cereals, is to the back of the house. It is a comfortable family home with a lived-in feeling. A cosy smaller lounge with open fire is used in winter; in summer, the large lounge is preferred. The bedrooms are of a good size, and breakfasts only are served in the dining room.

OWNER Mrs Elma Hunter OPEN May 31 – October 30. ROOMS 1 twin, 2 family; 1 en suite TERMS £16; reduction for children; single supplement £3

FEENY

Drumcovitt Barn
704 Feeny Road, Feeny, Co. Derry BT47 4 SU
Tel: 028 777 81224 Fax: 028 777 81224
Email: drumcovitt.feeny@btinternet.com

This impressive creeper house dates back 300 years, and was built on the land owned by the Fishmonger Company. A round-ended Georgian front was added in 1796, enlarging the house, adding two extra reception rooms and two bedrooms. The views here are stunning, stretching down a wooded valley to

Benbraddagh, across to Mullaghash. This is a working farm, and sheep and young stock graze in the adjoining pasture. The ambience is informal, friendly and relaxing. There are no en-suite rooms, but it is such a wonderful house, no-one seems to mind; the two bathrooms and an additional loo provide ample facilities. Many original features remain, such as the sandstone floor in the inner hall, pitch pine floors, window panes and shutters. Of special interest is the 300-year-old security. The spacious bedrooms have King size beds, TV, telephone and tea makers.

There is a library nook on the landing, and a comfortable drawing room with plenty of seating. Breakfasts, at which vegetarians are catered for if pre-arranged, and modestly priced home cooked dinners are served family style. Dinners should be pre-booked. Period furniture decorates the house, and guests return often for the charm, and friendship they found here. The Beech trees, and grounds, provide a great habitat for birds and butterflies, and quiet walks can be taken along the lanes. There are many standing stones and Danish Forts to be seen, and Banagher Dam with its surrounding slopes is an Area of Special Scientific Interest. The city of Derry is a 20 minute drive. Self catering cottages are available. Drumcovitt Barn is a non-smoking house. Visa accepted. Situated approximately half a mile from Feeny village.

OWNER Frank and Florence Sloan OPEN All year ROOMS 4 rooms, single, double, twin and family room. TERMS from £19 to £14; reduction for children MEALS dinner (if arranged)

LIMAVADY

Ballycarton House
239 Seacoast Road, Limavady, Co. Derry BT49 0HZ
Tel: 0287 77 50126 Fax: 0287 77 50990

Built in the 1800s, this lovely rambling farmhouse, is nestled at the foot of Binevenagh Mountains, and has wonderful views. It has been a bed and breakfast for over 35 years, ran all that time, by the present owners parents. It was taken over 5 years ago by Patricia Craig, who has completely refurbished the property, retaining its charm, character, and warm ambience. Patricia offers the same high standards people have enjoyed in the past. Tartan carpets greet guests as they enter, and the five large en-suite, well equipped bedrooms, are tastefully decorated in soft shades, and have pine furnishings. All rooms have TV, clock radio, hairdryer and tea makers. There is a conservatory and sitting-room, plus a dining room, which has William Morris wallpaper, and many items of interest. A fire burns in the sitting-room on chilly days, and the conservatory overlooking the view is a peaceful spot to relax and plan your days out.

This is the perfect combination of a great house, wonderful hospitality and good food. The imaginative breakfast menu includes French Toast, Pancakes American style, served with maple syrup, croissants, juice, fruit and a full Irish breakfast with home-made soda bread. Special diets are catered for at breakfast. Little wonder Ballycarton House is the recipient of "Ulster Guest House of the Year". Guests have use of the garden, which has a gazebo, and barbecue area. Non-smokers are preferred. When booking, ask for their directional map to be sent.

OWNER Patricia Craig OPEN All year ROOMS 5 /double/twin/ single; all en suite. TERMS from £19; reduction for children; single supplement £5

Ballyhenry House
172 Seacoast Road, Limavady, Co. Derry BT49 9EF
Tel: 028 77 722657

This large, bright and airy farmhouse is close to the sea between Limavady and Castlerock. It was built around the turn of the century by Mr Kane's grandfather, and the flat and fertile land extends to 140 hectares. The farm is managed by Rosemary Kane's two sons and their uncle; it is a very successful operation, and they have won a variety of awards. Guests are welcome to wander around the farm and watch daily activities.
  Rosemary Kane is a very friendly lady, who prepares excellent evening meals, if arranged in advance. The rooms are nicely proportioned and pleasantly decorated and furnished with some interesting antique furniture. A large en suite room has a double and a single bed and its own balcony, and a loft has been converted to provide a self-catering unit that sleeps six. Smoking in lounge only. From Londonderry left at traffic lights before entering Limavady the B69 road, farm is just over three miles on this road. From Coleraine 2 miles after Bellarena train crossing turn right onto Seacoast Road.

OWNER Rosemary Kane OPEN All year ROOMS 1 double, 1 twin, 1 family, 1 single; 1 en suite. TERMS £17; reduction for children; single supplement £4

Streeve Hill
Limavady, Co. Derry BT49 0HP
Tel: 028 777 66563 Fax: 028 777 68285
Website: www.hidden-ireland.com/streeve

Peter and June Welsh are warm and welcoming hosts, greeting guests with tea and biscuits, and create a relaxed and informal atmosphere in their home. Streeve, which means "running water" in Gaelic, was built by Conolly McCausland in 1730 and stands in secluded grounds on 500 acres of parkland, woodland and farmland. The three comfortable luxurious bedrooms, are furnished with antiques, have crisp cotton sheets, and lovely views. One very spacious room is ideal for families, all rooms have en-suite facilities. The drawing room has a log fire burning on cool days. The emphasis at Streeve is on good food. Breakfasts include a wide range of starters, with home-baked bread, fresh-squeezed juice, fruit, cereals followed by traditional fare, with free range eggs. Pre-arranged four-course candlelit dinner could include, chilled pimento soup, Irish salmon fillets with a herb crust, zucchini frites, cucumber and dill salad, rocket, new potatoes, Irish cheeses, and mouth-watering desserts. Fresh vegetables and fruit from the garden are used in season. Vegetarians are well catered for. Dinners are available June, July and August, (except Sunday and Monday). Peter cooks breakfast and June is the Master Chef for evening meals. Smoking is allowed in the drawing room only if other guests have no objection. No pets.

There are several golf courses close by and for garden enthusiasts arrangements can be made to visit Drenagh Gardens for a modest fee. American Express, Visa, Mastercard accepted. From Limavady take B119 sign-posted from Castlerock, follow estate wall on the right, past gate lodge, turn right at the end of the wall.

OWNER Peter & June Welsh OPEN February 1 – October 30
ROOMS 3 double/family; all en suite. TERMS £40–50 per person; reduction for children if sharing; single supplement £5
MEALS dinner

PORTSTEWART

Oregon Guest House
168 Station Road, Portstewart, Co. Derry BT55 7PU
Tel: 028 70 832826

About 1km from the sea, and within walking distance of the city centre, this well maintained and well-kept guest house lies on the outskirts of Portstewart, just off a fairly busy main road. The house has a high standard of furnishings and fresh, bright rooms, prettily decorated with floral curtains and bed covers. One of the double bedrooms has a corner bath, and some are on the ground floor. The small, cosy, panelled dining room, with fine china and flowers on the table, overlooks the sunny patio with a pond and a small fountain. The lounge is comfortable and breakfast and pre-arranged evening meals are served in the dining room, which is very bright and has windows all round. There is plenty of information for the visitor. Access, Visa, Mastercard, American Express accepted.

OWNER Mrs Vi Anderson OPEN February 1 – October 31.
ROOMS 4 double, 2 twin, 1 family, 1 single; all en suite
TERMS £22.50; reduction for children; single supplement £8.50
MEALS dinner

COUNTY DOWN

A county rich in monuments of antiquity, County Down has
been subject to many invasions throughout its history, the
fiercest of all from the Vikings in the ninth century.
Legend has it that St Patrick landed here in A.D. 432 at the place
where the Slaney River flows into Strangford Lough. During the
30 years between his arrival and death in A.D. 461, St Patrick
converted the pagan Irish to Christianity.

The Ards Peninsula, bordered by Strangford Lough to the
west and the Irish Sea to the east, is a narrow strip of land with
a bracing climate, reputedly the sunniest and driest part of the
North. It has some charming villages and towns that were first
settled by the Scots and English.

Bangor was a famous centre of learning from the sixth
century, until it was devastated by the Vikings in the ninth
century. It was from here that the missionaries St Columbanus,
St Gall and many others set off to bring Christianity to the rest
of Europe.

The breezy coast road runs from Bangor past
Ballycopeland – the only working windmill in Ireland – past the
pretty village of Kearney to the attractive town of Portaferry,
where the 8 km-long ferry ride to Strangford affords lovely
views of Strangford Lough. The Lough is a famous bird sanctuary
and wildlife reserve, and the small rounded hills, called "drumlins," that cover North Down are to be found in Strangford
Lough, appearing as small islands. Amongst the historic places to
visit are Castle Ward, built by the first Lord Bangor in 1765, and
Mount Stewart, the childhood home of Lord Castlereagh, a former British Foreign Secretary. Out of the Cistercian Abbeys in
medieval County Down, three were built around the Lough: Inch
Abbey, Grey Abbey and Comber.

Downpatrick, at the southern tip of Strangford Lough, is
an attractive Georgian town and contains the burial site of St
Patrick, which is in the graveyard of the cathedral.

The Mourne Mountains cover a small area, 22.5 km long
and 12 km wide, with 12 rounded peaks. The barren peak of
Slieve Donard, climbing steeply to 860 m, dominates this peaceful
land-scape, which is a paradise for walkers. From the summit you
can see the Isle of Man, the Belfast hills and Lough Neagh. There
are also two artificial lakes or reservoirs that supply Belfast with
water. These are surrounded by a huge dry stone wall over 2 m
high and 33 km long. The Mourne Wall Walk attracts thousands
of walkers from all over the world each June.

The coast south from Newcastle, a lively seaside resort, was notorious for smuggling in the eighteenth century. Newry was once a prosperous mercantile town with large town houses and public buildings, as well as the earliest Protestant church in Ireland, St Patrick's Church of Ireland.

BANGOR

Bethany House
58 Queens Parade, Bangor, Co. Down BT20 3H
Tel: 028 91 457733 Fax: 028 91 274178

The adjoining building to Hebron House, and under the same ownership, Bethany House is part of an attractive terrace of houses, set back from and above the sea front and harbour. Two of the rooms have sea views, and they all have TV and tea- and coffee-making facilities. Evening meals are available at certain times of the year. The accommodation is very simple and clean. No smoking, no pets. Most major credit cards accepted.

OWNER Phillip & Ilona Maddock OPEN All year ROOMS 1 family, 2 double, 1 twin, 1 single; 3 public bathrooms. TERMS £18–25 MEALS evening meals £12

Cairn Bay Lodge
278 Seacliff Road, Bangor, Co. Down BT20 5HS
Tel: 028 91 467636 Fax: 028 91 457728

Cairn Bay Lodge is a most interesting and substantial house, built in 1880, it stands in a large and beautifully maintained garden. It is set back from the shore with uninterrupted views of the sea. Its rather heavy woodwork and panelling in some rooms makes it a little oppressive, and there are all kinds of unusual pieces of furniture and décor. The drawing and sitting rooms occupy the front of the house, affording lovely views over Belfast Lough. The well equipped, spacious, comfortable bedrooms, each with hairdryer, trouser press, TV, tea- and coffee-making facilities, desks and some with telephones, have a yesteryear feel to them. There is a resident beautician, baby sitting service, and meals can be served if booked in advance. Visa and Mastercard accepted. Pets in cars only, no smoking. Cairn Bay is a quiet, peaceful place, and is just a five minute walk from the centre of Bangor at the southern end of town.

OWNER Christopher Mullen OPEN All year ROOMS 9 double/twin/single/family; all en suite. TERMS £28–35; single supplement £5; reductions for children MEALS dinner £14.50

Hebron House

59 Queens Parade, Bangor Co. Down BT20 3BH
Tel: 028 9146 3126 Fax: 028 9127 4178
Email: reception@hebron-house.com
Website: www.hebron-house.com

Hebron House is part of an attractive Victorian terrace of
houses, set back from and above the sea front and harbour. It is
comfortable and attractively decorated and provides good
service. The bedrooms have TV, telephones and tea- and coffee-
making facilities, and one room has a sea view. Evening meals are
available some of the time, and there is a combined TV lounge
and dining room. No pets. No smoking. Major credit cards
accepted.

OWNER Mrs Ilona Maddock OPEN All year ROOMS 1 double, 1
family, 1 twin. TERMS £18–22; single supplement £3–7; reductions
for children MEALS dinner £12

Shelleven House

61 Princetown Road, Bangor, Co. Down BT20 3TA
Tel: 028 9127 1777 Fax: 028 9127 1777

Shelleven House stands one street above the sea front in a small
terrace of Victorian buildings. The Westons, who are a friendly,
competent couple, acquired the building three years ago, and are
gradually refurbishing the rooms. Some of the bedrooms have
sea views, and some are on the small side. The comfortable
lounge is separated from the dining room by a slide-up door and
evening meals are available with notice. One bedroom is on the
ground floor. Shelleven House is fully licensed, and major credit
cards are accepted. There are some smoking areas.

OWNER Mary & Philip Weston OPEN All year ROOMS 11
doubles/twins/singles, all en suite. TERMS £22.50–25; single
supplement £7.50–15 MEALS dinner

CASTLEWELLAN

Slieve Croob Inn

119 Clanvaraghan Road, Castlewellan, Co. Down BT31 9L
Tel: 028 4377 1412 Fax: 028 4377 1162
Email: slievecroob@mcmail.com
Website: www.slievecroob.mcmail.com

Under Slieve Croob on a remote country lane this collection of
white washed buildings blend well into the landscape. Purpose
built, they provide one building containing the bed & breakfast
accommodation, and others for self catering and banqueting
facilities. The b& b guests have a lounge and the restaurant for
breakfast, lunch and dinner, and bedrooms that are spacious,

comfortably furnished and well equipped with tea- and coffee-making facilities, TV and telephones. With the mountain behind and the sea view in front the Inn is located in a spectacular position. Slieve Croob is well sign-posted from Castlewellan.

OWNER Laurence Kelly OPEN All year ROOMS 6 double/twin, I suite TERMS £30; single supplement £5; reductions for children MEALS lunch, dinner

DOWNPATRICK

Denvir's Hotel
English Street, Downpatrick, Co. Down
Tel: 028 4461 2012 Fax: 028 4461 7002

Established in 1642 this middle of the town old inn is a hub of activity. The bar has an unusually high ceiling and is almost square in shape, above which are six spacious, attractively furnished and decorated bedrooms. The dining room is quite separate from the bar and is a bright room with cheerful colours and gaily coloured tablecloths.

OWNER Ronnie Martin & Colin Magowan OPEN All year ROOMS 3 family, I double, 2 twin TERMS £25; single supplement £5 MEALS dinner

Havine
51 Ballydonnell Road, Downpatrick, Co. Down BT30 8EP
Tel: 028 44851242

This comfortable, eighteenth century, pebble dashed farmhouse, part of a farm of 50 hectares, is highly acclaimed and has received an award for hospitality. Mrs. Macauley is a most welcoming, friendly lady and tries to think of everything for her guests' comfort, including such items as sewing kits, dressing gowns and slippers. The bedrooms are small and cosy, with sloping wooden ceilings, and hairdryers, trouser presses and tea- and coffee-making facilities. There are two lounges, one with a TV, and one for relaxing or reading and which has all kinds of musical instruments for guests to use - which they do! Havine Farm is a place you will look forward to returning to. Pets in cars only, smoking permitted in the lounge. Located on the Downpatrick road three kilometres from Clough, turn right at Tyrella – the house is three kilometres on the left.

OWNER Myrtle Macauley OPEN All year ROOMS 3 double/twin/family, I public bathroom. TERMS £17.50–19

Tyrella House

Downpatrick, Co. Down BT30 8SU
Tel: 028 44851422 Fax: 028 4485142
 Email: tyrella.corbett@virgin.net
Website: www.hidden-ireland.com/tyrella

This large, elegant country house, with a porticoed, classical façade, stands in 120 hectares of parkland and farmland that stretches down to the sea and its private sandy beach. Most of the house dates from around the eighteenth century, with the Georgian front added in the early nineteenth century. The grounds include a private event course, and a point-to-point course which is used a couple of times a year. Horses are available for beach, forest or mountain rides, or guests are welcome to bring their own horses. Hunting can be arranged and tuition is available in cross-country riding and polo. Guests can also enjoy a game of croquet or tennis on the grass court. The house has a welcoming feeling, with a large hallway and stairs leading up to the three large bedrooms. Dinner (if pre-booked) is served by candlelight in the elegant dining room, and a cheerful fire is lit in the drawing room where coffee is served after dinner. Smoking permitted in hall only. Pets can be accommodated in the kennels or owner's car. Visa and American Express accepted. Advance booking essential. Tyrella's Gate Lodge with blue gates is seven kilometres from Clough on the Clough/Ardglass road.

OWNER David & Sally Corbett OPEN March 1 – November 30 ROOMS 1 double, 1 twin, 1 family; 2 en suite, 1 private bathroom. TERMS £40; single supplement £10 MEALS dinner £22.50

DROMORE

Sylvan Hill House

76 Kilntown Road, Dromore, Co. Down BT25 1HS
Tel: 028 92692321 Fax: 028 92692321

This listed Georgian house was built in 1781 and stands in beautiful gardens with mature trees and panoramic views of the Mourne and Dromara mountains. Jimmy and Elise Coburn are solicitous hosts, entertaining their guests either in their well lived in sitting room, or in the more formal dining room. They join their guests for dinner, which in summer is sometimes served in the conservatory. Mrs. Coburn is a gourmet cook, all breads and desserts are home made, and a special treat at breakfast is her elder flower marmalade. The three very large bedrooms, all with hairdryer and tea- and coffee-making facilities, overlook the garden, and the furnishings are a mixture of antique and traditional. Pets are accepted by arrangement. Smoking permitted downstairs. To find Sylvan Hill House, turn off the A1 onto the Lurgan road, take the first right (Kilntown Road) signposted to Moira, go two and a half kilometres to the top of the hill and the house is on the right.

OWNER Elise Coburn OPEN All year ROOMS 1 double, 1 twin, 1 family; 2 en suite, 1 private bathroom. TERMS £28 MEALS dinner £16 (including wine)

HELEN'S BAY

Carrig-Gorm
27 Bridge Road, Helen's Bay, Bangor, Co. Down BT19 1TS
Tel: 02891 853680 Fax: 02891 85368
Email: elizabeth@eves.fsnet.co.uk

Carrig-Gorm is a rambling, old, white house standing in its own grounds on the edge of Helen's Bay village. It is thought that the oldest wing of the house dates back around 300 years, and the newest, which includes the elegant drawing room, from 1870. The house exudes a warm, friendly atmosphere. Guests tend to sit around the open fire in the comfortable panelled hall, and also in the conservatory during fine weather. There are sea views from all bedrooms, which have TV, hairdryers and tea- and coffee-making facilities. Breakfast only is served in the dining room. There are lovely coastal walks and a Folk and Transport Museum. No pets and no smoking. To reach Carrig-Gorm take the A2 from Belfast, left at Helen's Bay sign, turn right after one and a quarter miles, fourth house on the left.

OWNER Elizabeth Eves OPEN All year except for Christmas ROOMS 1 twin, 1 single, 1 family; 1 en suite, 1 public bathroom. TERMS £25–30; reductions for children

HOLYWOOD

Ardshane Country House
5 Bangor Road, Holywood, Co. Down BT18 ONU
Tel: 028 90422044 Fax: 028 90427506

Ardshane means "hill of John" and is built on the 800-year-old campsite of King John's army. It is a large, Edwardian, brick family home standing in most attractive mature gardens, approached up a long driveway. It is a restful, spacious and elegant house, beautifully appointed with every comfort. There is a TV lounge and an elegant dining room with a marble fireplace. The bedrooms are large, with modern bathrooms, telephones, TV, hairdryers, trouser presses and tea- and coffee-making facilities. There is a croquet lawn for the enjoyment of guests, and the house is well suited for the disabled. Pets are accepted by arrangement. Non-smoking bedrooms are available. Ardshane is located at the Bangor end of Holywood off the main road.

OWNER Valerie Caughey OPEN All year ROOMS 3 double, 3 twin, 1 family, 1 single; 7 en suite. TERMS £32.50; single supplement £17.50; reductions for children MEALS dinner from £17

Braeside Country House

10 Brown's Brae, Croft Road, Holywood BT18 0HL
Tel: 028 90 426665 or 07977595347 Fax: 028 90 426665
Email: braeside@lineone.net
Website: www.braesidecountryhouse.com

At the very end of Croft Road, Croft House stands high up above the town of Holywood in its own grounds and gardens with lovely views over Strangford Lough. Built in 1850, it is an elegantly furnished country house, with a very pleasant drawing room and nice dining room. The Johnstons converted the garage end of the old stone house into a charming guest wing, with very simple, attractive bedrooms, and downstairs a self catering unit, which is sometimes used for bed & breakfast guests. Braeside is a mile from the centre of Holywood and close to golf courses and good restaurants. The centre of Belfast is 6 miles away. No pets, no smoking in bedrooms. Visa cards accepted

OWNER Jill Johnston OPEN All year ROOMS 3 double/twin; all en suite. TERMS £30; single supplement £10

Rayanne House

60 Demesne Road, Holywood, Co. Down BT18 9EX
Tel: 028 90425859 Fax: 028 90425859

Rayanne House, a substantial brick building dating from the nine-teenth century, stands in its own grounds and enjoys lovely views across Belfast Lough to Carrickfergus and the Antrim Hills. It offers a warm welcome, good food and a high standard of comfort and service. Anne continues to operate a professional and immaculate house, in spite of the tragic death of her hus-band, Raymond. She is constantly seeking to improve the already high standards. The bedrooms are charming, each one completely individually decorated and furnished with a lot of flair. They all have large bathrooms, and all the bits and pieces included you can imagine, as well as the more standard amenities of hairdryer, telephone, trouser press, TV and tea- and coffee-making facilities. The two sitting rooms and the dining room are comfortable, informal and filled with all sorts of china and knick-knacks. Breakfasts are memorable with a wide selection from the menu. No pets. Smoking in the lounge only. Visa and Mastercard accepted.

OWNER Mrs Anne McClelland OPEN All year ROOMS 9 double, twin, single, family; all en suite. TERMS £35; single supplement £20; reductions for children MEALS dinner

Heath Hall
160 Moyadd Road, Kilkeel, Co. Down
Tel: 028 41762612 Fax: 028 41764032

Heath Hall, a turn-of-the-century, stone built farmhouse has a modern appearance, and is set in 6.5 hectares of farmland with sheep and cattle. It has views of the sea and the Mourne Mountains. The house was completely renovated a few years ago, and some rooms have sea views. All three bedrooms have hairdryers and tea making facilities. The TV lounge has the original marble fireplace, and there is also a snooker room. The house was formerly run as a bed & breakfast by Mrs. McGlue's mother-in-law, and has a reputation for offering good value meals and accommodation. Lunch must be arranged in advance. Pets outside only. No smoking. Heath Hall is located on the B27, 2.5 kilometres north of Kilkeel.

OWNER Mary McGlue OPEN All year except for Christmas ROOMS 1 double, 1 twin, 1 family; 1 en suite, 1 private bathroom. TERMS £16–18; single supplement £2–4; reductions for children MEALS lunch

Barnageeha
Ardmillan, Killinchy, Co. Down BT23 6QN
Tel: 028 97541011

On the edge of the tiny village of Ardmillan, Barnageeha is reached up a winding driveway, crossing a small river. It is a long, low, modern attractive whitewashed building covered in creepers and climbing roses, right on the shores of Strangford Lough. The house is very comfortable and pleasantly furnished, has a relaxing atmosphere, and Margie Crawford is a delightful host. The large bedrooms are all en suite, and dinner can be provided if arranged in advance. The property comprises a small sheep farm and there is a tennis court for guests' use. But what attracts a lot of visitors is the bird watching, and with the proximity to the water, watchers can remain in the comfort of the house. Pets can be accommodated in the stables. It is advisable to get directions.

OWNER Margie Crawford OPEN All year ROOMS 3 twins/ doubles; all en suite. TERMS £25; single supplement £5 MEALS dinner

The Old Schoolhouse Inn

100 Ballydrain Road, Killinchy, Comber, Co. Down BT23 6EA
Tel: 028 97 541182 Fax: 028 97 542583
Email: info@theoldschoolhouseinn.com
Website: www.theoldschoolhouseinn.com

The restaurant was the original old school and has been whimsi-
cally decorated with knick-knacks and bottles, and decorated in
warm, dark colours. In matching brick a recent guest wing was
added, offering spacious, comfortable bedrooms, equipped to a
high standard, each one named after an American president of
Ulster descent. Avril is the head chef, and whilst the food is
based on French cooking, she likes to experiment with new
combinations. The Inn is next to Castle Espie, which has the
largest collection of wildfowl in Ireland, and Strangford Lough is
only a few minutes away. From Comber follow the signs for
Castle Espie and The Old Schoolhouse Inn can be found half a
mile beyond it.

OWNER Terry & Avril Brown OPEN All year ROOMS 12
double/twin; all en suite. TERMS £32.50; single supplement £8
MEALS dinner

Dufferin Coaching Inn

31 High Street, Killyleagh, Co. Down BT30 9QF
Tel: 028 4482 8229 Fax: 028 4482 875
Email: dufferin@dial.pipex.com
Website: www.dufferincoachinginn@co.uk

Halfway down the High Street of the historic town of Killyleagh
this atmospheric old inn lies between spectacular Killyleagh
Castle above and the shores of Strangford Lough below. The Inn
has been operating since 1803, and both it and the seventeenth
century castle were originally part of the Dufferin & Ava estate.
Kitty Stewart and Morris Crawford are an amazing couple with a
lot of energy, and they originally owned both the pub part of the
inn as well as the accommodation. Now this has been separated
and they own the bed & breakfast which has very attractive,
spacious, beautifully decorated bedrooms with large bathrooms.
Some have four poster beds. They also own the conference
facilities which have evolved from the courtyard at the back of
the building bordered by the old stables. The bed & breakfast
drawing room used to be the Ulster Bank. Morris is in the
building trade, and he and Kitty also run riding, sailing and golf
holidays. The pub offers entertainment and excellent food. The
Dufferin Coaching Inn is a lively spot with a great atmosphere
and comfortable accommodation.

OWNER Kitty Stewart OPEN All year ROOMS 4 doubles, 2 twins; all en suite. TERMS £32.50; single supplement £5 MEALS dinner

NEWCASTLE

The Briers
Middle Tollymore Road, Newcastle Co. Down
Tel: 028 437 24347 Fax: 028 437 26633

This 200-year-old former farmhouse, once part of Lord Roden's estate, is set in 0.75 hectares of grounds, which include a newly planted aboretum. The original house is a low, whitewashed building. It has a modern two storey addition, which is where the guests' accommodation is located. Here there are two ground floor bedrooms suitable for the disabled. The bedrooms are all en suite and have hairdryers, TV and telephones. Both lunch and dinner are available if arranged in advance. Smoking is allowed in the lounge. Pets are allowed outside only. Horseback riding and fishing are available close by. All major credit cards accepted. The Briers is sign-posted opposite Tollymore Forest Park.

OWNER Anne Bowater OPEN All year ROOMS 9 twin/double/family; all en suite. TERMS £25; single supplement £10; reductions for children MEALS lunch from £5, dinner from £8

NEWTOWNARDS

Ballycastle House
20 Mountstewart Road, Newtownards, Co. Down BT22 2AL
Tel: 028 427 88357 Fax: 028 427 88357
Email: ballycastle@breathemail.net
Website: www.ballycastlehouse.com
A warm welcome always awaits you at Ballycastle House, the comfortable home of the Deerings. The house was built over 150 years ago and is set in 16 hectares of lovely grounds that were once part of the Mount Stewart estate. The bedrooms have some interesting furniture, the guest lounge features the original fireplace, and a conservatory has been added.
Mr Deering collects and restores old farm machinery and tractors. The house is minutes from the sea, with lovely walks close by. Pets outside only, no smoking. Ballycastle House can be found one kilometre off the A20, turning left at the Ballywalter signpost, six kilometres south of Newtownards.

OWNER Margaret Deering OPEN All year except for Christmas ROOMS 2 double, 1 family; all en suite. TERMS £22; single supplement £5; reductions for children

Ballynester House

Cardy Road Newtownards Co. Down BT22 2L
Tel: 028 42788386 Fax: 028 42788986
Email: geraldine.bailie@virgin.net

Standing just above the village of Greyabbey, Ballynester House
was built by Geraldine Bailie's husband. It enjoys lovely views of
Strangford Lough and is surrounded by its own garden. The
house is well furnished and decorated, and the three guest
bedrooms are all on the ground floor. They all have TV, hairdryer
and tea- and coffee-making facilities. The two front rooms have
the water view, and the rear bedroom was the original master,
and has a large bathroom. Geraldine Bailie is a charming and
friendly person and keeps her home in immaculate condition.
Visa and Mastercard accepted. No smoking. There is an adjacent
self catering lodge. The house is sign-posted at the roundabout
at Greyabbey.

OWNER Geraldine Bailie OPEN All year ROOMS 1 double, 1
twin, 1 family; 2 en suite, 1 private bathroom. TERMS £25; single
supplement £5

Beech Hill Country House

23 Ballymoney Road, Craigantlet, Newtownards, Co. Down BT23
4TG
Tel: 028 9042 5892 Fax: 028 9042 5892
Email: beech.hill@btinternet.com
Website: www.beech.hill.net

This long, low, whitewashed house was built 40 years ago by
Victoria Brann's grandmother in the Georgian style. It stands on
a slight rise surrounded by its own farmland (which is let out)
with lovely views over the north Down countryside. The
grounds include a croquet lawn. Beech Hill has a very pleasant
country house atmosphere with the public rooms leading from
one to another. The elegant dining room and comfortable drawing room are tastefully furnished with antiques, and beyond is
the conservatory, which is used for breakfast. The bedrooms are
on the ground floor. The beds are made up with Irish linen and
all the rooms have TV, hairdryers, telephones, trouser presses
and tea- and coffee-making facilities. Nearby are Mount Stewart
House and Gardens, Rowallane Gardens, Dundonald Motte and
Greyabbey, with its herb garden and antiques centre. Visa and
Mastercard accepted. Pets by arrangement and smoking is
permitted in the drawing room. Beech Hill is only ten minutes
from the centre of Belfast, and can be reached by taking the A2
and one and a half miles from the bridge at the Ulster Folk
Museum turn right up Ballymoney Road signed to Craigantlet.
The house is one and three quarter miles on the left.

OWNER Victoria Brann OPEN All year ROOMS 1 twin/double, 2 double; all en suite. TERMS £32.50; single supplement £10

Edenvale House

130 Portaferry Road, Newtownards, Co. Down BT22 2AH
Tel: 028 91 814881 or 07798741790 Fax: 028 91 826192
Email: edenvalehouse@hotmail.com
Website: www.edenvalehouse.com

Approached up a long driveway, Edenvale House is a small Georgian country house located above Strangford Lough. It stands in its own grounds surrounded by fields, and is immaculately kept, both inside and out. Diane Whyte is a welcoming host, and the atmosphere is informal and relaxed. The house has been beautifully furnished and decorated with great taste, and there are lovely views from the first floor rooms. One of the bedrooms now has a four-poster bed and a dressing room with room for a single bed if needed. Guests generally prefer to have breakfast, which includes fried potato bread and hot home-made bread, in the large kitchen at the big kitchen table. Diane's daughter looks after the livery business, and guests are welcome to bring their horses. The beautifully kept stables and barn lie to the side of the house, and within the half a hectare of gardens is a croquet lawn. Mountstewart House is a three minute drive away. Children and pets are very welcome. Smoking restricted. Most cards except American Express accepted. Edenvale House can be found three kilometres from Newtownards on the Portaferry road.

OWNER Diane Whyte OPEN All year except for Christmas ROOMS 1 double, 1 twin, 1 family; all en suite. TERMS £27.50; single supplement £7.50; reductions for children

The Narrows

8 Shore Road, Portaferry, Co. Down BT22 1JY
Tel: 028 42 728148 Fax: 028 42 728105
Email: info@narrows.co.uk
Website: www.narrows.co.uk

The Narrows stands at the very end of the Ards Peninsula, and right on the shorefront overlooking the "narrows" and village of Strangford on the opposite side of Strangford Lough. It is owned by Will and James Brown, two brothers who returned to their father's family home in 1992 and skilfully and sympathetically transformed a series of derelict buildings into a place of charm and rustic simplicity. The original house contains most of the bedrooms, which are simply decorated and furnished and have telephones, TV and tea- and coffee-making facilities, and every room except the single has a sea view. Behind is the old renovated stone byre, which has a sauna (free for guests). The restaurant building is new and very cleverly designed, still retaining its big arched entranceway, allowing cars to be driven into the small courtyard. Upstairs is a conference/function room with big windows on each side overlooking the sea or charming walled garden. Here weekend workshops are sometimes held on such subjects as painting, basket making and stonewalling (some of the garden walls were rebuilt by students - nothing like being paid to have the work done!). The restaurant, offering deliciously cooked local food, with a strong emphasis on seafood, is very popular. The floors and furniture are pine, there is a small bar in the corner, the day's menu is posted on a blackboard, and every table enjoys views of the water. Will's wife, Sarah, is the pastry chef, and she is also responsible for the décor in the house. Some of the paintings around the house are hers; paintings and weavings by local artists also hang on the walls. Equally welcoming to families and functions, The Narrows is a great place for a break in this beautiful and interesting area of Ireland. Pets by arrangement. Smoking permitted in the sitting room/bar area. All major credit cards, except Diners, accepted.

OWNER Will Brown OPEN All year ROOMS 13 double/twin; all en suite. TERMS £45; single supplement £15; reductions for children MEALS all meals

The Cuan

Strangford Village, Co. Down BT30 7ND
Tel: 028 44 881222 Fax: 028 44 881770
Email: enquiries@thecuan.fsnet.co.uk
Website: www.thecuan.com

This quite extensive long, low building comprises bars,
restaurant, a traditional fish and chip shop, and bed and breakfast
accommodation. Peter and Caroline McErlean, the very
delightful, friendly owners, gradually acquired the buildings over
the last few years, and opened the different pieces along the way.
Now it seems they own almost one side of the charming square,
which is where the ferry to Portaferry comes and goes from.
The bedrooms are well furnished and equipped, and one is
suitable for less able visitors. There are four golf courses within
ten miles, excellent sea angling, lovely walks and, reached by
ferry, 'Exploris' a sea aquarium.

OWNER Peter & Caroline McErlean OPEN All year ROOMS 2
family, 7 double/twin; all en suite. TERMS £29.95–34.95; single
supplement £5; reductions for children; MEALS dinner

COUNTY FERMANAGH

County Fermanagh is lake or land – one third of the county is
under water – and is traversed by the Erne River, which meanders its way across the forested county into a huge lake dotted
with drumlins. A paradise for fishing, boating and other water-
related activities, Lough Erne is a magnificent 75-km-long waterway offering uncongested cruising opportunities with 154 islands
and many coves and inlets to explore. It has an interesting mix of
pagan and Christian relics and traditions that have withstood the
centuries.

The medieval town of Enniskillen is built on a bridge of
land between Upper and Lower Lough Erne. The town's origins
go back to prehistory, when it was on the main highway between
Ulster and Connaught. The County Museum, housed in the
Castle keep, displays the brilliant uniforms, colours and
Napoleonic battle trophies of the famous Inniskillings Regiment,
which fought at Waterloo.

Amongst the many islands to visit, Devenish is particularly interesting, with its perfect twelfth-century round tower, tiny
church and remains of a fifteenth-century Augustinian abbey. In
the cemetery of Boa, the largest island, are two ancient stone
Janus idols, thought to date from the first century. Belleek is
famous both for its fishing and its china, which comes mostly in
the form of objets d'art. Two of Northern Ireland's most attractive Georgian houses are to be found in Fermanagh – Castle

Coole, a neo-classical mansion with Paladian features, built in 1795 for the Earl of Belmore, and Florencecourt House, seat of the Earls of Enniskillen, which has wonderful rococo plasterwork.

Corralea Lodge Guest House
Belcoo, Co. Fermanagh
Tel: 028 6638 6325

The Lodge stands in a superb location on 14 hectares of a forested nature reserve on the shores of Lough Macnean, with glorious views over the lough and to the hills beyond. When the Catteralls came here nearly 25 years ago, the farmhouse was derelict, and they built a new house amidst this breathtaking scenery. The bedrooms, all on the ground floor, have patio doors, enabling guests to step outside and enjoy the view. The property has its own private landing stage and boats are available for hire. Sika deer roam the estate and in 1970, 37,000 trees were planted. The lounge is large and the separate dining room is where breakfast and evening meals can be served, if booked in advance. The dining room is non-smoking. Guests may bring their own wine to dinner. This is the perfect place for bird-watching, painting and walking. Upper Lough Macnean has the reputation of being the most pollution-free lake in Northern Ireland and the best place for pike in western Europe.

OWNER Mr & Mrs Peter Catterall OPEN March 1 – October 31 ROOMS 2 double, 2 twin; all en suite TERMS £20; reduction for children; single supplement £5 MEALS dinner if booked

Ardess House
Kesh, Co. Fermanagh
Tel: 013656 31267 Fax: 0135656 31267
Email: dorothy.pendry@lineone.net
Website: ardesshouse.co.uk

Ardess House is a Georgian stucco building situated at the top of a hill in secluded grounds and gardens where peacocks stroll and Jacob sheep graze in the paddocks. It was built in 1780 as the rectory for the church opposite and has lovely views. The Pendrys bought it in 1984 and have done a great deal of work on restoring the house, and are continuing to upgrade the property. Dorothy Pendry was a teacher in a girls' school in Belfast and did weaving and spinning as a hobby. The basement has been converted into small workshops, where courses on different crafts are taught. The students who attend the courses get full board in the house, though even those not attending courses can partake of evening meals if they wish. Guests are also welcome to join in the activities in the craft centre. The kitchen is the preferred place for breakfast, but there is a dining room as well, and a drawing room. The bedrooms have been freshly decorated and good-sized bathrooms have been added. The former are large, airy rooms, with high ceilings and wonderful views and they are furnished with antiques. The house has been awarded a British Airways Tourism Endeavour Award. Non-smokers are preferred. Pets by arrangement. Follow the signs to Kesh; turn off onto the B72 before you reach the village. Access, Mastercard, American Express accepted.

OWNER Dorothy Pendry OPEN January 15 – December 15
ROOMS 3 double, 1 twin; all en suite TERMS £25; reduction for children; single supplement £5 MEALS dinner

COUNTY TYRONE

The least populated of the six counties in Northern Ireland, Tyrone is in the heart of Ulster and is bordered to the north by the Sperrin Mountains, bare hills with fertile green valleys. The main towns are Omagh, the county town, Cookstown and Dungannon, which has a textile industry and crystal factory. The meaning of the Beaghmore stone circles, consisting of seven Bronze Age stone circles and cairns, is still unknown. The Ulster-American Folk Park at Camphill, Omagh, which recreates the America of pioneering days and the Ireland those pioneers left, grew up around the cottage where Thomas Mellon was born in 1813.

Also in County Tyrone is the ancestral home of President Woodrow Wilson. The farm is still occupied by Wilsons, who will show callers around the house.

BALLYGAWLEY

The Grange
15 Grange Road, Ballygawley, Co. Tyrone BT70 2HD
Tel: 028 855 68053

Dating from 1720, the Grange had a thatched roof until recently. It now has the appearance of a more modern house, with white stucco and new windows. It stands in a lovely, walled garden of lawns surrounded by flower beds. Mrs. Lyttle is very friendly, and the house has a pleasant, lived-in feeling. The attractive lounge has a piano and TV. The dining room, from which stairs lead to the first floor, has lots of character and is full of knick-knacks. There are sideboards decorated with silver and china. There is one ground floor bedroom. Pets outside only, smoking allowed in

TV lounge. The Grange is on the edge of Ballygawley a few metres from the roundabout.

OWNER Ella Lyttle OPEN April – December ROOMS 2 double, 1 twin; all en suite. TERMS £17–18; reductions for children

Killycolp House
21 Killycolp Road, Cookstown, Co. Tyrone BT80 8UL
Tel: 028 867 63577 Fax: 028 867 63577

This attractive house built in 1736 is surrounded by farmland, which is now mostly leased out and overlooks Tullyhogue Fort, where the kings of Ulster were crowned. The bedrooms are bright and attractively decorated, except for the twin which is on the small side, and most have nice views. There is a double room on the ground floor and the rooms have TV and tea- and coffee-making facilities. Guests have use of a sitting room, and breakfast is served in the entrance hallway. Killycolp House is sign-posted off the A29 south of Cookstown.

OWNER Mrs. Elizabeth McGucken OPEN All year except for Christmas ROOMS 1 family, 1 twin, 1 double; all en suite. TERMS £20; single supplement £6; reductions for children

Grange Lodge
7 Grange Road, Dungannon, Co. Tyrone BT71 7EJ
Tel: 02887 784212 Fax: 02887 784313
Email: grangelodge@nireland.com

This attractive Georgian country house is set in 1.25 hectares of pleasant gardens. It is a spacious house with well proportioned reception rooms which include a large drawing room, a cosier, smaller study with a TV and a panelled snooker room with a

piano. The Browns, who also own a retail business in Dungannon, are superb hosts - friendly, welcoming and perfectionists in maintaining their very high standard of accommodation and food. The bedrooms are pretty and comfortable and all have TV, hairdryers, telephones and tea- and coffee-making facilities. A stay here would not be complete without sampling Norah Brown's cooking, which is superb both in the extremely high standard of the food itself and the way in which it is presented. Dinner for house guests is served in the elegant dining room, at separate tables covered in white tablecloths and decorated with pretty flowers and candles. Non-residents are accommodated in a newly added dining room, which is completely self contained with its own entrance. Dinner must be booked in advance. Pets outside only. No smoking. Access, Visa and Mastercard accepted. To reach Grange Lodge from the M1 junction 15 on the A29 Armagh road, turn left at sign Grange, then right and house is first white walled entrance on the right.

OWNER Norah & Ralph Brown OPEN February 1 – December 20 ROOMS 3 double, 1 twin, 1 single; all en suite TERMS £39; single supplement £16 MEALS dinner from £25

MOY

Charlemont House
4 The Square, Moy, Dungannon, Co. Tyrone BT71 7SG
Tel: 028 87 784755 or 784895 Fax: 028 87 784895

Charlemont House, a lovely Georgian townhouse, occupies a corner site in the central square of the small town of Moy, which lies halfway between Armagh and Dungannon. The McNeice family has been associated with inn-keeping in Moy for many generations, and also runs Tomney's Bar and Lounge and Moy Reproductions, located just a few doors down the square. The bar is completely authentic, with small, dark rooms and a great atmosphere. The house has elegant proportions and is an amazing place, full of Victorian furnishings and furniture. The lounge has old floral wallpaper, pinkish chintzes, black and pink patterned carpeting, black furniture (including a piano), romantic pictures and all kinds of glass and china. The breakfast room, in the basement, is less flamboyant with an Aga cooker and pottery adorning the high shelf around the room. The property stretches right down to the River Blackwater at the back, reached through a courtyard. Guests can sit here on fine days, surrounded by old coach houses, then go through an archway to a pretty, partly walled, compact garden with more tables and chairs. No pets, smoking in the lounge only. Visa accepted.

OWNER Mrs Margaret McNeice OPEN All year ROOMS 9 double, twin, single, family; 3 en suite, 3 public bathrooms. TERMS £20; reductions for children

Muleany House
86 Gorestown Road, Moy, Co. Tyrone BT71 7EX
Tel: 028 87 784183

Muleany House was purpose-built some 15 years ago and is a substantial, porticoed whitewashed building. Mrs Mullen is a most friendly, chatty lady, who does her own baking and enjoys meeting her guests. The good sized bedrooms have tiny shower rooms and additionally there are two public bathrooms with bathtubs. Two bedrooms are on the ground floor. Well suited for families, Muleany House offers a baby-sitting service, laundry facilities and a large games room with pool table, small organ and open fire. There is also a smaller lounge with TV, and a dining room where evening meals are served, if ordered in advance. There are two self catering units in the grounds. Most major credit cards accepted. No pets, no smoking in the bedrooms or dining room. The house can be found about 1.6 kilometres from Moy by taking the B106 to Benburb, then the right fork towards Ballygawley.

OWNER Joanne Mullen OPEN All year except for Christmas ROOMS 9 double/twin/family/single; all en suite. TERMS £19.50; single supplement £5; reductions for children MEALS dinner £10-15

Bankhead
9 Lissan Road, Omagh, Co. Tyrone BT78 1TX
Tel: 028 82 245592

This small farmhouse is at the end of a long private road and has pleasant views over farmland with the Drumragh River just below. It was built by the Clements in 1970 and is part of an 11 hectare beef and sheep farm. The bedrooms are furnished simply, and are fresh and bright. They are all on the ground floor. There is a small, neatly kept TV lounge with an open fire, and the dining room has a TV and sitting area. The terrace is pleasant for sitting outside on fine days, and guests have use of the garden. Pets outside only. Smoking is not permitted in the bedrooms. Bankhead can be found off the A5 towards Omagh by crossing the Drumragh River and turning left immediately into Lissan Road.

OWNER Sadie Christina Clements OPEN All year ROOMS 2 double, 1 twin, 1 public bathroom. TERMS £15; reductions for children MEALS light supper

Ballantine's B&B

38 Leckpatrick Road, Artigarvan, Strabane, Co. Tyrone
Tel: 028 41 882414 Fax: 028 41 882414

This family home has a friendly atmosphere and stands in its own garden with lovely distant views of farmland and hills. It is a modern house with three small bedrooms, sharing two bathrooms. There is a TV lounge with an open fire, a conservatory and the dining room has one table, where evening meals are served if arranged in advance. The Ulster American Folk Park is 24 kilometres away. No smoking. Pets outside only. The house is located by turning off the B40 opposite Leckpatrick Dairy and it is the first on the right.

OWNER Jean Ballantine OPEN January – November ROOMS 1 double, 1 twin, 1 single; 1 private bathroom, 2 public bathrooms TERMS £15; reductions for children MEALS dinner from £7.50

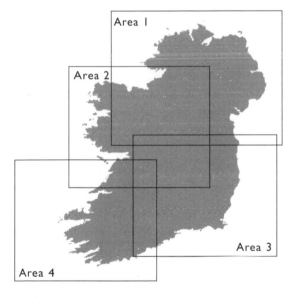

Area 1

Area 2

Area 3

Area 4

Area Maps

Area 1

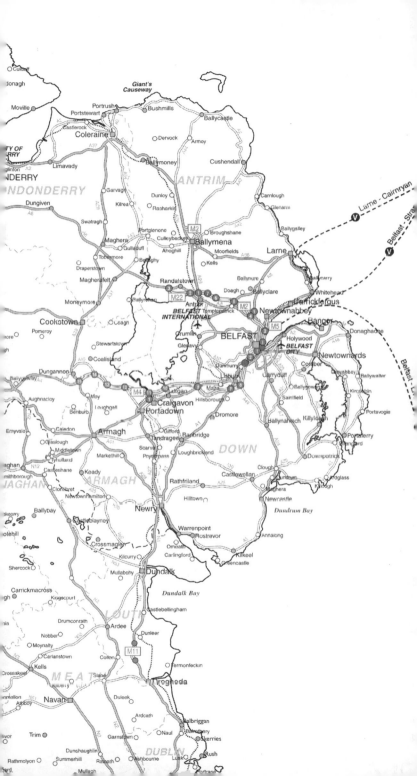

Area 2

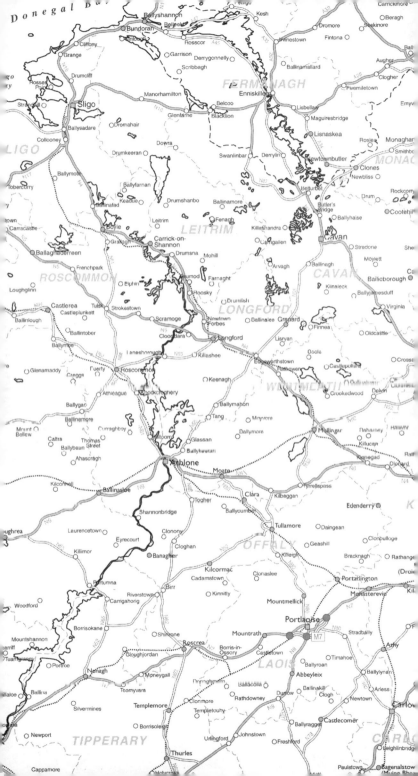

Area 4

Index

Killorglin	98	Newbliss	232
Killuin	122	Newcastle (Co. Down)	292
Killybegs	150	Newcastle West	179
Killyleagh	291	Newport	190
Kilminchy	237	Newtownards	292
Kilmore	123	Newtownforbes	230
Kilrush	133		
Kiltegan	43		
Kinsale	68	Oldcastle	35
Knock	188	Omagh	301
		Oughterard	171
Laghey	151		
Lahinch	134	Portaferry	295
Leenane	169	Portmarnock	27
Letterkenny	152	Portrush	271
Lifford	153	Portstewart	282
Limavady	280		
Limerick	178		
Liscarney	189	Rahan	234
Lisdoonvarna	134	Ramelton	155
Listowel	98	Rathnew	44
Longford	229	Redcross	46
Louisburgh	189	Richill	275
		Riverstown	197
		Rosslare	125
Macroom	70	Rosslare Harbour	126
Maddoxtown	221	Roundstone	172
Mallow	71		
Maynooth	211		
Midleton	71	Salthill	173
Millstreet	74	Schull	75
Moate	253	Shanagarry	76
Monasterevin	212	Shillelagh	46
Mountnugent	206	Skibbereen	77
Moville	155	Sligo	198
Moy	300	Sneem	99
Moycullen	170	Spiddal	175
Muckamore	270	St Margaret's	28
Mullinahone	247	Strabane	302
Mullingar	254	Stradbally	111
Multyfarnham	257	Stradbally	238
		Straffan	212
		Strangford	296
Navan	34	Strokestown	241
Nenagh	248		
New Ross	123		